John Campbell & Charlotte Dawson

Trials of Life and Law

David William Otterman

John Campbell & Charlotte Dawson: Trials of Life and Law
Copyright © David Otterman 2014

Cover: Remnant oak tree at Aberscross, Scotland, birthplace of John Campbell. Photo by Barbara (Campbell) Otterman

All rights reserved. No part of this publication may be reproduced, stored in a retrieval system, or transmitted in any form or by any means, electronic, mechanical, photocopying, recording or otherwise, without the prior written permission of the author.

National Library of Australia Cataloguing-in-Publication entry

Creator:	Otterman, David William, author.
Title:	John Campbell & Charlotte Dawson: trials of life and law
ISBN:	9780994195005 (paperback)
Subjects:	Campbell, John.
	Dawson, Charlotte.
	Pioneers--Australia--Biography.
	Women convicts--Australia--Biography.
	Frontier and pioneer life--Australia--History.
	Australia--History--1788-1851
Dewey Number:	920.0994

Published by David Otterman with the assistance of InHouse Publishing
Unit 2/75 Parramatta Road
Underwood, QLD, 4119
Phone: (61) 7 3208 7576
publishing@inhouseprint.com.au
www.inhousepublishing.com.au

Printed and bound in Australia by InHouse Print & Design.

Contents

Introduction 5
Author's Note 8
Chapter 1	*Sutherland* 13
Chapter 2	*Tenant Farming in the Highlands* 28
Chapter 3	*Clearance* 39
Chapter 4	*The Voyage* 43
Chapter 5	*Hobart 1823 -1829* 64
Chapter 6	*Charlotte Dawson - Lincolnshire* 72
Chapter 7	*Trial* 84
Chapter 8	*Gaol* 98
Chapter 9	*Transportation* 123
Chapter 10	*Sydney* 138
Chapter 11	*John Grant, James South and Mary McQueen* .. 159
Chapter 12	*Service and The Factory* 170
Chapter 13	*Marriage* 192
Chapter 14	*Morpeth* 198
Chapter 15	*Disaster* 205
Chapter 16	*Canadian Rebels* 219
Chapter 17	*Van Diemen's Land* 228
Chapter 18	*Charlotte's Revenge* 236
Chapter 19	*Free Again* 246
Chapter 20	*Final Trials* 257
Chapter 21	*The Past Dismissed* 261
Acknowledgements 266
Bibliography 267
Index 271

For Barbara

Our fathers toiled for bitter bread
While idlers thrived beside them,
But food to eat and clothes to wear
Their native land denied them.
They left their native land in spite
Of royalties' regalia,
And so they came, or if they stole
Were sent out to Australia

Freedom on the Wallaby, Henry Lawson

Introduction

In 2004 Barbara (Campbell) Otterman found a revealing essay in the Raymond Terrace and District Historical Bulletin of March 1984. The article entitled 'The Campbells Are Still Coming' by Royal W. Campbell not only made known to Barbara the names of her great-great grandparents, John Campbell and Charlotte Dawson, but also revealed that Charlotte had been transported to Australia as a convict on the Ship *Harmony* in 1827. Royal had discovered Charlotte's convict past only a few months before he wrote the article. There was little detail about these two pioneers in the essay and so began a ten year search for information culminating in this book.

This is the story of John Campbell and Charlotte Dawson, the people they met, the circumstances and events which shaped their lives. It is a small part of the larger story of Australia. John and Charlotte were common ordinary people caught up in the circumstances of their time. Although social change was progressing they lived in a time when the rights, interests and moral opinions of the privileged were still paramount to those of the common individual. They did not shape history; they lived only with its consequences. Some aspects of the story are raw and confronting, but the facts exist even though they had been lost or conveniently forgotten through the passage of time. With the gradual release of records into the public domain a previously brief, imprecise oral history can be revised and expanded.

It is difficult, if not entirely wrong, to judge these people based on our perception of values. We live in a different age. We have not suffered the struggle to survive which confronted them. Fortunately the shame of having a convict ancestor has all but disappeared. As early as the 1820s, even though the taint of convict parentage was stigmatic, there was recognition that the class of inhabitants who had been born in the colony afforded a remarkable exception to the moral and physical character of their parents.[1] More recently, Alison Alexander, in Tasmania's Convicts, How Felons Built a Free Society, writes '...there is no discernible difference between those of convict descent and others. Its main consequence is on individuals, giving them an interest, perhaps pride, occasionally still shame.' [2]

By 1988, the bi-centenary of permanent European presence on the continent, it was desirable to have a convict in the family tree; even more so if they were on the First Fleet. The recognition of their achievements promoted a sense of worth outweighing by far the burden of their crimes. These were the people who built Australia. They provided the labour for its infrastructure, the enterprise for its economy and they inspired a free, egalitarian approach to its society.

As well as relieving Britain of a growing petty criminal class, which could not be accommodated in domestic penal facilities, transportation to Australia gave the new colonies of Van Diemen's Land and New South Wales a young, cheap work force and an ever expanding presence on the island continent. Charlotte and her co-felons convicted in Lincolnshire were ordinary members of a working class which were often driven to petty theft to supplement an income insufficient to provide the necessities of life. They were young; ideal candidates for the transportation system.

John Campbell, removed from his Highland home, emigrated from Scotland to Van Diemen's Land in 1823 as a free man. Five years later he came north to Sydney and eventually settled on a small farm near the Green Hills (Morpeth) in the Hunter River Valley of New South Wales. Inevitably he came into contact with convicts and in conflict with the legal system.

A certain amount of historical, social and geographical information is included to give some perspective to the story. However, the bulk of the work deals with individuals who were either directly or indirectly associated with John and Charlotte; mainly people who they met and knew.

In writing the book, the trap of never ending research was always present. As each new fact emerged new questions were raised, followed by trips to archives and libraries in New South Wales, Tasmania, Queensland, Scotland and England; a travel program repeated several times. And still questions remain.

John and Charlotte faced much more adversity during their lives than oral history has recorded. There are undoubtedly more facts to be discovered. Certainly additional facts will emerge, perhaps in conflict with known facts, perhaps to change the story slightly, definitely to enhance it. Such facts are welcome additions and can only enrich the story of a remarkable couple.

Notes to Introduction

1 Thomas Keneally, *Australians, Origins to Eureka*, Allen & Unwin, Crows Nest, 2010, p.286.
2 Alison Alexander, *Tasmania's Convicts, How Felons Built a Free Society*, Allen & Unwin, Crows Nest, 2010, p.264.

Author's Note

Quotations from historic sources have been transcribed as written without alteration to give the reader a more precise view of documentation from the period. Misspellings have been left intact to avoid the overuse of the mannerism (sic). Where the original quoted source is in handwritten script the transcribed text is italicized. For clarity, ship's names and medical terms in Latin have also been italicized.

Weights, Measures and Currency

Rather than convert to units currently in use, units of weight, measure and currency have been stated in their original form. The older terms may not be familiar to some readers therefore explanatory notes are included here to assist comprehension.

Dry Volume

Boll

> The basic unit of dry capacity in Scots measure was the boll (from the word 'bowl'). A quarter of a boll was a firlot (a 'fourth lot'). A quarter of this was a peck. A quarter of a peck was a lippie (from the Anglo-Saxon leap, meaning a 'basket'). Sixteen bolls made a chalder or chaldron (from the French chaudron, meaning a 'kettle').
> Lippies, pecks, firlots, bolls and chalders varied depending on what was being measured:
> For wheat, peas, beans, meal etc. (Scots = Imperial = Metric)
> 1 boll (or 4 firlots) = 3 bushels 3 pecks 1.944 gallons = 145.145 litres
> For barley, oats, malt etc.
> 1 boll (or 4 firlots) = 5 bushels 3 pecks 0.600 gallons
> = 211.664 litres

Linear Measure
    1 mile = 1,760 yards = 5,280 feet = 1.609 kilometres
    1 rod = 5.5 yards = 16 feet 6 inches = 5.029 metres
    1 yard = 3 feet = 36 inches = 0.914 metres
    1 foot = 12 inches = 0.305 metres.
    1 inch = 2.54 centimetres

Square Measure
    1 acre = 0.405 hectares

Weight
    1 pound (lb) = 16 ounces (oz) = 0.454 kilograms
    1 stone = 14 pounds = 6.350 kilograms

Currency
    Pounds (£), shillings (s) and pence (d) Sterling.
    The notation used in this text for one pound, one shilling and one pence is: £1 1s 1d

    In the context of the period of time in this book: £1 = 20s and 1s = 12d

    The comparative value of one currency to another has changed enormously over time due to fluctuations in the relative value of a currency and the endless march of inflation. Therefore the value of £1 equalling today's value of approximately 2 Australian dollars (AUD$) is meaningless in the context of the first half of the 19th century. From 1800 to 1850 the purchasing power of £1 in terms of today's value ranges from £66 (AUD $132) to £87 (AUD $174).[1]

    The ring dollar or holey dollar was produced in New South Wales in 1813 to combat the scarcity of coinage. A central plug, known as a dump, was cut out of a Spanish dollar and stamped with the value of fifteen pence. The remaining ring coin, known as a ring dollar or holey dollar, was given the value of 5 shillings. At a total value of 6s 3d, the two coins were worth 25% more than the value of the Spanish dollars from which they were made.

Temperature

Celcius (C) and Fahrenheit (F)
0 degrees Celsius (0°C) = 32 degrees Fahrenheit (32°F)
Conversion: °F = ((°C/5) x 9) + 32
°C = ((°F-32)/9) x 5

Abbreviations in the text and notes

ADB	Australian Dictionary of Biography
Adm	Admiralty
AJCP	Australian Joint Copying Project
AOTAS	Archives Office of Tasmania
CM	Caledonian Mercury
CO	Colonial Office
EEC	Edinburgh Evening Courant
HO	Home Office
HRA	Historical Records of Australia
LA	Lincolnshire Archives
LRSM	The Lincoln, Rutland & Stamford Mercury
MM&HRGA	Maitland Mercury & Hunter River General Advertiser
MUP	Melbourne University Press
NAUK	National Archives of the United Kingdom
NLS	National Library of Scotland
NRScot	National Records of Scotland
NSW LPI	New South Wales Land & Property Information
QSA	Queensland State Archives
SG&NSWA	Sydney Gazette & New South Wales Advertiser
SRNSW	State Records Authority of New South Wales
TAHO	Tasmanian Archives and Heritage Office

1 Lawrence H. Officer and Samuel H. Williamson, "Five Ways to Compute the Relative Value of a UK Pound Amount, 1270 to Present," Measuring Worth, http://www.measuringworth.com/ukcompare/ accessed 18 November 2013.

Chapter 1

Sutherland

Sir George Gipps, Governor of New South Wales, read the petition without interest. He was uncomfortable. The humid January day and his stiff uniform of office added to his discomfort, subverting his concentration. He did not know the petitioner John Campbell. Perhaps Campbell was one of the sordid mob that had confronted him at Morpeth the previous year. The incident had marred an otherwise pleasant visit to Maitland.

One paragraph, the last in the petition, briefly caught his attention.

> *Maitland January 13th 1840 I hereby certify that I have known Petitioner upwards of Eight years and always found him an Honest and industrious man and am of the opinion that he must have been brought into his present circumstances through Elgin and Nugent tried with him. James Norris, Agent for the Steamers Morpeth*[1]

The character reference, one of six, made no impression on him. His decision was immediate, his declaration brief.

> *I regret to say that I see nothing in this case to lead me to think that I can properly interfere with the sentence of the Law. GG Jan 22*

With these words, Gipps sealed John Campbell's fate; seven years servitude in Van Diemen's Land.

For John Campbell the decision was disastrous. All hope of reprieve was gone. Filled with apprehension he wondered what would happen to his wife and his infant son. In his head he traced the journey that led him to this time, this horrible place. The reflection firmed his resolve. This would not be the way his life ended. A free man from Scotland he would be free again.

...

Above the Strath Fleet valley in northeastern Scotland lie the ruins of Aberscross, an abandoned Highland village west of the coastal town of Golspie. All that remains of this once thriving community are broken lines of boulders, the remnant foundations of houses and garden fences, partially obscured in the long grass.

At Aberscross the highland area rises abruptly from the north side of the valley to a height of 150 metres above sea level. A stream traverses the area on its journey to the River Fleet dividing the village into Easter and Wester Aberscross. Its banks steepen as it descends the upland slope. Before it reaches the river flats it merges with a smaller stream from the northeast and together they form a narrow gorge.

It is from this feature that the area derives its name, the Pictish words *aber* meaning 'meeting of two burns' and *sgor* meaning 'deep cleft'. The resulting name, Abersgor (anglicised to Aberscross), implies a history of habitation from ancient times and several stone circles and small standing stones on the site demonstrate this ancient connection.

From Wester Aberscross the view to the east along Strath Fleet is spectacular. Highlands confine both sides of the river as it flows through marshy and alder covered ground towards Loch Fleet and onward to the broad expanse of the North Sea. The valley is cultivated from opposite Aberscross to its upper reaches to the west. Its regular shaped farm paddocks of green and yellow contrast strongly with the meadows and pastures of the wilder, rocky, purple heather and brown bracken clad highlands on either side. The changeable weather, soft sunshine and scudding white clouds against a blue sky one minute and gale force winds and driving rain the next, make this a wild and beautiful place.

John Campbell, born in the Parish of Golspie, Sutherland, in 1798, spent his early years at Aberscross where a group of tenant farmers and their families eked out a subsistence living. The meager income from farming, depleted by rents paid in money and victuals to the Sutherland Estate, was insufficient to ease their impoverishment. But even though making a living was difficult in the bleak landscape of the eastern highlands, they were a hardy folk who loved the land and their way of life.

Invaders from Scandinavia had colonized Sudrland (South Land) in the 9th century. With Caithness and the Shetland and Orkney islands it became part of the Jarldom of Orkney. The Norsemen intermixed to a certain extent with the indigenous Pict inhabitants but constantly came into conflict with the Scots Gaels to the south and west. In 1165 William I 'the Lion', grandson of King David I, succeeded to the Scottish throne. After a series of strategic battles had effectively diminished the Norse Orcadian influence on the mainland, William gave the lands of Sutherland to Hugh Freskin as payment for military services. Hugh was the grandson of Freskin of Moravia, a Flemish Knight, who had received Duffus in Moray from King David I in return for his services against the Norsemen. Hugh Freskin's son, William, took the name Sutherland for the family name and was created the first Earl of Sutherland by Alexander II about 1235.

The remainder of the Freskin family adopted the surname Morray (Murray) and populated the hills and glens of southeastern Sutherlandshire, particularly in the Parishes of Dornoch, Rogart and Golspie. They became the principal vassals of the Earl of Sutherland, charged with the defense of the shire against the enemies of the Earl, noteably the MacKays of Caithness and the Sinclairs of Strathnaver. The chieftains of the Murrays erected a small castle at Aberscross overlooking the entrance to Strath Fleet, but by the end of the 17th century the castle had fallen into ruin and there is no evidence of its existence remaining today.

In 1514 the Earldom passed by marriage to a branch of the Gordons of Huntly who consolidated their hold on the title. The seventeenth century saw the earls not only move into the reformed Protestant religion but also become one of the leading covenanting families in Scotland during the Civil Wars of the 1630s and 1640s. In the early 1740s the family was officially reconciled with MacKay and together they fought for the government in 1745, William the 16th Earl being present at Culloden.[2]

Situated along the coast, immediately north of the village of Golspie, is Dunrobin Castle, the seat of the Earls of Sutherland. Besieged by tourists, it majestically faces the North Sea from its cliff top position. A fort-like building had stood there from at least the early part of the 13th century and William, the first Earl of Sutherland, died there in 1248. William was buried in the south aisle of the cathedral church at Dornoch which then became the usual burial-place of the Earls of Sutherland. Additions to Dunrobin Castle were made in the 16th century and extensions in 1785. A complete re-modeling commencing in the mid 1800s changed the castle-fort to a house in the Scottish Baronial style. But viewed from the seaward side, the medieval 'fairytale' façade of the castle can still be seen.

When John Campbell was born, the Sutherland Estate (which comprised its castle, Dunrobin, and about 1 million acres occupying most of what is now the county of Sutherland) was the inheritance of Elizabeth Gordon (1765 – 1839), second daughter of the Earl and Countess of Sutherland. She had just turned one year old when her parents, having gone on retreat to Bath for the sake of their health, died of "putrid fever" in June 1766. Their elder daughter Caroline had died earlier that year and they had no son.

Elizabeth's right of succession was vigorously contested by Sir Robert Gordon of Gordonstoun and George Sutherland of Forse. The House of Lords finally decided the matter in the girl's favour in 1771. However, the succession of a young child meant that a group of administrators handled the legal and business affairs of the estate. They were the Duke of Athole; the Earl of Elgin; Thomas Miller, the Lord Justice-Clerk; Sir Adam Ferguson of Kilkerran; Mr James Wemyss of Wemyss; Sir Alexander Dalrymple of Hailes; Alexander Boswell of Auchinleck; and John Mackenzie of Delvine. The day to day management of the estate was placed in the hands of a manager, Captain James Sutherland who, in part due to his isolation, acted unilaterally on many local matters. Factors under Sutherland were initially James Campbell and later John Fraser.[3]

Raised by her maternal grandmother Elizabeth Hairstanes ('Lady Alva' 1717 – 1806), Countess Elizabeth's education and upbringing in London and Edinburgh were directed towards an aristocratic life. She was not taken to Sutherland until the age of seventeen but soon afterwards became ambitious and determined to improve the Sutherland Estate into a paying property. In 1785 she married George Granville Levenson Gower (1758 – 1833), son of the wealthiest man in England, Earl Gower, the Marquess of Stafford.[4] The marriage connected her relatively poor family and large landholding to the richest family in the country. On becoming the Marquess of Stafford in 1803, her husband was able to employ vast amounts of money from his substantial interests in English estates and canals to his wife's Highland property.

The new wealth enabled the Countess to realise her aspirations towards the reorganisation of her territory. Her plan for the Sutherland Estate incorporated two ideas: the conversion of large portions of the estate to sheep farming and, in parallel, the establishment of fishing and manufacturing industries at specific places along the coast. Sheep farmers from the south, willing to pay much higher rents for the highlands and glens than the existing tenants and wadsetters, would improve income and implement more productive agricultural practices. The Highland people's cattle and meal farming methods were outdated subjecting them to periods of famine and poverty. Cleared from the highlands to accommodate the sheep, they would be re-settled on or near the coast where they would be gainfully employed in fishing and kelp harvesting and their living conditions would be much improved.

As in the rest of Europe, the population of Sutherland was increasing at a great rate presenting an unsustainable future for the Highlanders' way of life. The Countess was of the opinion that the resettlement plan would be successful and preserve the Highland people. This sharply contrasted with the plans of Scottish peer Lord Selkirk who, as a precaution against potential insurrection arising from the forced removal of the people from their traditional lands, favoured wholesale emigration to the British colonies, principally to Canada.[5]

Successive possessors of the estate had pursued an interest in improvement from at least the 1720s if not earlier. The earliest record of non-native sheep on the estate is described in a claim made for losses to Jacobite forces in east Sutherland in the spring of 1746. Lieutenant John Gordon claimed that the rebels had killed and carried off twenty one wedders of the English breed worth five shillings sterling each at Aberscross and Golspietower.[6]

The culture of the Scottish Highland clans had changed over the centuries and radically subsequent to the Jacobite uprising of 1746. From a system where a clan and its chief collectively possessed the lands, the social and economic structure had changed to a system where the chieftain possessed the lands and its resources in his own name. The chieftainship became a legalised heritable title. The clan chiefs had eventually become absentee landlords more interested in financial survival than in the wellbeing of their people who were left without any legal title to land.[7]

As can be imagined, the removal of people from their traditional lands, particularly in order to replace them with sheep, was bound to be traumatic in spite of the well meant intention to improve both the lot of the people and the productivity of the land. There were also numerous hindrances to the planned improvements including foremost the existing land tenure system. Large leases or tacks were given out as a right to half-pay officers who sublet to large numbers of 'tenants at will'. The tenants had little or no security of tenure and their land use was subject to the will of the tacksmen. Many of these subleases were operated on the old runrig system where land was not enclosed and was shared in common inhibiting any individual tenant raising his own standard above that of his co-tenants.[8]

In 1802 John Fraser died and the Countess appointed Captain David Campbell as factor of the estate. He was a cattle breeder of note and had farmed extensively in the Highlands. Although the small tenant farmers seemed to have been happy and contented under Campbell's management, he was unpopular with the tacksman class. He was reluctant to progress the interest of tacksmen who had made offers for portions of the estate and was negligent in drawing up lists of lands and numbers of people to be removed and accommodated elsewhere. It became apparent that Campbell was not suitable for the task of modernizing the Sutherland Estate. On Whitsunday 1807 he was replaced by Cosmo Falconer, an Edinburgh lawyer.[9]

The Sutherland clearances began in earnest that same Whitsunday when the first of the old tenancy leases expired and the first of the big sheep farms was let at Lairg, about 20 kilometres west of Aberscross. Approximately 300 people were removed, some to Strathnaver, some to Dornoch and a few to the new village of Golspie. This first round of clearances was not as smooth as it should have been and many people chose to emigrate to North America as an alternative to the unattractive, inadequate and overcrowded accommodation offered along the coast and elsewhere. In spite of all the forward planning, the lack of co-operation from the people and the lack of sufficient resettlement facilities were a disappointment to the Countess. She lost confidence in her managers, in particular Falconer, who had shown little enthusiasm for the task and had become dejected at his inability to get anybody to do anything.[10]

In 1810 Falconer was dismissed and, on Whitsunday 1811, two energetic and dynamic agricultural entrepreneurs from Morayshire, William Young and Patrick Sellar, took charge as joint managers to provide a stronger guidance, new initiatives and a more enthusiastic approach. Both the Countess and Earl had visited Young's Inverugie property in Aberdeenshire and had been highly impressed with the improvements he had put in place and his development of the Village at Hopeman.

For Young, a man of unlimited optimism and ideas, the development of one of the largest estates in Scotland backed by seemingly unlimited supplies of money was a golden opportunity. For Sellar at the age of 28 and the younger of the two men, the position was less attractive. A potential to be regarded only as the older man's clerk or to assume blame for any failed plans was inherent in the position due to Young's overly ambitious and impatient nature. The position also meant giving up a qualified position in his father's well established legal practice. However, Sellar's greatest interest was in farming and, as he had already invested in one of the properties on the estate, he decided to accept the position.

Young and Sellar had seen the potential for farm development in the Golspie parish when, in 1809, they visited Falconer to discuss the possibilities associated with establishing a packet boat service between Burghead and Littleferry near the entrance to Loch Fleet.

Before returning to Moray they made an offer for the Culmaily area along the coastal plain south of the village of Golspie and north of Loch Fleet. At that time the River Fleet was tidal as far inland as Pittentrail, with Morvich, the next tenancy west of Aberscross, considered to be at the mouth of the river and the sea loch extending from there to the North Sea.

The ferry crossing at the narrow seaward end of the loch was hazardous and unsuitable for progressing development of resources in Sutherland. Young envisaged the formation of a mound across the landward end of the loch between Cambushmore on the south side of the loch and Craigton Rock (now called the Mound Rock) on the northside. Such a structure would provide a barrier preventing tides from penetrating the upper reaches of the strath, confine the river to a more manageable course and make available new land for cultivation. However, the risky job of constructing an embankment across a tidal loch with a base of unknown nature was unattractive to professional contractors. Young and Sellar were finally forced to undertake the construction themselves. Work began in the summer of 1815 and was planned to be completed during that season. But the project was not completed until June 1816. On the 26th of that month the Earl and Countess crossed safely on their way to Dunrobin thereby avoiding the tedious and frequently dangerous crossing at Littleferry.

Neither Young nor Sellar considered themselves to be Highlanders. Typically, they held the small tenant farmers of the Highlands in contempt. They considered the Sutherland Estate to be particularly backward primarily due to the misapplication of labour and mismanagement of the land. Under their management implementation of Lady Elizabeth's ideas was accelerated and expanded into a great exercise in social and economic planning.[11]

Removals and the letting and establishment of big sheep farms stocked with Cheviot sheep proceeded at a great rate. Clearances commenced in the parishes of Assynt, Kildonan and Clyne in 1812 and in Farr (Strathnaver) 1814, and continued in Golspie, Rogart, Dornoch and Loth. Several thousand people were displaced and there was, as could be expected, a considerable amount of resistance, some of it formidable. Young complained that everything he did had to be done as at the point of a sword and that both rich and poor were hostile to every plan of improvement preferring to remain a century behind. The Countess was equally dismayed and felt that since their efforts had been resisted by force, the people should be brought to reason by the same means.

Sellar, as under-factor to Young, was zealous in his tasks of collecting rents, serving writs of removal and debt, evicting debtors and prosecuting poachers and illegal distillers. He became known as a hard and unfriendly agent. When he acquired territories in Strathnaver, which he intended to convert to a grand new sheep farm, his part in the clearances was no less harsh eventually leading to an indictment on various charges including culpable homicide. It was alleged that in several inland townships he had maliciously and cruelly set fire to crops, houses and barns and had acted brutally during the removals causing deaths and injuries.

Sellar's trial commenced on 23rd April 1816 before the Circuit Court of Justiciary in Inverness with Judge Lord Pitmilly presiding and a jury of fifteen men, none of whom was from Sutherland. A large number of witnesses from Strathnaver were examined under oath but their statements were often contradictory and failed to give any support to the serious charges. Sellar, with his own legal background and represented by a legal counsel of three, was well defended. He claimed he had acted entirely within the law and his actions were humanitarian in all respects. Describing his participation in the alleged events in mitigating terms he testified buildings had been destroyed only where absolutely necessary. He was also adamant that he had given explicit instructions to guarantee the preservation of crops and that there should be no harsh treatment employed in removing the people. The jury did not hesitate in returning a unanimous verdict of not guilty. Although the verdict was a clear triumph for Sellar, it was deemed to be unjust resulting in Sellar being stamped in the minds of the Highlanders as a tyrant, oppressor and murderer.[12]

Lord Stafford and the Countess were well informed of their managers' policies, but primarily due to their lack of direct contact with their tenants, they were unaware of the excesses carried out in their name. Consequently they became hated by some of the displaced tenants and branded as monsters.

Under Young's management average annual income on the estate increased threefold, but expenditure increased ninefold resulting in annual deficits. Sellar's misgivings about William Young were eventually realized following several problems stemming from verbal agreements Young had entered into and his failure to keep his younger partner fully informed. It was decided that their private interests should be separated. Sellar offered to give his share of Culmaily to Young if he could have Morvich for himself, or the other way round if Young preferred to have Morvich. After much deliberation, Young went to live at Rhives and Sellar gained sole possession of Culmaily. Morvich was taken over by Lord Stafford for himself but later came under Sellar's occupation.

Young also came under criticism for the failure of the mound scheme to produce many acres of arable land, the drained bed of the loch proving unsuitable for cultivation. Today the area of the loch immediately above the mound is mostly marshland, largely populated with alders and birdlife, but the regions of the strath previously subjected to tidal flooding are now extensively used for agricultural purposes. Although Young's achievements were admirable, his inability to control spending on projects had become unacceptable. In August 1816 he resigned. James Loch, an Edinburgh lawyer, who had been appointed financial adviser to Lord Stafford in 1812, then took charge of the Sutherland Estate management. His protégé Francis Suther, a Lowland Scot, was brought in as factor to complete the last of the great clearances.[13]

On 24 May 1816 Sellar wrote a note at Culmaily concerning Sutherland in which he described the people as being barely civilised, 'shut out from the general stream of knowledge and cultivation' living 'in turf cabins in common with the brutes' and 'fast sinking under the baneful effects of ardent spirits'[14]. In the letter he railed against the illicit production of whisky and associated loss of tax payments to the government and applauded the rightful endeavours of Lord and Lady Stafford to bring the people 'from the inaccessible country where alone this mortal complaint rages, to the accessible coast where with proper care it can't exist'[15]. In describing the situation in detail in each parish he says of Golspie:

> What I have ventured to Prophecy as to Dornoch has already taken place as to GOLSPIE except in Wester and Easter Aberscross, Strathlundie and Scottery districts, the inhabitants of which inaccessible places all live by smuggling whisky. All that remains to be done is to bring these families into Golspie or Brora, laying Aberscross to Morvich, Strathlundie to Culmaly and Scottary and these grounds along the Brora Lake and river to the Dunrobin Glen pasturage. Nature has pointed these things out and they are scarcely to be avoided without compromising the interest of the Noble Family and their people. [16]

In spite of Sellar's contempt for the illegal trade in whiskey the industry was a necessary evil. Profits from the trade often provided the only means for the small tenant farmers to honour their rental payments. In most cases the tacksmen and rent collectors turned a blind eye to the activity. An enforced end to it would have robbed the Estate of much of its lease revenue.

Later, on 31 May 1816 in the final part of the essay, Sellar complained about the lack of specific trades amongst the people and suggested it was the reason for their lack of productivity.

> ... in no country of which I have yet read or heard is there in every one person such an accumulation of offices as in the highlands of Scotland. Every man is a Quarrier, mason, woodman, carrier, square wright carpenter, cooper, turf cutter, thatcher, wood destroyer, currier, tanner, shoemaker, saddler, shepherd, wool comber, spinner, farmer, cattle dealer, distiller, poacher, and God knows what, and yet with all this bountiful provision for every man of them, are they not de

facto (but as Lord and Lady Stafford well know) de Jure beggars.[17]

He pointed out that his sentiments reflected those of the Scottish economist and moral philosopher Adam Smith, in his work 'The Wealth of Nations' quoting:

> ... every country workman who is obliged to change his work and his tools every half hour, and to apply his hand in twenty different ways almost every day of his life renders him almost always slothful lazy and incapable of any vigorous application even on the most pressing occasions.[18]

Again Sellar's solution was to remove the people to the coast where they could acquire specific trades and be employed more productively in the coal, salt, lime, kelp harvesting and fishing industries. They would also benefit from developed infrastructure along the coast.

James Loch's feelings were much the same. In 'An Account of Improvements On The Estates of the Marquess of Stafford' written in 1820 he comments on the lack of productivity and the crude state under which the land in each town was held. Classed according to quality, the land was divided into as many lots as there were occupiers and held on the runrig or common field system.

> Such being, until very lately, the condition of the estate of Sutherland the effect was to scatter thickly, a hardy but not an industrious race of people up the glens and over the sides of the various mountains; who taking advantage of every spot which could be cultivated, and which could with any chance of success be applied to raising a precarious crop of inferior oats, of which they baked their cakes, and of bear, from which they distilled their whiskey, added but little to the industry, and contributed nothing to the wealth of the empire. Impatient of

regular and constant work, all the heavy labour was abandoned to the women, who were employed, occasionally, even in dragging the harrow to cover in the seed. To build their hut, or get in their peats for fuel, or to perform any other occasional labour of the kind, the men were ever ready to assist; but the great proportion of their time, when not in the pursuit of game, or of illegal distillation, was spent in indolence and sloth.[19]

Loch blamed the tacksmen for perpetuating this system, through their own lack of resourcefulness and their comfortable reliance on the minimal amount of exertion required on their part to contribute to the maintenance of the estate. He continued:

So long as the system, just described, remained in full force, no attempt could be made to improve or meliorate the situation of these poor people. To better their condition, however; to raise them from such a state of continual poverty and occasional want; to supply them with the means, and to create in them the habits of industry, was, and is the bounden duty of the owners of every such property. And it was not less their duty to do so, because the same arrangement, which was calculated to produce this salutary effect, was at the same time the best suited to increase the value of their property, and to add to the general wealth of the community.

... None felt the full extent of this obligation more than the proprietors of the estate of SUTHERLAND. But such an attempt was one not to be undertaken without much consideration; and when fully determined on, it was not a matter to be easily accomplished.[20]

In reference to accusations of brutality and harsh treatment raised during implementation of plans for improving the economy of the estate, Loch again blamed the tacksmen.

> --- it is from individuals of this class, and persons connected with them, that those false and malignant representations have proceeded, which have been so loudly and extensively circulated. Actuated by motives of a mere personal nature, regardless of the happiness of the people, whose improvement it was the great object of the landlord to effect, they attempted to make an appeal in favour of a set of people who were never before the objects of their commiseration, in order that they might, if possible, reduce them, for their own selfish purposes, to that state of degradation from which they had been just emancipated.[21]

But Loch was trying only to deflect criticism away from himself. He could not escape the fact that his henchmen had implemented overly harsh measures during the clearances.

These were the prevailing attitudes of the land owners and the socio-economic conditions under which John Campbell was born and raised. As is so often the case, 'The best-laid schemes o' mice an' men gang aft agley'[22]. The intention of the Sutherland family to improve the prosperity of their estate and the well being of the people was admirable. But the idealism associated with their plans was always going to be overshadowed by the trauma of displacing a people who preferred to stay where they were and maintain their rugged lifestyle. This was the same situation confronting people elsewhere in Europe during the industrial and agricultural revolution. But the Highland experience was aggravated by its critical lack of employment for surplus labour in local industries forcing a large proportion of the displaced population to emigrate.

Notes to Chapter 1

1. SRNSW: NRS 905 Colonial Secretary's Correspondence, Letter 40/775, [4/2513], Reel 2245.
2. Anne Marie Tindley *The Sutherland Estate, ,c.1200-1920: a Short History*, Glasgow Caledonian University, 2009, pp.2-3.
3. Margaret Wilson Grant, *The Golspie Story*, The Northern Times Limited 1983.
4. George Granville Leveson-Gower, Marquess of Stafford, a liberal reformer, had considerable influence, becoming the 1st Duke of Sutherland six months before his death in 1833. A statue to his memory erected in 1834 on Ben Bhraggie above the town of Golspie, dominates the surrounding landscape as far as the eye can see. On the base of the statue, in bold letters, is painted the word 'Monster".
5. Eric Richards, *The Highland Clearances*, Birlinn 2008, Chapter 8.
6. Malcolm Bangor-Jones, *Sheep farming in Sutherland in the eighteenth century*, AgHR,II, pp181-202.
7. James Donaldson, *Fairwell to the Heather*, Hawthorn, Vic., 2006, p10.
8. *The Golspie Story*, op.cit., pp.105-106.
9. Ibid., pp.108 & 112.
10. Richards, *The Highland Clearances*, op.cit. p.164.
11. Ibid., p.166.
12. Ibid., pp.181-189.
13. Ibid., pp.199-200.
14. R.J Adam, *Sutherland Estate Management: Papers*, Vol. 1, p.176, Scottish History Society, Edinburgh, 1972.
15. Ibid., Vol.1, p. 179.
16. Ibid., Vol.1, p.182.
17. Ibid., Vol.1, pp.184-185.
18. Ibid., Vol.1, p186.
19. James Loch, *An Account of Improvements On The Estates of the Marquess of Stafford*, p51, Longman, Hurst, Rees, Orme & Brown, London, 1820.
20. Ibid., pp.59-60.
21. Ibid., pp.61-62.
22. Robbie Burns, To a mouse, 1795.

Chapter 2

Tenant Farming in the Highlands

History generally deals only with those who have attained a level of authority or have done great deeds or misdeeds. Unfortunately historical accounts about the lives of common individuals are minimal. The few records publicly available for the Sutherland tenant farmers are found in the papers of the Sutherland Estate kept in the National Library of Scotland. These generally consist of lists of names of tenants for each parish and their rental payments, but give no information about their families other than the rare document stating the number of people in each family. However, from the few records that do exist, including the more formal accounts of the population and the geography and agriculture of the area written at the time, a glimpse of the way of life in the early part of the 19th century on a small tenancy in the Highlands can be seen.

Aberscross, part of the Estate of Skelbo during the 18th century, came into the Parish of Golspie in 1808 when a disposition of the Estate by A. MacKenzie four years earlier was finally settled in favour of the Countess of Sutherland.[1] At the end of the 18th century the community consisted of the tenanted farming areas Easter Aberscross and Wester Aberscross. To the west lay the tenancy of Morvich; to the east the round, dark grey dome of the Mound Rock, an outcrop of Early Devonian conglomerate rising from near sea level on its east side like a great, rock bubble to a height of more than 200 metres. To the south, the river, occupying the Strath Fleet valley below, flowed into Loch Fleet, and from there into the North Sea. To the north was higher ground around Aberscross Hill (270 metres above sea level) and Ben Lunnndaidh (446 metres) with Loch Lunndaidh nestled in the upland valley between the two hills.

The Statistical Account of Scotland,[2] compiled by Sir John Sinclair from written reports submitted by parish ministers between

1791 and 1799, gives an insight into the geography, population and produce of each parish at that time. The Reverend William McKeith, in his submission for Golspie,[3] described 'Abermoss and Morvick' as 'being about 50 acres each.'

Prices for provisions in the parish were:

> Beef and mutton 2½ pence the pound in their season, and 3d at least in spring; geese 1s 6d; ducks 6d; chickens 4d; pork 2½d; butter 12s = 1£ English; cheese 4d and of better quality 5d and 6d; barley 12s 6d; oats 9s 6d.
>
> All these kinds of provisions could be bought 20 years ago at half the present prices.

Obviously inflation had been running at an average rate of 5% per annum.

For labour in the parish:

> Some labourers get 8d and 9d; but most 6d in summer, and 5d in winter. Carpenters and masons 1s 6d; tailors 1s. A common labourer, when married, gets 4 bolls bear-meal, at 10 stone weight, and 2 bolls oat meal at 8½ stone weight, land for potatoes and kail-garden, and about £2 10s in money, which, with some small earnings of his wife in spinning, or farm work, or partly both, maintain their family pretty well. The wages of a male servant, including perquisites, are equal to £3 Sterling, and of female servants about £1 10s a year.

The population of the parish was about 1700 and there were 363 houses in the parish with an average of 5 people in each household. However, among these there were 42 households with only one person and several houses with only 2 people. Annual births averaged 1 for every 26 people, marriages 1 in 26 and deaths 1 in 36. Each marriage produced an average of 7 children.

Subsequently in 1812 the Board of Agriculture published a report by Captain John Henderson on the agriculture of the County of Sutherland as of the year 1807 with an addendum for 1811. An appendix included historical observations and descriptions of some of the changes that had taken place in the intervening years.[4] The report contains interesting and valuable information about the people and geography of Sutherland, forms of land tenure, farm buildings, methods of farming used, and the types of animals and crops raised. Although it refers to the county as a whole, much is pertinent to Aberscross.

In his report Henderson stated that the small tenant farmers used the old Scotch plough for turning the sod and described the implement as 'made of birch or aller, with the head and mouldboard of the same materials, having a thin plate of hammered iron on the bottom and land side of the head. This plough, exclusive of the ploughshare and sock plates, costs about 5s to 15s and is often made by the tenant who uses it.'[5] The plough was pulled by four small garrons (native horses) abreast or two small ponies and two cows, all abreast, with a driver. Harrows with wooden teeth were also handmade. They were dragged along by a man and were less effective in reducing the soil than a steel toothed harrow used elsewhere.

For carting manure or fuel a small wooden conical basket cart with wheels three inches thick made of ash plank and about two and a half feet in diameter was used. A small pony dragged the load, about half a cubic yard, to the field where the basket was unloaded from the cart, overturned and then replaced on the cart.

The houses of the small tenant farmers were very basic and to quote Henderson 'mean and wretched'[6]. Dwellings, consisting of a single room, were used for accommodating both people and livestock. The habitation was inclined or built on a slope with the family living at the upper end and the animals tethered with bindings made of birch withes tied to stakes in the walls at the lower end where they reaped the benefit of the warmth from the hearth.

Referred to as 'black houses', the crudest had mud or turf walls. The more substantial dwellings were generally built with double drystone walls. The outer wall was thicker than the inner wall and the space between was filled and packed with earth and rubble. Most were built long, low and narrow to facilitate construction of the roof which was made of wooden rafters covered with divots of turf and thatched with barley straw, bracken fern or reed. As there were no eaves the walls remained damp for much of the year. The floor generally consisted of packed earth, although flagstone was often used and there was a central hearth for the fire. There being no chimney, the smoke from the hearthfire, which burned day and night, winter and summer, made its way through the thatched roof either directly or through small holes cut in the roof. One door provided entrance and exit for both humans and animals and there were no windows.

The animals were housed at night in winter and sometimes in the summer if the weather was inclement. Conditions inside the houses were obviously unsanitary, particularly when winter weather forced the cattle to be confined inside for long periods. The stench would have been overwhelming to anyone unaccustomed to those conditions. Once a year, in the springtime, the interior midden was removed and spread on the fields.[7]

Attached to the house, generally on the down-slope side, was an enclosed garden area or kailyard. Here kail (cabbage), potatoes, turnips, and other kinds of garden vegetables were grown mainly for consumption by the occupants of the house. At Wester Aberscross the remnants of some house foundations and attached garden enclosures are still visible and in all cases the house was located upslope from the enclosure.

The traditional small tenant farming community consisted of a core of lower, more sheltered arable land and an upper area of hill pasture. A dyke or wall made of stone surrounded the arable land which in most Highland areas was an irregular, discontinuous area interspersed with patches of grass, stone outcrops and boggy ground. Stock grazed on the arable land between growing seasons, adding manure to the ground. However, once the growing season was under way, usually in May, the animals were taken to the hill pastures for two to three months.[8]

According to Henderson's report, cattle, sheep and grain were the staple commodities raised by the Sutherland tenant farmers for food, clothing and income from sale.

THE inhabitants near the coast-side live principally upon fish, potatoes, milk, and oat, or barley-cakes. Those in the interior, or more Highland part, feed upon mutton, butter, cheese, milk, and cream, with oat or barley-meal cakes, during the summer months. They live well, and indolent, of course are robust and healthy. In winter the more opulent subsist upon potatoes, beef, mutton, and milk; but the poorer class live upon potatoes and milk, and at times a little oat or barley cakes. In times of scarcity, in summer, they bleed their cattle, and after dividing it into square cakes, they boil it, and eat it with milk or whey, instead of bread.[9]

Crops consisted of bere (pronounced and often written 'bear' and sometimes referred to as 'big'), oats, rye, peas and potatoes, although perhaps not all of these were grown at Aberscross. Bere, a very old form of barley with a six row seed head, was brought to Britain in the 9th century. It grew well on soils of a low pH in areas where there was a short growing season with long hours of daylight. Sown in the spring and harvested in the summer, it was used principally for making whisky or ground into beremeal for bread, biscuits and bannock. The Highlanders often bought quantities of the grain from the coastal farmers if their own small portions of land were of insufficient size to produce the necessary amount to sustain them throughout the whole year.

The cattle were generally black in colour, well shaped and had short legs. Only a few were kept by the smaller tenant farmers and were valued as a source of milk, butter and cheese and important stock products such as hides, leather, horn and bone. Each farmer, depending on the size of his acreage, had from a dozen to 100 head of the native breed of sheep. The sheep were small with good wool, mostly white but sometimes black or grey. The tenants' wives made blankets and tartan plaids of the white and black wool and other items of clothing for themselves and their families. The grey wool was used to make stockings and mittens.[10]

As well as wool, the native sheep provided milk (made into cheese) and meat, both products used for household consumption as part of the subsistence economy. Cheese and sheep were also sold at local markets and there was possibly a regional trade in sheep. Lambs and wethers were often included in the rents and paid in kind to the estate.[11]

The native sheep, however, were soon to disappear from the area and the Highland population with them:

> In the winter of 1806 and spring of 1807, this breed of sheep almost all died of the rot and scab. The introduction of sheep-farming upon a large scale in this county, has compelled many of the tenantry to emigrate, and those who remain are so circumscribed as to pasturage, that they cannot think of renewing their former flocks of the aborigines. These sheep weighed from 28 to 36 lb. the carcass, or four quarters; the wool of from nine to twelve of them, made a stone of 24 lb.; they were collected in cots at night in the winter time, but seldom got any food except what they picked for themselves, even during a storm of snow. One cartload of their dung was reckoned equal to three of cattle or horsedung, for manure.[12]
>
> The decrease of population, is entirely owing to the progress of sheep farms in the county. Although the produce of this county did not maintain the inhabitants for time immemorial, yet as it is a Highland district, and their staple commodity being black cattle, they at all times had the means of purchasing corn from the neighbouring county of Caithness; and as many of the young men went into the army, and the women occasionally, during the harvest, to the southern counties of Scotland, the county might be called a nursery of brave, hardy Highlanders, not over-peopled; yet an agriculturist from the south of Scotland would be apt to

conclude that there were more people in it, than could be well employed in Agriculture. The climate is so healthy, that one medical man is all that can earn a livelihood from his profession in the whole county.[13]

Life at Aberscross involved much of what has been described above. From the records for the Sutherland Estate we can ascertain that two of the tenant farmers living at Wester Aberscross between 1800 and 1819 were John Campbell and Donald Campbell. They were brothers, probably born in the late 1760s or early 1770s. Both men were married and had children.

They were not the only Campbells in the Parish of Golspie but, including George Campbell at Morvich, they were the principal farmers with that family name in the parish. Other Campbells in the parish were Alexander, a tradesman and subtenant of John Polson at Easter Aberscross, Alexander of Culmaily, a tradesmen and Donald, a taylor in the Glenn. There were also a number of Campbell families in the neighbouring parish of Rogart.

The Scottish birth records for the late 18th and early 19th century are incomplete and those which do exist are brief in their description of parentage often giving only the father's name. According to the census of 1811[14] the household of John Campbell of Wester Aberscross comprised 2 males and 3 females. This is enigmatic as the only records discovered so far reveal that John Campbell and his wife Lilias Mann (or Munroe) had at least three sons and only one daughter at the time of the census.

James, christened 7 November 1796;[15]
John, christened 5 September 1798;[16]
Marian, born ca 1801;[17] and
Donald, born ca 1808. [18]

In the 1811 census, Donald Campbell of Wester Aberscross, occupation agriculture, was head of a household consisting of 5 males and 2 females (1 family). Four children are known from birth records for Golspie.

Ann baptised 20 April 1801;[19]
William born 22 February 1805;[20]
Hugh born 29 June 1807;[21] and
Margaret born 20 October 1811.[22]

Margaret, born in October 1811, would not have been present at the time the census data was gathered in May of that year. Donald's wife and Ann account for the two females and Donald, William and Hugh, three of the males at the time of the census, leaving 2 males unaccounted for in the list of births above.

The John Campbell of our story was most likely the son of John Campbell, farmer of Wester Aberscross, and his wife Lilias Mann. John's Australian death certificate of 1870, states that he was born in Golspie, Sutherlandshire. His occupation was recorded as farmer and carpenter. His father's name was Donald of unknown occupation; his mother's name, also unknown.[23] But no record has been found to show that Donald Campbell of Wester Aberscross had a son named John.

An age at death of 70 years old on John's death certificate appears to be a rounded guess since from other Australian documents it can be estimated that he was born between the 12th of February and 21st of September 1798.

The informants on the death registration were neighbours and they may not have known all the correct details. Donald appears to have been John's uncle. Alternatively, although equally conjectural, it is possible the 'Donald' stated on John's death certificate was his brother rather than his father or uncle. Donald, son of John Campbell (senior) and Lilias Mann, born ca 1808, died in the Parish of Dornoch in 1866.[24] Dornoch is given as John's place of origin on at least one Australian record[25] and he may have resided there with the family before departing for Australia.

John Campbell (senior) and Donald Campbell were listed as rent paying tenants at Wester Aberscross from 1802 to 1816, the period for which some detailed records exist.[26] They along with William MacDonald, James MacLeod and Robert MacDonald maintained their tenancies throughout those years, whereas the other tenancies at

Wester Aberscross changed, most notably between 1803 and 1807, possibly due to the death or departure of an individual tenant. The MacDonalds' antecedent is recorded as having occupied Wester Aberscross and having paid rent along with other tenants as far back as 1740[27]. It is possible the Campbell families were resident there at that time as well. In contrast to their namesakes in the Western Highlands, the Campbells and MacDonalds seem to have lived in harmony at Aberscross.

Donald Campbell's rental payments averaged £1 3s money and 2 Bolls victuals each year. It can be assumed that the 2 Bolls victuals consisted of bere grain, the rental record for 1812-1813 specifically noting the victual crop paid as being 'bear'. An additional rent of 18 shillings, 6 and 2/12ths pence was paid in 1808 probably to compensate for the fact that only £1 2s 2d was paid in 1807. The loss of native sheep combined with poor harvests in 1806 and 1807 perhaps explains a slightly lower rent for 1806, the shortfall in rent paid for 1807, and the consequent additional payment in 1808.

Initially John Campbell paid the same rent as Donald Campbell, but from 1807 shared his rent with Robert Gordon. In general they paid a combined sum of £2 7s 6d money and 4 Bolls victuals per annum. This came to an end in 1810 and from 1811 they paid separately, John Campbell's rent being £1 3s 9d money and 2 Bolls victuals each year.

Money was not easily acquired, and often it was not until crops had been harvested and sold at the end of summer that sufficient money was available to pay the annual rent. Fortunately rents were due to be paid on Martinmas (11 November), after the harvest had been gathered and a portion sold. But payment meant depleting both grain stores and money needed to survive during the winter.

The Campbells were most likely involved in distilling, smuggling and selling whisky. Two elderly second generation Australian female descendants described their grandfather as having been a whiskey distiller. It seems unlikely that this refers to employment at the Clynelish distillery established in 1819 at Brora ten kilometres north of Golspie. Rather it indicates that he distilled whiskey for himself and whatever other purposes he desired. The clear water of the Aberscross burn with its cloak of oak trees, the home grown supply of bere and the unobstructed view up and down the strath would have been ideal for this clandestine yet lucrative activity.

On different occasions in Australia, John stated his occupation as a carpenter and a farmer, suggesting he had a number of skills consistent with the tenant farmers of the Highlands. Sellar may not have applauded the variety of skills but they would have been of particular value to a young man in Australia during the first half of the 19th century where his versatility would have given him a broader range of employment opportunities.

Notes to Chapter 2

1. James Loch, *Dates and Documents relating to the Family and Property of Sutherland,* 1859 , p 49.
2. Sir John Sinclair (ed.), *Statistical Account of Scotland,* (20 Vols.) William Creech, Edinburgh, 1791 - 1799.
3. Ibid., Vol.9, pp. 26-32.
4. Capt. John Henderson, *General view of the agriculture of the County of Sutherland with observations of the means of its improvement,* M. McMillan, London, 1812.
5. Ibid., p56.
6. Ibid., p45.
7. James Hunter, *The Making of a Crofting Community,* pp112-113, Donald, Edinburgh, 1976.
8. Robert Dodgshon, *The Age of the Clans, The Highlands from Somerlad to the Clearances,* pp29-32, Birlinn, 2002.
9. Capt. John Henderson, op.cit. p.120.
10. Ibid., pp.103-104.
11. Malcolm Bangor-Jones, 'Sheep farming in Sutherland in the eighteenth century', *The Agricultural Historical Review,* 50, II, p.182.
12. Capt. John Henderson, op.cit. p.104.
13. Capt. John Henderson, op.cit. p.119.
14. Highland Council Archives, M/SUTH/12/5/b-c, Transcribed by Malcolm Bangor-Jones, 1977.
15. NRScot, Scotland's People, Births and Christenings, Rogart Parish, OPR 055/000 0010 0030.
16. Ibid., Golspie Parish OPR 051/00 0020 0035.
17. NRScot, Scotland's People, Deaths, Rogart Parish, 1870 SD 055/00 0001.
18. Ibid., Dornoch Parish, 1866 SD 047/00 0008.
19. NRScot, Scotland's People, Births and Christenings, Golspie Parish, OPR 051/00 0020 0039.
20. Ibid., OPR 051/00 0020 0042.
21. Ibid., OPR 051/00 0020 0046.
22. Ibid., OPR 051/00 0020 0052.

23 Registry of Births, Deaths and Marriages New South Wales, Death Certificate Registration Number: 1870/005643.
24 NRScot, Scotland's People, Deaths, Dornoch Parish, 1866 SD 047/00 0008.
25 AOTAS CON35/1 p131.
26 NLS, Sutherland Papers, Dep. 313/2123; 2124; 2129; 2130; 2131; 2132; 2135; 2136; 2137 and 2141. No records were found for the years 1804 to 1806, and 1817, 1818.
27 Ibid., Dep. 313/2113.

Chapter 3

Clearance

In 1819, Donald Campbell, his family and young John Campbell were cleared from Wester Aberscross, their names included in the list of removals for Golspie drawn up by James Loch in June of that year.¹ In total fifteen tenants and their families were removed from Wester Aberscross and their destinations recorded as follows:

Tenants' name			*Whither gone*
Donald Campbell	married	7 children	Latheron in Caithness
John Campbell	unmarried		unknown
Robert Gordon	married	4 children	Latheron in Caithness
John Grant	married	9 children	Bishop Field Dornoch
John Gunn	married	4 children	Proncy ----d----
Rob McDonald	unmarried		America
Wm. Mc Donald	married 7 children		Dornoch moor
Widow John MacKay	3 children		Caithness
Jn. McKay Jun. lately Willm married 2 children			Lives wi. his mother-in-law parish of Rogart
Jas. McLeod married 5 children			Swordale parish of Creech
John McPherson married 4 children			at present in Kinnauld but looking out for a place
Hugh Munro married 2 children			Golspie
John Munro married 4 children			Latheron in Caithness
Angus Sutherland married 6 children			Latheron in Caithness
Widow Christy Sutherland 3 children			Glasgow

John Polson remained on Easter Aberscross, the 19 year lease granted to him by William Young not due to expire until 1828. The subtenants on his tack supposedly had been removed in 1808.

The Aberscross people were not keen to move. They were, however, resigned to their fate. In January 1819 James Loch had written to Lady Stafford about the progress of the clearances in Sutherland.

> ... *the Kildonan people have taken some lots at Helmsdale, but the Strathbrora people and Aberscross people have as yet taken few lots at Brora, which would surprise me, if I were not by this time accustomed to the prickliness of their temper and resolution. Some few of them have taken lots at Rosshire, but the bulk of them I believe will settle. One thing is clear, which is that they have made up their minds to move as they have not ploughed any of their land, and this is the most important matter.*[2]

The removal was not without incident. Suther, of his own accord, had adopted a policy of burning, authorising the constables accompanying the clearing parties to set fire to the houses after the people had been ejected to prevent them from returning to occupy the buildings. Loch was appalled that a practice that had been at the heart of the charges against Sellar had been brought back into practice. He had, however, instructed Suther, in January 1819, to destroy buildings' timbers and not leave them in the possession of the people in order to prevent them from returning and resettling the community.[3] Possibly frustrated by the people's recalcitrance, Suther had obviously taken the most expedient method of carrying out the instruction.

On 3rd June 1819 Loch wrote to Suther congratulating him on the completion of the removals.

> *Your letter of the 25th ... I have received this morning and it gave me great pleasure to find that your removals were so satisfactorily completed at last. Your explanation that the burning of the timbers was more necessary than I expected and therefore cannot be helped how much I could have wished it otherwise.*[4]

Eric Richards in his account of the Highland clearances relates a statement made by one of the clearing officers, J. Campbell of Lairg, regarding his involvement in the clearances at Aberscross in Strathfleet. Campbell recollected that three crofters resided near the Mound Wood. 'The wife of one of them named Mcdonald, was about to give birth to a child'. The factor, along with half a dozen servants, went to burn down the houses:

> They burned the rest of them; and this crofter's was the last. He pleaded hard to be left in the house till his wife was well. The factor did not heed him, but ordered the house to be burned over him. The crofter was in the house, determined not to quit until the fire compelled him. The factor told us the plan we were to take – namely, to cut the rafters and then set fire to the thatch. This we did, but I shall never forget the sight. The man, seeing it was now no use to persist, wrapt his wife in the blankets and brought her out. For two nights did that woman sleep in a sheep cot, and on the third she gave birth to a son. That son, I believe, still lives, and is in America. That is only one instance. I could give many more did space permit.[5]

The victims in this case were William MacDonald and his wife noted in Loch's list of removals. They subsequently went with their seven children to Dornoch moor where the reception lots were described as improvable muir-lands but considered by most to be impossible to drain and inappropriate for cultivation.

John Campbell, of unmarried status in the removal list, was almost twenty one years old. John Campbell Sr, his wife and siblings were not on the list having left Wester Aberscross, possibly to settle at Dornoch, before the 1819 clearance. Young John held out until the bitter end. The reference to his whereabouts being unknown implies that he had decided to seek a new life. He had not accepted the offer to take up one of the small plots on the muir-lands or on coastal land with its attachment to the fishing and kelping industries. He was intent on improving his skills as a farmer and carpenter, and he would be his own man. Despite the recent trauma, in his mind's eye the future looked bright.

Notes to Chapter 3

1. NLS, Sutherland Papers, Dep. 313/1015, p.65.
2. Ibid., Dep. 313/1146, Letter from Loch to Lady Stafford, 16 January 1819.
3. Ibid., Dep.313/1139, Letter from Loch to Suther, 14 January 1819 (wrongly dated 14 June 1819).
4. Ibid., Dep.313/1139, Letter from Loch to Suther, 3 June 1819.
5. Eric Richards, *The Highland Clearances*, pp. 209-210, Birlinn, 2008.

Chapter 4

The Voyage

As the ship *Greenock* moved out of Leith Roads into the Firth of Forth, John Campbell must have felt a mixture of emotions; a pang of sadness at leaving his homeland contrasting with the excitement of embarking on an adventure and the start of a new life in a strange and distant land. It was the 3rd of May 1823 and John, with 61 other passengers, was on board the first ship of The Australian Company of Edinburgh and Leith to make passage to Van Diemen's Land and New South Wales. He had taken advantage of the requirements for skilled artisans in the colony and had most likely secured steerage passage as a bonded carpenter or farm worker.

It had, no doubt, not escaped John Campbell's notice that in Scotland the increased availability of education in English and better opportunities for young people with a knowledge of the English language, combined with the influx of southerners, meant that old customs, the former way of living and the Gaelic language were in decline. Internationally, the American War of Independence, the French Revolution and Napoleonic Wars heralded the rise of the common man. Social change was evolving all over Britain.

The first three decades of the nineteenth century were years of turmoil economically, socially and politically. At the end of the Napoleonic Wars in 1815, the introduction of the Corn Laws and revisions to the Poor Laws, designed to safeguard the wealth of the landed gentry, resulted in the poor being even more impoverished and degraded. Discharged sailors and soldiers could find no work. Artisans and workers seeking relief from high prices and low wages attempted to form unions. By the 1820s the prospect of emigration to a new land was becoming very attractive.

During the intervening years since the Campbells had been cleared from Aberscross, John had made his way to Dornoch and Edinburgh working at odd jobs, but mainly increasing his knowledge and skill as a carpenter to gain employment. Finding work was not an easy task. Although the national wealth of the country and the prosperity of most of the people were increasing steadily, the unprecedented growth of the economy made it susceptible to cycles of speculative booms and severe depressions. Since the end of the Napoleonic Wars, there had been periodic depressions initially resulting from the loss of markets for an overexpanded manufacturing capacity stimulated by wartime demands. New markets were required not only for the country's products but to maintain its shipping industry and investment interests. Population movement from rural areas to industrial centres provided a workforce but also created huge unemployment problems during times of commercial depression. Fluctuations in agricultural prices, high rents, and the scarcity of new farmland added to economic uncertainty in rural areas. All these pressures combined to channel the flow of emigration, trade and investment into new areas including Australia.[1]

Canada, for settlement, and the West Indies and Cape of Good Hope, for commercial interests, had been the destination of most Scottish emigrants since the end of the American Revolutionary War. At the beginning of the nineteenth century, Upper and Lower Canada and Nova Scotia were the preferred destination for emigrants with regular sailings from the Clyde to North America beginning as early as 1818. Public interest in Australia had increased steadily following reports in the Scots Magazine on the flourishing state of the colony and by 1822 the first important phase of Scottish emigration to Australia had begun. In June 1822 the Scots Magazine published an article entitled 'Van Diemen's Land: View of the present state of the settlement with the prospects held out by it to British emigrants'. Considering the commercial distress and lack of available agricultural land in Scotland at the time, the article was influential in encouraging emigration. Van Diemen's Land was reported to be the favoured resort of the emigrant in preference to New South Wales owing to its climate, fertility, mineral wealth and prospects for securing land. Furthermore the convict stigma attached to New South Wales and the remoteness and wildness of its grazing lands presented a less attractive venue for the respectable settler.[2]

In 1822 a book, designed as a handbook for people intending to emigrate to Australia, was published in Edinburgh. The fact that the work received favourable notices in the journals and newspapers indicates that it became well known over a broad spectrum of the population. Its author was James Dixon who in 1820 had commanded the ship *Skelton* on its voyage from Scotland to Australia with a large contingent of Scots emigrants. In his laboriously entitled 'Narrative of a Voyage to New South Wales and Van Diemen's Land in the ship "Skelton" during the year 1820, with Observations on the state of these colonies, and a variety of information calculated to be useful to Emigrants' he asserts 'If a man can live at home, let him do so. If he must emigrate, Australia is the best quarter he can choose.' Dixon had remained in Van Diemen's Land for six weeks before continuing on in the *Skelton* to Sydney, where he spent five months. He gave a lengthy, detailed and favourable account of the interior as far west as Bathurst and emphasised the great future which he believed the wool industry would have.[3]

The pressure of local conditions in certain parts of Scotland, the inducements of land and labour offered by the authorities, articles and reviews in quarterly magazines, glowing reports in newspapers, and publications such as Dixon's 'Narrative', all combined to swing part of the tide of Scottish emigration towards Australia. Notices portraying New South Wales and Van Diemen's Land in a favourable light and featuring the improving prospects for wool growers were published in the Edinburgh Evening Courant, the most widely read of the capital's newspapers. Centred mainly in Edinburgh and Leith, the Australian trade not only provided the opportunity for farmers, merchants and professionals to emigrate but also for artisans and mechanics to pursue their occupations in the Australian colonies. Between 1819 and 1822, two hundred and thirty three applications were received by the Colonial Office.[4]

Under these prevailing circumstances, the Australian Company of Edinburgh and Leith was formed by a group of Edinburgh and Leith business men, principally the same men who had founded the Commercial Bank of Scotland in 1810. The company was designed as a trading concern as well as a shipping company and its prospectus emphasised both emigration and the potentialities of the colonial market. It recommended the system of emigrant colonization which appeared to be 'the simplest and most efficacious plan of relieving the inconveniences occasioned by a redundant population, and which has, at the same time, an effect of creating employment for labour and capital, by opening new channels for disposing of manufactures and engaging in commerce'.[5] Paid up capital in the initial offering of the company was 1 million pound sterling consisting of 10,000 shares at £100 each. The response of the local investors to the prospectus was immediate and enthusiastic and within two weeks about a third of the capital had been subscribed.[6]

On 29 November 1822 an article in the Edinburgh Advertiser reported:

> AUSTRALIAN COMPANY.
>
> A PUBLIC JOINT STOCK COMPANY, under the designation of the AUSTRALIAN COMPANY, has been recently formed in this metropolis, for the purpose of facilitating the Trade and Maritime Conveyance between this COUNTRY and AUSTRALIA, comprehending New South Wales, Van Diemen's Land, and other Islands, under the jurisdiction of the Governor of New South Wales.
> Australia is universally acknowledged to possess superior inducements for its colonization by British subjects. The most obvious attractions are:—The very small number, and inoffensive disposition of the aboriginal inhabitants—the healthiness of the climate—the capabilities of the soil for the easy production of the necessaries and luxuries of Life—the abundance of coal and most valuable minerals—and the suitableness of its rivers and harbours for commerce.
> The want of a regular and secure means of conveyance between the mother country and these settlements, has hitherto operated as a great obstacle to the advantageous intercourse which would

otherwise have existed. The difficulties of communication being removed, and a wide field to British enterprise laid open, by the institution of the present Company, and the complete security afforded that due precaution shall be taken to insure the comfort of passengers, and safety of property intrusted to the care of the company, great national advantage, it is confidently contemplated, shall result from this Establishment.

The Company's Office, Bridge Street, LEITH, will be opened in a few days meantime, reference for farther information is made to Mr. WILLIAM ALEXANDER, writer to the signet, the law agent for the Company, at whose Chambers, No. 6, Elder Street, printed copies of the prospectus may be procured.

Edinburgh November 29, 1822[7]

The lack of skilled craftsmen, a serious impediment to colonial development at the time, inspired the company to set up registries in Leith and Hobart where both prospective employers and intending emigrants could enrol, thus launching the first workable scheme where indentured or bonded artisans could obtain steerage passage.[8]

For its purposes, the company required ships large enough to carry sufficient cargo and passengers to make the voyages profitable but small enough to be easily loaded and unloaded at Leith and the less than satisfactory wharfs at Australian ports. The company's aim was to provide four regular traders to Hobart and Sydney each year.

The company's first ship, the *Greenock*, a vessel of 442 tons with two decks and quarter galleries, had been built in 1818. It was purchased from John Scott and Sons, an important shipbuilding and shipowning firm in Greenock. According to Lloyd's Register of 1823, the *Greenock*, surveyed in April of that year, was a First Class vessel constructed of first quality material and sheathed in copper. She carried proved iron cables and drew 17 feet of water when fully loaded. A second ship, the Triton (405 tons) was purchased from the same firm and a third ship the *Portland* (385 tons) was purchased in the summer of 1823. The fourth and largest ship, the *City of Edinburgh* (454 tons) was built in Leith in 1824. Initial investment for the four ships is estimated to have been about £25,000.[9]

The *Greenock's* first voyage to New South Wales and Van Diemen's land was advertised in the Edinburgh Evening Courant on 23rd December 1822. The sailing was scheduled for about the 1st of February 1823 from Leith. A commander had not yet been selected.

> FOR NEW SOUTH WALES AND
> VAN DIEMEN'S LAND,
> *The Australian Company's Ship*
> GREENOCK,
> — — - , Commander,
> *To sail from Leith about 1st February*
> The Greenock is a fine Vessel, three years old, and 442 tons register; has a large and convenient Cabin, and is seven feet between decks, which will be neatly fitted up for the steerage; will have a Supercargo and Surgeon on board.
> For freight or passage, apply at the Company's Offices here.
> R. BROWN, Manager.
> BRIDGE STREET, LEITH,
> Dec. 17, 1822.[10]

However, the forecast departure date was not realised, possibly due to the difficulty in engaging a captain and in February 1823 the *Greenock* was advertised as about to sail on the first of April. The advertisement in the Edinburgh Advertiser on 21 February stated:

> FOR VAN DIEMAN'S LAND, AND
> NEW SOUTH WALES,
> To call at the Cape of Good Hope.
> The Australian Company's Ship
> GREENOCK
> Joshua Richmond, Commander
> To Sail about the 1st of April
> The Greenock is a fine ship, of 442
> tons register, three years old, and fitted up in a most

convenient and commodious style for Cabin
and steerage passengers.
She will carry a Supercargo and Surgeon
For freight or passage apply at the Company's
Office here; to Messrs. FLEMING and HOPE, Glasgow; and to JOHN HOLMES and Co. Greenock.
ROBERT BROWN, Junr.
LEITH, 15th Feb. 1823[11]

By 5 March her cargo had been fully engaged and there was only room for a few more passengers.[12] Further notices stipulated that four joiners, two masons, two bricklayers and two blacksmiths were required for Van Diemen's Land and New South Wales[13] to supplement the mechanics, tradesmen and farm workers already contracted to go out on the vessel. Normal fares were fifty guineas for cabin passengers and twenty four pounds for steerage passengers, but free passage was offered to indentured or bonded artisans.[14]

There was further delay, possibly due to the difficulty in securing the required complement of emigrants or goods, supported by the fact that Robert Brown did not enter the ship in the Leith Register of Shipping until the 23rd of March. Furthermore the ship was not surveyed until sometime in April. On the 12th of April the Caledonian Mercury reported:

> Emigration – We have lately had an opportunity of inspecting the ship Greenock, Captain Richmond, which we understand, will soon proceed to Australia, being the first belonging to the Australian Company. We shall venture to say, that a more complete or finer ship never sailed from the port of Leith, nor one in which elegance, convenience, and comfort for passengers have been more anxiously studied by those under whose management and direction she has been fitted out. This company appear to have been peculiarly fortunate, not only in their purchase of this beautiful ship, but also in the choice of Captain Richmond, whose polite and accommodating manners, added to his well-known

professional knowledge, particularly qualify him for his situation. It is with pleasure we learn, that this vessel goes out a bumper ship with goods and passengers. We trust that the trade of Leith will derive much benefit from the public spirited exertions of the many highly respectable individuals of whom this Company is composed.[15]

Finally on 3rd May 1823 the *Greenock* cleared out from Leith[16] for Cape of Good Hope, Van Diemen's Land and New South Wales under the command of Joshua Richmond with 62 passengers on board, and a cargo including cows and bulls. Among the passengers were John Wyld the company's agent for Van Diemen's Land (nephew of James Wyld, one of the principals of the Australian Company) and Alexander Warren agent for New South Wales.[17] The appointment of Wyld as the agent for Van Diemen's Land emphasised its importance to the company's operations. Also on board were John Campbell, and significantly John Tyre, who kept a journal of the voyage, a copy of which resides in the Mitchell Library in Sydney, Australia.[18]

The Australian Company's ships were run along lines similar to those of more superior merchant vessels like the East and West Indiamen or the Western Ocean packets. Their Captains were designated 'Commanders' and the ships carried surgeons and were armed, if only moderately. The conditions for steerage passengers were remarkably good. Curtained births were provided, passengers were allowed access to the quarter deck and the allowance of provisions was generous and included sugar, butter and spirits. Fresh provisions purchased at the Cape of Good Hope meant the passengers did not suffer for the lack of food during the whole voyage. Supplies of wines and spirits could be purchased from a steward assigned to serve the steerage passengers. In spite of tensions which could develop on long voyages, relations between passengers and the ship's officers were good and it appears that cabin passengers and steerage passengers associated freely and both were allowed to go ashore at ports of call. Both passengers and crew attended religious services, held each Sunday.[19]

Leaving Leith, the *Greenock* cleared Leith Roads on the 4th of May, sailed out of the Firth of Forth into the North Sea and south-southeast along the east coast of Scotland and England. Unfortunately the first few days of Tyre's journal are illegible in the microfilm copy but by the afternoon of the 7th of May the ship was off the coast at Sunderland in a fair breeze from the west and making four miles per hour.[20] Views of the river Tyne and a vast array of collier ships had been seen early in the morning. At 11 o'clock a howling scream startled the passengers and they came running to see a mastiff dog strangling a little pig. The captain was quickly on the scene and, fastening a stone around the transgressor's neck with a rope, threw the dog overboard.

The next day a sudden squall with gale force winds knocked the vessel over on her side sending chests and dishes tumbling. A distant view of Yorkshire, described as a barren and mountainous country, was followed by a most beautiful view of Scarborough Castle perched on a hill almost surrounded by sea. To the south lay Scarborough town, its tall roofed houses prominently displayed. The rocky shore of Flamborough Head was also passed that day and Bridlington town and Bay. Vast quantities of wild ducks skimmed the surface of the sea, adjusting their elevation to the rise and fall of the waves. About mid day, a London Steamer passed the *Greenock* and the passengers hailed it with three cheers, their salute obligingly returned by the occupants of the steamer.

Overnight the breeze freshened and the ship made great speed at about 8 knots per hour. Little did John Campbell realise that he was sailing past the home country of his future wife. About mid morning the ship was off Yarmouth Roads and stood well out to sea to avoid the dangerous, shifting sandbanks near the coast, allowing only a distant view of Nelson's monument and Yarmouth Harbour with its many vessels.

Over the next seven days progress was slow in an almost constant headwind as the *Greenock* struggled into the Strait of Dover. The ship stood well out from shore affording only glimpses of the coast of England. During this time a passenger asked a widow named Mary why she had chosen to leave her native country. She replied *'Indeed, sir, to tell the truth, its because the tea is cheap and ye ken yourself auld* wives is very fond of a dish of tea'. On Sunday the Reverend Mr Ross 'made exercise in the morning and in the afternoon'.

On the 16th of May a distinct view of the coast of France could be seen to the south and the beautiful town of Calais with its church steeples, towers and substantial buildings. The pleasant view of the coast, however, was clouded by the remembrance of the *'late bloody and warlike plains of France'* and their deceased Emperor Bonaparte who had looked with vexation towards England's territories from this very point of land, the 21 miles of sea between the two countries thwarting his ambitions.

At 3 o'clock next morning anchor was dropped in the Downs off the town of Deal amongst approximately 140 other ships lying along the coast, waiting for favourable winds to take them into the English Channel. Deal lies on the Channel eight miles north-east of Dover and proximal to the notorious Goodwin Sands. The water between the town and the sands, provided a naturally sheltered anchorage which may have helped the passengers to get their 'sea-legs' in preparation for their long and arduous voyage. Despite the absence of a harbour the town was a significant shipping and military port with goods and people transited from ship to shore in small tender craft. Strongly built batteries pointing towards France were observed along the coast as well as a barracks hospital and Kings Stores.

Anchor was weighed at nine o'clock in the morning of the 17th and in a fair breeze under sunny skies the ship sailed off with more than 100 other sails. On the deep blue sea, against a background of white chalk cliffs, blue sky and billowing white clouds, the view presented the most beautiful sight many of the passengers had ever seen. By 11 o'clock Dover Castle and town were passed; by seven o'clock that evening they were off the prominent white cliff at Beachy Head.

On Monday 19th of May the ship dropped anchor in Spithead, between Portsmouth and Ryde on the Isle of Wight, to take on fresh water, ballast and provisions. Its arrival, from the Downs under Captain Richmond, was reported in the London Morning Post of the 21st of May.[21] The town of Ryde, could be seen, beautifully situated on higher ground on the coast, surrounded by glens and woods decked in their summer attire. At 8 o'clock in the morning the next day, 18 passengers, John Tyre amongst them, went ashore in a small boat and visited the harbour and suburbs of Portsmouth, the shipping docks and hulks. They returned to the *Greenock* at 7 pm.

The ship remained at anchor, taking on provisions and was finally ready to sail on the 25th of May. However, at roll call two passengers, James Hunter, a mason and Alexander Robertson were missing. Robertson, formerly a sailor, was well educated and was going out as a clerk. Apparently he was a 'bit of a lad' and having spent all his money in Portsmouth, had received credit by pawning some of his personal belongings. The men did not return to the ship and their sea chests were sealed with black wax.

There were other reasons, unknown to our eye witness, why Robertson did not return to the ship. He apparently made his way back to his father's house at Pathead, Scotland arriving about the end of August or beginning of September and on 28th September 1823 married Ann Reid at Dundee. Robertson had become acquainted with Reid in 1822. On 12th March 1824 his wife gave birth to a fully developed male child which became the focus of an action for maintenance at the insistence of the mother, with Robertson's concurrence, against the alleged father David Jobson. The case was found in favour of the mother but there remained some question as to when Robertson had actually returned home.[22]

Back in Portsmouth the *Greenock* was prepared to sail. But, tragically, on the 26th of May at 2 o'clock in the morning John MacKeracher, a child of Mr and Mrs Malcolm MacKeracher, died. Later that morning, there being no wind to commence the voyage, the child's father and seven passengers conveyed the boy's body in a small boat to Portsmouth for burial. The parents, although grief stricken, were relieved that their little son had been buried on land rather than '*on the restless ocean*'. Finally, at 4 o'clock in the afternoon of 27th May 1823, the ship weighed anchor and set sail. Another ship carrying two hundred convicts bound for Sydney departed at the same time. The convict ship was soon left behind, to the relief of the passengers who had heard that the worst characters, so far transported that year, were on board.

Water and other rations were commenced next day with the expectation that if the allowances were adhered to the whole voyage would be very comfortable. Land was out of sight shortly after midday. The weather had started to warm considerably and everyone put on the lightest clothing possible. To the bemusement of the passengers a young sailor was given eight lashes for disobedience, the punishment seeming to be more a reprimand than real punishment. They were soon out of the English Channel and on the 31st sailing past the mouth of the Bay of Biscay at 9 miles per hour.

The 1st of June brought some excitement and anxiety. About 6 pm, passengers strolling on the deck noticed a brig making course directly for the *Greenock* on her larboard (port) side. The brig shifted its sails continuously until it had fallen in directly behind. It then hoisted more sail to catch up. Swinging to the starboard side for further observation, it slid behind and continued to follow in a '*lurking*' fashion. Suspicion was aroused that she was a pirate.

As it was Sunday all on board were called to public worship and about 10 am the service commenced. But before Reverend Ross could conclude his sermon, a loud report from a large gun on the brig followed by a second loaded shot alarmed the worshipers. Mr Ross concluded his sermon immediately and retired to his cabin. All passengers were startled into action. The Captain using his spyglass determined the brig to be French built but flying the Spanish flag. She had about 60 men on board. Richmond then ordered the ship's two large guns to be made ready for action and all firearms, cutlasses and swords brought forward. Within 10 minutes all able bodied passengers and sailors were on deck, armed and ready to do battle. About 40 persons armed themselves with muskets and the rest carried pistols or swords. One of the passengers, a former sergeant, carried out drill exercises with those who had muskets in preparation for an anticipated attack from the brig. The *Greenock* took on a daring and warlike appearance. With firm resolution and steadfast determination the brave Scotsmen '*stood forward with undaunted courage to shew that Scots Sons had a spirit of boldness to fight their way whether on land or sea*'.

The brig came up fast under full sail until she was within half a mile astern. Then, suddenly, she reefed in her sails and retreated to everyone's astonishment and relief. Three cheers were given and the captain proclaimed that they were afraid to come closer when they smelled the oatmeal cakes and knew their quarry was from a brave land. There was still some consternation that she would return under cover of darkness. A sharp lookout was kept all night. By 10 o'clock the next morning they were well clear of danger. However, as a precaution, all passengers were summoned to the quarter deck at 11 am to attend drill practise scheduled for one hour each day during the fortnight.

The ship continued in fair wind and weather, sailing at 8 or 9 miles per hour. For some time another brig followed her but without incident. On the 7th of June in the morning Madeira was sighted rising like black clouds from the sea, its white houses bold against the dark background. As the ship sailed southwest the temperature continued to increase and the Surgeon ordered the passengers to take their beds on deck as often as possible for the sake of their health. Fine wind and weather continued. Groups of flying fish were observed, about 30 yards from the ship, leaping from the ocean to soar with rapid beating wings at a height of 10 to 20 feet above the surface of the water.

The Tropic of Cancer was crossed on the 12th of June in the company of a ship to the starboard and a brig to the larboard, both directly abeam of the Greenock. Subsequently the vessel's course was shifted from southwest to south to pass within view of the Cape Verde Islands allowing the Captain and Mate to determine the accuracy of their navigational calculations. A group of bottle nosed porpoises cavorted in front of the bow as the ship sailed along at 7 knots. In the evening on the 18th of June, the anniversary of the Battle of Waterloo was celebrated *'with mirth and a flowing glass'*. Fair wind and weather continued. But with heavy showers and squalls gradually becoming more frequent, the wind eventually shifted unfavourably ahead. At one point a brig steering the same course as the *Greenock* approached to within 200 yards. Suddenly a squall came up and she disappeared out of view.

An English brig, the Luna, bound for Rio de Janeiro, South America, came up close alongside on the 27th of June and was given latitude and longitude coordinates to check navigational calculations.

With the wind still ahead little progress was being made and opportunity was taken to catch a dolphin and a bonito. A week later the wind was still ahead. The passengers complained that they had nothing to amuse themselves with other than catching fish. Finally on the 4th of July the South East Trade Wind kicked in and the ship began to make progress again. Fishing continued and more bonitos were caught, their number around the ship resembling shoals of herring.

At 10 o'clock on Wednesday the 9th of July 1823, the Greenock crossed the equator in fair weather and a fine fresh southeast breeze. At 8 o'clock in the evening the crew and passengers were hailed by Neptune in a loud voice from the bow calling 'Ship Ahoy'. The Captain answered him in a booming voice through his speaking trumpet. Together they proceeded with a long ceremonial discourse, after which a tar barrel was set alight and tossed overboard. This signalled Neptune's departure declaring that he would be back on board tomorrow to see his children. The next morning all the sailors were up at 4 o'clock making preparations for Neptune's return. A sign was hung up over the entrance that led to Neptune's shaving stool:

ANTONIO KADUZAR BARBER
X FROM AFRICA X
Superintending to NEPTUNE

The sign attracted much attention from the passengers and the sailors spent a pleasant day being shaved.

Over the next two weeks the southeast winds continued to blow; the weather remained fine with occasional showers and squalls; sermons were preached on the Quarter Deck on Sundays; fish were still being caught; the odd brig was sighted and work continued as usual.

On the 22nd of July the wind shifted more favourably to the east and the ship reached 6 miles per hour. The weather becoming cooler, the passengers were forced to put on their shoes and stockings. Everyone was in good health and the passengers stayed up past their usual bedtime of 9 o'clock to see the full moon and the eclipse, which totally obscured the moon about 12:30 am. Fortunately it was a clear night allowing a full view of the whole astronomical event. The ship was at 13.5 degrees south latitude and closing on the coast of South America. Depth soundings were taken frequently. When 30 fathoms was recorded on the evening of the 25th course was shifted to the south to direct the ship away from land. At 1 degree off the Brazilian fishing village of Caravelas, it was in danger of running aground on the cluster of coral islands and shoals of the Abrolhos Archipelago.

With wind continuing from the southeast and ahead, progress was slower over the next few days. The weather and seas became rougher and the wind whistled through the rigging. A large whale about 25 feet long was sighted and a shark, about 6 feet long (estimated to be 2 years old) was caught.

At midday on the 2nd of August, with a favourable wind from the east-northeast, the ship crossed the Tropic of Capricorn. The next day being Sunday, the minister delivered his sermon between decks due to heavy foaming seas washing over the ship. A week later no sermon was given, the ship heaving in a heavy swell. In winds from the northeast, north and west the ship made good progress with speeds of up to nine and a half miles per hour although the seas were variable, one day being calm with a heavy swell, the next rough and confused. The weather also was very changeable alternating frequently from clear skies to clouds, rain and storms. The temperature was getting colder. A water spout, rising up to the clouds, appeared straight ahead of the ship on the morning of the 12th of August and course was altered to avoid it. Position was recorded at 32 degrees South; 24 degrees West.

The voyage continued much the same for the next three weeks with the wind improving steadily, except for the occasional calm day or day of head wind. The course now was east-southeast and speeds of up to 10 knots per hour were achieved. Reverend Ross was flung across the vessel while giving Tuesday prayers when the ship suddenly rolled and the lights went out. He immediately stopped singing and concluded the meeting with a short prayer. By the 24th of August the ship was at 36 degrees; 33 minutes South and 0 degrees; 40 minutes West. All on board were in good health and on calm days both cabin and steerage passengers took exercise around the vessel. On the 27th the wind and sea being quite calm, seven passengers, the first mate and two hands, each with a gun, took the jolly boat to shoot fowl that had been flying about the ship. They returned with 7 Cape pigeons. In the afternoon they bagged another two birds.

The crew began preparing the boat for the Cape of Good Hope and on the 1st of September land was sighted straight ahead to the great joy of the passengers. Coming up towards the land from the southwest, not knowing exactly where they were, they passed the Cape of Good Hope and sailed across the mouth of Simons Bay (False Bay). Turning westward the ship stayed close upon the land during the day until they sighted Table Mountain. They then made for Table Bay, hauling up close to the wind to do so and in the afternoon of Thursday, 4th of September, cast anchor.

About an hour later, the Inspecting Surgeon for the Colony came on board to see if there were any sick before granting liberty to go ashore. The next morning the ship was towed nearer to the shore and after breakfast the Captain and a few cabin passengers went onshore to Cape Town. On Saturday, the 6th of September, a party of passengers including John Tyre went ashore. Tyre and two companions walked to Simon's Town, a distance of about 22 miles, the first 8 miles of their journey taking them through pleasant vineyards. Returning to Cape Town on Sunday they were unable to get back to the ship, the wind blowing so hard it prevented them from leaving the land. As they sat resting, three of the *Greenock's* passengers came by with a local Scotsman who invited them all to his home for dinner. He gave them as much wine as they could drink and although he had no accommodation for his guests, showed them where they could get good lodgings.

Prospects for returning to the ship were no better the next day as the wind blew stronger than the day before. The 'Table Cloth', the white cloud that spills over Table Mountain, hung heavy on the mountain. They spent the day travelling around the harbour and had a pleasant walk through the plantation leading to the Governor's House.

Originally established by the Jan Van Riebeek and Dutch settlers in 1652 to supply Dutch trading ships with fresh fruit and vegetables on their voyages to and from the East Indies, the Company's Gardens were later extended in the direction of Table Mountain and a zoo established at the top end of the extension. Following the British annexation of the Cape in 1806, the gardens were re-established as The Governor of Cape Town's gardens and the southern entrance to the zoo, the 'Lion Gateway', was built. Government House, built by the Dutch in 1700, was renovated and enlarged numerous times including a complete makeover to Georgian style by the British who extended the building on both sides. Now known as De Tuynhus (The Garden House) it is used as the Cape Town office of the Presidency of the Republic of South Africa. In 1823 the Governor was Lord Charles Somerset.

Continuing on, our intrepid travellers saw three young lions, an old lion, a jackal, a tiger, two land turtles and some large African fowls at the zoo. Passing through more rich vineyards, and orchards of oranges, lemons and other fruits, they came upon a spring from which they drank heartily and with relish, the water tasting as good as wine. The vineyards and spring were part of Oranjezicht Farmstead owned by the Van Breda family. Several springs and the Stadtsfontein (City Fountain) were located on the Oranjezicht Farm (now Homestead Park) which extended from the Gardens to the base of Table Mountain.

On returning to town they again met up with the Scotsman, now considered to be an old friend. He once again provided them with their dinner, tea and as much wine as they could drink. After a cheerful, happy evening they retired to their lodgings.

They were back on board Tuesday morning having hired a boat about 7 am. The wind had settled and the cloud was almost gone from the top of the mountain. About midday they spotted a whale blowing and in an instant two whale boats came out from the port to catch it. The boats followed the whale for some time, carefully watching its movements. Then one of the boats launched its harpoon. Blood gushed from the whale and it made out to sea dragging the boat behind it, leaving a trailing wake of red foaming water. On Wednesday they heard that the whale had been taken.

The ship was in great confusion with casks and packages lying on deck, goods taken out of the hold to send ashore and livestock, vegetables and casks of fresh water brought on board. The only other ship in the bay was the *Jupiter*. Bound for New South Wales it carried the wives of the Radicals who had been transported to Australia on the ship Speke for their part in the uprising at Bonnymuir near Glasgow in 1820.

The Radical War or Scottish Insurrection of 1820, resulted from Radical demands for reform in the United Kingdom of Great Britain and Ireland beginning in the early years of the French Revolution. Repressed during the long Napoleonic Wars, artisans, particularly weavers in Scotland, again sought reform after the wars. Their actions, regarded as revolutionary by an unsympathetic government, culminated in a week of strikes, unrest and inevitably, on the 4th of April, armed conflict at Bonnymuir. The leaders James Wilson, Andrew Hardie and John Baird were executed. Nineteen accomplices were transported for life to the penal colony of New South Wales but in August 1835 they were granted absolute pardon.

Confusion continued on the Greenock over the next week. The ship was towed nearer to Cape Town and more casks of fresh water, sheep, pigs, beef, mutton and other fresh provisions taken on board. On Thursday the 18th several passengers went ashore for the African Club Races, a vast crowd of people, carriages and gentlemen on horseback assembling at 2 o'clock for the first of four races. The first race, a two horse affair, run over two and three quarter miles, had a winner's bet of 1000 Rex Dollars (£100 sterling).

The horses were swift and well matched. Neck to neck near the end of the race, the riders applied their whips without spare, Lord Somerset's horse winning by half a head. The remaining races were not nearly as exciting or well contested. A few of the passengers remained on land and walked to the foot of Table Mountain the next morning returning to the ship in the afternoon.

Finally on Tuesday the 23rd the ship was ready for the final leg of John Campbell's voyage. The chain cable was shortened, the signal flag hoisted and three shots fired from one of the large guns to let everyone know that departure was imminent. Three new passengers (two cabin and one steerage) from Cape Town joined the voyage.

Early the next morning the anchor was weighed, the sails unfurled, the flag hoisted and the Greenock was on its way to Van Diemen's Land in a moderate breeze.

However, the wind quickly became unfavourable blowing ahead. It took four days to reach the entrance to Table Bay, finally clearing the land on the 29th of September. Constant fair winds, under cloudy skies with occasional showers, propelled them into the southern Indian Ocean at a rate of about 5 knots per hour. More whales were sighted and 6 albatross, each slightly smaller than a goose but with a much larger wingspan of about 10 feet, were caught with a hook and line off the stern of the ship. The weather was cold at 39 degrees south latitude and the ship was making good progress running due east.

All was not smooth sailing. For three days the wind was so strong and violent that only three sails were kept up in *'seas mountainous and foaming along with tremendous fury, wave after wave lashing against our ship and the low howling wind making a terrific noise whistling through the blocks'*. At times the ship was allowed to drift. Conditions improved for awhile and a south-easterly course at 7 knots was maintained, but worsened again. In strong wind from the southeast, the captain was forced to keep the ship on short sail, hard upon the wind.

The passengers were uneasy and no doubt seasick from the constant rolling and pitching of the ship as she alternately drifted on the huge swells or sailed hard into the wind. Cloudy skies prevailed with only the occasional bright spell. Then the wind abated and for several days blew from the west and west-southwest, ship speed varying from 1 to 5 knots. By the 21st of October the ship was sailing southeast in a good westerly breeze at 9 to 11 knots in the vicinity of 40 degrees South and 47 degrees East.

Over the next three weeks the westerlies remained favourable, except for the odd day of head wind, as the ship sailed east at 40 degrees south latitude. The weather was cold, the skies remained cloudy with frequent rain showers and visibility was poor. About halfway between Africa and Australia, the ship passed to the south of the Islands of St Paul and Amsterdam. Unseen in the cloudy conditions, the only evidence of their existence were large accumulations of seaweed.

Clear skies and warm sunshine were received with relief on the 10th of November at 42 degrees 50 minutes South latitude; 112 degrees East longitude. Under continued fine weather the crew busied themselves painting and tarring the vessel and on the Thursday 20th of November land was sighted ahead. On Friday the Greenock sailed into the mouth of the Derwent River and at about three o'clock dropped anchor close in on the town of Hobart.

The passengers were relieved to see a fine looking country and a town with a good number of houses, but were disconcerted about the amount of forest covering the countryside around the town. Realisation gradually dawned revealing that some of the books, newspaper articles and advertisements they had read about Van Diemen's Land were not entirely factual. The diversified landscape of gentle hills, expansive plains and lush valleys described in the promotional literature was not evident at first inspection. The extensive grasslands of the interior were nowhere to be seen.

Although pleasant enough, the place appeared undeveloped and very basic. After a voyage of almost 7 months, they were relieved to be finally at their destination, but overwhelmed by a feeling of isolation at the end of the earth. A few of the cabin passengers went ashore that day including John Wyld and Alexander Warren, agents for the Australian Company. The next day all passengers disembarked. It was Saturday the 22nd of November 1823. John Campbell had arrived in Australia.

Notes to Chapter 4

1. David S. MacMillan, *Scotland and Australia 1788 – 1850: emigration, commerce and investment*, pp14-15, 24, Clarendon, Oxford, 1967.
2. Ibid., p.45.
3. Ibid., pp.50-52.
4. Ibid., pp.55-58.
5. Ibid., pp.152-153.
6. Ibid., p.160.
7. *Australian Company*, The Edinburgh Advertiser, Friday, November 29, 1822, p.1, col. 4.

8. D. MacMillan, 'Scottish Enterprise in Australia, 1798-1879', *Studies in Scottish Business History,* Peter L. Payne (ed.), Cass &Co., London, 1967, p. 330.
9. MacMillan, *Scotland and Australia 1788 – 1850,* pp.170-171.
10. *For New South Wales and Van Diemen's Land,* Edinburgh Evening Courant (EEC), Monday, December 23, 1822.
11. *For New South Wales and Van Diemen's Land,* The Edinburgh Advertiser, Friday, February 21, 1823, p.119, col. 4.
12. *For New South Wales and Van Diemen's Land,* EEC, Thursday, March 6, 1823.
13. *For New South Wales and Van Diemen's Land,* EEC, Thursday, March 6 and Thursday, March 13, 1823.
14. MacMillan, *Scotland and Australia 1788 – 1850,* p.170 and footnote 5, p.170.
15. *Emigration,* Caledonian Mercury (CM), Edinburgh, Saturday, April 12, 1823, p.3, col.3.
16. *Leith Shipping,* CM, Edinburgh, Monday, May 5, 1823, p.3, col.4.
17. Ian H. Nicholson, *Shipping Arrivals and Departures, Tasmania Vol.1, 1803 to 1833,* Roebuck, 1989, p.92.
18. Journal of John Tyre, Mitchell Library, B806 CY reel 1256.
19. MacMillan, *Scotland and Australia 1788 – 1850,* p.219-222.
20. Most of the description of the voyage is paraphrased from Tyre's journal.
21. Ship News, London Morning Post, 21 May 1823.
22. The Scottish Jurist, Vol. IV, 1832, pp.465-467, Anderson, Edinburgh, 1832.

Chapter 5

Hobart 1823 -1829

Hobart was abuzz. The arrival of a ship load of goods in a community often lacking necessary materials, not to mention luxury goods, was indeed an event. Equally the arrival of sixty two new free settlers in the community of about 3,400[1] people was cause for excitement. The Hobart Town Gazette and Van Diemen's Land Advertiser of Saturday, 22nd November 1823 announced in the shipping news:

> Arrived yesterday from Leith, touching at the Cape of Good Hope on her passage, the Australian Company's ship Greenock, Captain Richmond.

and reported in the general Hobartown news column:

> Alexander Warren and John Wyld, Esqrs. Agents for the Australian Company in these Colonies, the former for New South Wales, and the latter for Van Diemen's Land, have arrived by the Company's ship, the Greenock; on board which vessel are the following passengers:-
> Mr. and Mrs. John Macleod and child, Mrs. and Mrs. Hill and child, Mr. and Mrs. MacKersey, Mr. Hugh L. Torrance, Mr. W.N. Grey, Mr. F. Schulz, Mr. W. Combe, Mr. Wm. Mackie, Dr. Radfrord, Mrs. Radford and child, Mr. and Mrs. Lang and family , Mrs. Mary Livingstone, Mr. John Tyre, Mr. John Wylie, Mr. John Francis, Mr. Wm. Murray, Mr. George McKirdy, Mr. Wm. Aird, Mr. Adam Cummings, Mr. John Turnbull, Mr. Wm. Smith, Mr. James Corbett, Mr. Alex McKay, Mr. William

Lockhead, Mr. and Mrs. Mackeracher, Mr. and Mrs. Anderson, Mr. Wm. Hamilton, Mr. Sinclair Williamson, Mr. C. Wilkie, Mr. A. Duff, Mr. D McKenzie, Mr. and Mrs. Bain, Mr. C. Gardiner, Mr. J. Scott, Mr. R. McPherson, Mr. A. Rassel, Mr. A. Vailance, Mr. N. Allan, Mr. A. Brooks, **Mr J. Campbell**, Mr. J. Thomas, Mr. J. C. Anderson, Mr. W. Hill, jun. Mr. Thomas Davies, Mr. W. Charelson, and Mrs A. Mitchell, making 62 persons, including children.

The cargo for Van Diemen's Land had been, 'selected expressly for the market', and represented the products of Scotland's rising industries and trades. It was unloaded and the merchandise stored in the commercial premises of Walter A. Bethune, a Scottish merchant in the colony who made his stores available until the company could build its own premises.[2]

The largest consignment consisted of food items, smoked hams, mess beef and pork, Irish butter, wines, spirits (principally whisky), barrels of beer, ale and porter. There were also large quantities of pitch and tar, grass and clover seeds, leather and iron goods. Leather items included shoes, boots, saddlery, and piece-leather. Iron goods consisted of boilers with furnaces for steam engines, grates, ovens, stoves, anchors, horse ploughs, plough-irons and iron cartwheels. Textiles included muslins, calicoes, ginghams, shawls, scarfs, linens and assorted tartans. There were, paints, cottons, pianofortes, tobacco, snuff, cart-bodies, gunpowder, and Cape wines and Madeira. An extensive collection of books, included copies of Sir Walter Scott's recent works. Four Ayrshire cows and two Ayrshire bulls, landed as livestock in this first shipment, reflected advances in stock-breeding in contemporary Scotland.[3]

The list of imports is impressive and even more so considering the further 10 casks of whisky, 84 casks (of beer?), 50 cases of wine and other sundry merchandise sent on to Sydney when the *Greenock* continued her voyage on 25th December 1823. Obviously spirits, wine, ale and porter figured prominently in the ship's cargo, reflecting the keen colonial demand!

Hobart, now approaching its 20th year, had grown rapidly from the initial settlement in 1804. At the beginning of 1821 the residential area of Hobart consisted of a total of 594 houses comprising 9 stone houses, 245 brick houses and 340 wooden houses.[4] The wooden buildings were constructed of various materials such as split palings or logs, the most basic built of wattle- and-daub and turf. There were most likely a few more houses when John Campbell arrived towards the end of 1823, but these statistics from census data gathered in October and November 1820 give an idea of the size of the village about that time. Block sizes were large covering a quarter acre, resulting in the village occupying about three times the space of an English village of equivalent size.[5]

Commercial and government buildings, built of stone or brick, were more substantial. They included Government House and a guard house on the waterfront, the Government Commissariat Store, the Angelsea Barracks composed of the Officers Quarters and a drill hall, a General Hospital and Dispensary and 3 commercial store buildings (including Walter Bethune's store) on Hunter Island. A Court House was under construction as well as several other commercial buildings, most notably the Scotch and Thistle public house and the Cascade Brewery.

These buildings served a European population in Hobart which, at the end of 1823, numbered 3,479 souls, comprising 1,070 people who had come free to the colony or were born in the colony, 431 free by pardon or completion of sentence, 172 conditionally emancipated and 1,806 convicts. Of the free and conditionally emancipated adults 688 were male and 397 were female. Among the adult convicts, 1,485 were male and 219 female. In all of Tasmania the European population stood at 10,009 including 4,519 free persons and 5,490 convicts.[6]

Although the food stores brought by the *Greenock* seem commonplace they were regarded as luxuries to a population that fed principally on fresh and salted mutton, damper and potatoes washed down with copious cups of tea laced with sugar, the latter two items obtained from India. There was almost a complete absence of dairy foods but there was an abundance of kangaroo and a favoured meal had become 'steamer', fresh kangaroo roasted or steamed in its own gravy with a piece of pork or salt rashers of pork. Kangaroo tail soup was also on the menu and most people considered kangaroo to be as good as any venison.

Similarly, the clothing materials the *Greenock* had brought were in great demand. European clothing for the most part was worn only by a minority in Hobart – officers, senior government officials and the well-to-do free immigrants. In general, the convicts and poorer settlers in the colony resigned themselves to supplementing the minimal cloth garments they had with kangaroo skins.

In spite of these rude elements in their lifestyle, by the mid 1820s Hobart society was taking itself very seriously becoming 'very good', as William Parramore, attorney and sometime private secretary to Lieutenant Governor Arthur, wrote in 1824, 'We have a great many gentlemanly men and hardly ever see a dag, except in the sea captains and farmers'.[7] As a result of the increase in free immigration, particularly during the second decade of the 19th century, the divide between convict and free became more rigid, impacting adversely on the social status of convicts and those who were now free but had a convict past. Generally speaking, however, in this frontier culture, society was more accepting than in the established societies of England. Women, small in number, as the population statistics for 1823 exemplified, were extremely vulnerable. But their minority position provided them with a good degree of choice in partners. In a male dominated society, women found it necessary to live with a man, whether in or out of marriage, for protection if for no other reason. Living alone was a more difficult option. Convict women often married or lived with soldiers, officials or male convicts in the colony and commonly initiated separations either amicably or acrimoniously. Many unmarried couples lived together openly in committed relationships and children born under these circumstances were generally accepted by society as were the women who bore them. [8]

There was little prospect of John Campbell finding a wife in Hobart. Fortunately, whether bonded to the Australian Company or not, there was no shortage of work. As a carpenter (or as a farmer) his labour was in demand. During the 1820s the storehouse for the Australian Company and warehouses for other commercial enterprises were built on Hunter Island. Walter Bethune built an elevated causeway with stone walls, to link the island with the town and over the following decades the island was extensively developed with commercial buildings.[9] Housing was required for the expanding population and attendant on that requirement, churches, shops and other buildings desired or deemed necessary for the community. The Australian Company's Store completed in 1826, was described as 'one of the most substantial and well constructed (buildings) in the Colony'. It occupied about 90,700 cubic feet, consisted of four levels and included spacious offices and a dwelling for the storekeeper.[10]

From 1820 Van Diemen's Land had become an attractive destination for a small but influential group of wealthy free settlers who believed the empty native grasslands offered hope for a more prosperous future. Indeed the park-like lands, the brilliant skies, the pure rivers and the fresh air provided much promise to the settler of unfettered imagination.

By the end of 1823 the best agricultural land in Van Diemen's Land had been taken up. Grants had placed over 500,000 acres under the control of Europeans and the demand for agricultural labourers, especially experienced farm hands was high. From the distinct areas around the administrative centres of Hobart and Launceston, settlement had spread outward along the major river systems. By 1823 the two areas had joined to form an unbroken stretch of granted agricultural land extending through the Midlands of Tasmania between the Central Plateau to the west and the mountains of the north east.[11]

All was not a tranquil, bucolic pastoral scene. European expansion was increasingly seen by the indigenous population as an invasion of their land and attacks by Aborigines on property and persons invited retaliation from the settlers and government with disastrous consequences for both populations. Bushranging gangs of escaped convicts launched raids against settlers' homesteads, robbed travellers along the roads and even robbed settlements around Hobart Town. Bushranger crimes were mainly against property and murders were uncommon, but the threat of assault against persons and property was ever present.

One of the most serious bushranger insurrections, led by Matthew Brady, was confronted by Lieutenant-Governor Arthur, between 1824 and 1826. Brady, of Irish descent was transported to Hobart in 1821 for forgery. In 1824 he escaped in a boat from Macquarie Harbour with a gang of 14 men and commenced a series of daring raids that became legendary throughout the colony. His attacks targeted the social pretensions of the free settlers and symbols of state oppression, namely aspiring gentry and soldiers. His exploits earned him enormous popularity with the general populace but disdain from the colonial officials. Brady was captured in 1826 and he and four of his gang were executed before a crowd of spectators who took to 'singing and by the time the fourth verse had concluded five bushrangers were dead'[12]

Nor was the farming landscape that picture of an English countryside that had been embedded in the minds of the settlers arriving at the beginning of the decade. Instead of the rustic beauty and quiet order of the English farm, fields of grain were unfenced, the seed sown amongst deformed, black stumps of trees hewn down to clear the land. There were no green hedges or flowering meadows. Dwellings were crude, mean structures made of sod, logs or mud and thatched with straw, their surroundings unkempt, strewn with heaps of wool, bones, sheepskins and carcasses of sheep and kangaroo strung up on trees. The inhabitants of these places were a mixture of dirty men, dogs and natives.[13]

This was by no means the description the prospective settler had read in the books and articles about the colony prior to his departure from Britain. To make matters worse, the cost of provisioning a farming operation with livestock and implements was very expensive to the point of being almost prohibitive.

Despite the initial shock and disillusion, the influx of settlers during the 1820s wrought vast changes and much improved agricultural practices to the colony. When John Campbell arrived in 1823, the predominant breed of sheep was a cross of Teeswater, Leicester and Bengal sheep mainly raised for meat. Merinos, introduced in the 1820s, aroused great interest in sheep grazing for the production of wool and the number of sheep in the colony grew quickly. By 1830 it was estimated more than 680,000 sheep were grazing compared to about 170,000 in 1820. Cattle numbers also increased and by 1829 it was estimated that there were about 100,000 cattle in the colony. By the end of the decade the export market for wool and meat was well established.[14]

Crops consisted principally of wheat, barley and oats, with wheat being the principal grain sown and cultivated. Care was needed to produce premium crops, yields varying from year to year depending on conditions. Although less attractive than grazing due to the larger amount of work required, grain crops presented good returns for those prepared to do the work. Mills were needed to produce flour to be turned into edible products for local consumption and by 1827 nineteen watermills and three windmills were operating in Van Diemen's Land. Barley, hops and to a lesser extent wheat, were used in brewing beer and were in great demand aided by the fact that distilleries were forbidden in the colony but breweries encouraged. Other cultivated crops for human consumption included peas, beans, potatoes and turnips. English grasses, vetches and turnips were also grown for animal feed and soil improvement.[15]

During John Campbell's five years in Van Diemen's Land the colony had grown from just over 10,000 people to almost 17,000 of which about 9500 were free settlers and 7500 were convicts. Women were still vastly outnumbered, there being a little over 3050 free females and about 725 female convicts.[16] Whether he had served out his bond, had run out of work, or was simply keen to seek out new opportunities, early in 1829 John set out for Sydney, New South Wales on board the '*Henry*'[17].

Notes to Chapter 5

1. CO 284/45, AJCP reel 1194, Yr. 1823, p.122-123 (38-39).
2. David S. MacMillan, *Scotland And Australia 1788 – 1850: emigration, commerce and investment*, pp194, Clarendon, Oxford, 1967.
3. Ibid., p194-195.
4. HRA, Series III, Vol. 4, p. 637.
5. Leslie L. Robson, *A History of Tasmania*, Vol.1, p.123, Oxford University Press, Melbourne, 1983.
6. CO 284/45 AJCP reel 1194; Yr. 1823 p122-123 (38-39).
7. James Boyce, *Van Diemen's Land*, Black, Melbourne, 2008, p160.

8   Ibid., p131.
9   Frank Bolt, *Old Hobart Town Today: a photographic essay*, Waratah, Hobart, 1981, p.45.
10 HRA, Series III, Vol. 6, pp. 362-363.
11 Sharon Morgan, *Land Settlement in Early Tasmania: Creating an Antipodean England*, Cambridge University Press, Melbourne, 1992, pp19 and 21.
12 James Boyce, op.cit., p.136.
13 Boyce, op. cit., p.140.
14 Sharon Morgan, op. cit., pp.59 and 67.
15 Morgan, op. cit., pp.82- 83 and 87.
16 CO 284/51 AJCP reel 1194, Yr. 1828.
17 SRNSW: NRS 905, Colonial Secretary's Correspondence 1832 – 1842, Letter 40/1168, [4/2486.2], Reel 1841.

Chapter 6

Charlotte Dawson - Lincolnshire

October was not a good month for Charlotte Dawson. It was the month in which she was born but it seemed her birthday always lead to some sort of trouble. At 24 years of age Charlotte was in a difficult position. Arraigned along with Mary McQueen, James South and John Grant on charges of stealing, she was to be tried at the Lincoln Michaelmass Quarter sessions at Kirton in Lindsey. They had been caught on the 17th October 1826 with stolen goods; a checked apron and a woman's shift, the property of John Fidell of Elsham, and a checked handkerchief, the property of his sister, Sarah Fidell. Arresting constables Richard Lawson of North Killingholme and William Thompson of Glanford Brigg wasted little time committing them to trial. Being so close to the date of the next the Quarter Sessions, their names were last on the list of 22 persons to appear at court on the 20th of October.

They were a peculiar looking quartet to say the least. John Grant, a Scot from Edinburgh, was a stonemason and cutter by trade. He was 24 years old and the smallest in stature at 5feet, 1¾ inches tall. He had a dark ruddy complexion, brown hair and hazel grey eyes. He was hairy-chested and had a defective right eye and a crooked little finger on his left hand.[1] James South originally from Wiltshire was 21 years old and worked as a brickmaker and plasterer. At 5 feet, 5½ inches in height, he was the tallest in the group. He had dark brown hair, brown eyes and two flesh moles under his right jaw.[2] Mary McQueen was 5 feet, 2¼ inches tall with brown hair, grey eyes and a sallow freckled complexion.[3] At 18 years old, she was the youngest in the group. And Charlotte Dawson, 24 years old, 5 feet, 3½ inches tall, was of fair complexion with brown hair, dark brown eyes and was '*in mouthed*'. She could read but subsequent records show that she could not write. She was of the protestant religion and she worked as a farm servant, in doors.[4]

What relationship these four people had is a matter for speculation. It seems that John Grant and Charlotte Dawson being the same age may have been an unmarried couple and James South and Mary McQueen of similar status. But they may have been just casual friends or workmates at Elsham or one of the other estates in the district. All four came from the village of North Killingholme, but the two men were not local and probably had become acquainted with the women either through work or while living in the village.

No birth record has been found for Charlotte. It can, however, be ascertained from later documents that her birthday was on the 3rd of October and her age at the time of the trial gives a birth year of 1802. Parish records for North Killingholme show a Dawson family resident in North Killingholme consisting of parents John and Mary and their children[5]:

>William – born – 12 January 1794
>Elizabeth – christened – 10 April 1796
>Robert – christened – 5 August 1798
>Harriet – christened – 18 June 1801
>Charles – christened – 24 October 1802
>Mary – christened – 25 March 1804
>Thomas – christened – 2 December 1809

Charlotte was probably a relative of this family.

The committal for trial was listed in the Lindsey Calender, Kirton, Michaelmas Sessions for October 20, 1826[6]:

> 19. James South 21
> 20. John Grant.......................... 24
> 21. Charlotte Dawson................ 24
> 22. Mary McQueen................... 18

Committed the 17th of October, 1826. Charged upon the oath of Thomas Fidell, of Elsham, labourer, with feloniously stealing, taking, and carrying away one checked Apron and one woman's

Shift, of the goods and chattels of the said John Fidell. Also upon the oath of Sarah Fidell of the same place, spinster, with feloniously stealing, taking, and carrying away on checked Handkerchief of the goods and chattels of the said Sarah Fidell.

John Hildyard, Clerk,
John Uppleby, Esq.

The fact that two separate charges were made, one for John Fidell and one for Sarah Fidell, meant that they would all have to face two trials. As there was little time available to place this case into the upcoming Sessions, court Clerk, John Hildyard quickly drafted the bonds of prosecutors and witnesses. Any delay would have meant the accused felons would have to be remanded in custody until the next quarter sessions or until a passing magistrate could attend their trials.

The prosecutor's bond for John Fidell and witness bond for his wife, Thomasin Fidell[7] read:

> *Lincolnshire Lindsey* To wit
> Be it remembered, that on the *Seventeenth* Day of *October* in the Year of our Lord One Thousand Eight Hundred and *Twenty Six John Fidell of Elsham in the said Parts and County Laborer* personally came before me *John Hildyard Clerk* one of His Majesty's Justices of the Peace for the said *Parts* and
> acknowledged himself to be indebted to our Sovereign Lord the King in the Sum of *Twenty Pounds of lawful British Money*
> UPON CONDITION that if the above-bound *John Fidell* shall personally appear at the next *General Quarter Sessions of the Peace* to be holden at *Kirton in and for the said Parts* and then and there prefer a Bill of Indictment against *James South late of North Killingholme in the said Parts Laborer, John Grant late of the same place Laborer, Charlotte Dawson late of the same*

place Spinster and Mary McQueen Late of the same place Spinster for the feloniously taking and carrying away one checked Apron and one Shift the Property of *the said John Fidell And also if Thomasin Fidell, the wife of the said John Fidell shall also then and there shall personally appear* and shall then and there give Evidence concerning the same, to the Jurors, who shall enquire thereof on the Part of our said Lord the King: And in case the same be found a true Bill, then if the said *Thomasin Fidell* shall personally appear before the Jurors, who shall pass upon the Trial of the said *James South, John Grant, Charlotte Dawson, and Mary McQueen* and give Evidence upon the said Indictment, and not depart without Leave of the Court; Then this Recognizance to be void.

Taken and acknowledged before me,
John Hildyard
      (Ball, Printer, Brigg)

The apron and woman's shift were undoubtedly the property of his wife, Thomasin but a wife's property was deemed to belong not to her but to her husband. Therefore her husband brought the first prosecution. Sarah, his sister was unmarried and the handkerchief was hers alone.

A similar bond was lodged for Sarah Fidell to appear and present a Bill of Indictment.[8]

The bonds of witnesses, Sarah Fidell[9] and William Thompson[10] for John Fidell, and Richard Lawson[11] and William Thompson[12] for Sarah Fidell were similar. Richard Lawson's bond stated:

Lincolnshire Lindsey To wit
Be it remembered, that on the *Seventeenth* Day of *October* in the Year of our Lord One Thousand Eight Hundred and *Twenty Six Richard Lawson of North Killingholme in the said Parts and County Constable* personally came before me *John Hildyard Clerk* one of

His Majesty's Justices of the Peace for the said *Parts* and acknowledged himself to be indebted to our Sovereign Lord the King in the Sum of *Twenty Pounds of lawful British Money*

UPON CONDITION that if the above-bound *Richard Lawson* shall personally appear at the next *General Quarter Sessions of the Peace* to be holden at *Kirton* in and for the said *Parts* and then and there give evidence as he knoweth, upon a Bill of Indictment to be exhibited *by Sarah Fidell of Elsham in the said Parts, Spinster* to the Grand Jury against *James South late of North Killingholme in the said Parts Laborer, John Grant late of the same place Laborer, Charlotte Dawson late of the same place Spinster and Mary McQueen Late of the same place Spinster for the feloniously taking and carrying away one checked Handkerchief* the Property of *the said Sarah Fidell* and in case the said Bill be found a true Bill, then if the said *Richard Lawson* shall then and there give Evidence to the Jurors that shall pass on Trial of the said *James South, John Grant, Charlotte Dawson, and Mary McQueen* upon the said Bill of Indictment, and not depart without Leave of the Court; Then this Recognizance to be void, otherwise of force.

Taken and acknowledged before me,
John Hildyard

(Ball, Printer, Brigg)

The village of North Killingholme is situated south of the Humber River and about 16 kilometres northwest of the Lincolnshire coastal town of Grimsby. In 1821 the parish including South Killingholme contained 89 houses and 438 inhabitants. By 1831 the population had grown to 480 and so in 1826 would have been about 450 people.[13] Manor Farm House, an L-shaped brick house and its two associated granges dating from the early to mid-16th century, and the church of St Denys (Church of England), initially built in the 12th century,14 are the main remaining historical features of the village. These landmarks would have been familiar to Charlotte and her companions in crime.

The ruins of Thornton Abbey, three kilometres northwest of the village, also would have been familiar to them. Founded as a priory in 1139 by William le Gros, the Earl of Albermarle, it was raised to the status of Abbey in 1148 and became one of the Augustinian Order's richest houses. Following the Dissolution of the Monasteries in 1539, it became a college of secular canons, part of Henry VIII's scheme for a system to replace the monasteries. Six years later, this too was dissolved and the site was granted to the Bishop of Lincoln. Over the following centuries the site was plundered for building materials until Lord Yarborough purchased and protected it in 1815. Some years prior to Yarborough's purchase, while a part of the ruins was being dismantled, a human skeleton was found, with a table, a book, and a candlestick. It was assumed to have been the remains of the fourteenth abbot who for some crime was 'sentenced to be immured; a mode of punishment not uncommon in monastic institutions'.15 Today, the remains of the abbey are the finest in Lincolnshire, while the 14th century gatehouse is not only one of the largest in England but is also an important early example of brick architecture.

Elsham, where the crime was committed, is a small village located about 14 kilometres southwest of North Killingholme. In 1821 it consisted of 57 houses and 383 inhabitants, and was the seat of William Thompson Corbett, Esquire, Justice of the Peace In the Parts of Lindsey and Deputy Lieutenant of the Subdivision of Brigg.16 His home, Elsham Hall, a small country house built about the 17th century and its surrounding estate came to him through his mother, granddaughter of William Thompson of Elsham. In more recent times Elsham was the site of a military airfield, used in both World War I and WWII. Requisitioned as an Anti-Aircraft HQ during WWII, Elsham Hall was left empty after the war. Lacking care and maintenance, almost one third of the total edifice was ruined, including two wings one of which housed the servants' quarters and billiard room. In the late 1940s the two damaged wings were demolished. Subsequent renovations have restored Elsham Hall to a modern mansion and its stables and gardens have been converted into a country park.

Elsham village was once home to a hospital begun by Beatrice de Amundeville for poor brethren. Her son, Walter, completed and committed it to a friar and regular canons of the Augustinian order. After dissolution Henry VIII granted the site to Charles, Duke of Suffolk in 1538. The local church, All Saints, dating from the 12th century is a landmark and retains some original Norman features. Two weather worn relief carvings on the buttresses either side of the arched entrance, date from the 13th century.

Lincolnshire is the second largest county in England. The population in 1826 comprised an equal number of males and females totalling 283,358 people distributed in 50,670 families and creating a population density of 87 inhabitants per square mile. Approximately 70% of the families were chiefly employed in agriculture. The Wapentake (group of Parishes) of Yarborough, in which North Killingholme and Elsham were located, had a population of 16,840 people (8,314 males and 8,526 females) distributed in 3541 families 63% of which were employed in agriculture. There were 1,003 families employed in trades and manufacturing, and 318 families 'not comprised in the previous classes'.[17]

The topography of Lincolnshire, although of relatively low relief, displays a variety of land forms featuring hills and valleys, steep cliffs and softly undulating plateaux, and low lying wet marshes and scrubby heathlands. These features create the various geographical regions in the County: the Fens, an area of marshland in the southeast and along the coast; the Lincolnshire Wolds, part of the chalk belt of eastern England in the northeast; and the Limestone Scarp (60 to 90 metres high). The 'backbone' of Lincolnshire, the Limestone Scarp extends the length of the western portion of the county and represents the northeastern end of the limestone belt which sweeps across England in a great curve from the Cotswolds to Yorkshire.

Agriculturally, the land was very productive with light loamy soils for the production of corn and green winter food, and marshland possessing excellent pasturage for cattle and sheep in summer. North Killingholme, located in the fens on the coastal plain east of the Wolds, was just one of many farming settlements in the area.[18] Today industrial plants along the Humber River estuary overshadow the patchwork quilt of farm fields surrounding the village.

In 1826 the produce of the county consisted principally of sheep, beef cattle, horses, and grain. The sheep were large, and their wool was long and thick, particularly suited to the manufacture of worsted and coarse woollen products. Large quantities of wool were sent annually to the mills of Yorkshire. Furthermore, sheep brought from other districts to the Lincolnshire marsh land yielded fleeces of greater weight and longer staple, than on their former pasture.

The cattle were a large, well shaped breed which through breeding and better feeding had replaced a previously prevalent large boned breed. There was virtually no dairying in the region. Horses bred in the northern part of the county were generally considered to be superior both for saddle and harness, while the southern part produced very excellent draught horses.

For ages most of the marsh land and fens, had been used for grazing. Drainage and enclosure in parts of the fens and marshlands had caused a material change in produce. A considerable portion of these areas became subjected to cultivation and production of oats, wheat, beans, peas and woad. Much of the high land was also devoted to tillage, and produced a great variety of grain. As land increased in value, was enclosed and put under the plough, rabbit warrens, formerly numerous and extensive in the county, all but disappeared and with them the commercial trade in rabbit skins.

Lincolnshire did not escape the vast changes in agriculture, manufacturing, transportation, economic policies and social structure that swept through Britain between 1750 and 1850, the era of the Industrial and Agricultural Revolution. Agriculturally, land was enclosed and drained for more organised and intensive farming methods. As a result larger and more efficient farms were developed, leading to increased output and large economic gains. More land came under cultivation, more food became available for the growing population, and more employment was generated in the countryside.[19]

The first half of the nineteenth century saw an enormous increase in productivity on Lincolnshire farms. Cattle and sheep were able to be bred by selection. As improvements created more arable land, barley, wheat and oats, turnips and potatoes were cultivated and the county became less of a pastoral area. Lincolnshire remained primarily an agricultural county with few industrial occupations to attract the labourer away from the farm and raise the level of wages.

From about 1821 people in Lincolnshire started to leave the county for the industrial towns. But until 1851 most of the rural population remained, maintaining a moderate level of growth in population between 1821 and 1831. This was still a world of manual labour and improvements in farming actually demanded more labour, not less. The area of farmland, considerably expanded by cultivation of commons and reclaimed wasteland, increased labour requirements. The work of enclosure itself created employment in making fences, hedges, new roads and building new farmhouses and barns. Crop rotation and higher crop yields required more labour for cultivating and harvesting. At times, the shortage of labour was so acute that even women and children were required to work on farms and large numbers of itinerant Irish workers were recruited during periods of high seasonal activity. It was not until after the middle of the nineteenth century that machines became commonly used on the land and started to make an impact on levels of farm employment.[20]

These changes in agricultural practice made a huge impact on the way of life of the farming classes. At the beginning of the eighteenth century, agriculture was carried out over most of the country on an open field system which can best be described as belonging to a village community of shareholders who cultivated the land. The structure of the village under this 'common' system comprised arable fields, common meadowlands and wasteland. The arable fields belonging to different owners were divided into narrow strips, cultivated on a uniform system by agreement, and open to pasturage after harvest. Similarly the meadowland was divided into lots distributed amongst the owners of the strips and was open to pasturage once the hay had been removed. The waste commons, varying from woodland to roadside strips and village commons were open to pasturage year round. This all changed during the eighteenth and early nineteenth century as land enclosure replaced the common system.[21] As an example, the Parish of Killingholme was enclosed during the period from 1776 to 1779.

The consequent benefit available to those people displaced from the land and forced to move following enclosure, was work. Many became gainfully employed on the larger farming estates. Others migrated to the newly forming cities of the Industrial Revolution. Of detriment was the social dislocation enclosure caused, the loss of the former communal, mutually-supportive way of life, and its replacement by capitalist farming. A portion of the population was disadvantaged and security of work was diminished.

Relevant to the size of the labour pool was its location within an 'open' or 'closed' parish. While open parishes had many owners, a closed parish belonged entirely to one owner. Until the Reform of the Poor Law in 1834 each parish was responsible for supporting its own poor and in general a mass of labourers most of whom were underpaid. A single landowner in a closed parish was required to meet the high rate of poor relief on a pro rata basis and therefore was keen to keep the number of labourers on his property to a minimum. Cottage accommodation rents were kept high or cottages were pulled down to reduce the workforce if the owner could draw sufficient labour from populous, neighbouring open villages. This practice often created overcrowding in poor conditions in the open parishes and compelled labourers to live at a great distance from their work. It also created an extremely mobile work force of labourers who would serve one or two years before moving on to another farm.[22] We can assume that Charlotte Dawson and her companions were part of this mobile workforce, the two women working as domestic servants and the men employed as tradesmen.

During the Napoleonic Wars, living standards had fallen as commodity prices rose dramatically and wages remained relatively static. The government raised hundreds of millions of dollars through taxation or in loans but none of this money was spent on the education of labourers' children or on any form of social assistance. Falling prices and employment after the end of the war in 1815 were no less traumatic causing distress and class conflict. Farm prices, after reaching their war-time peak in 1812, gradually fell to a low point in 1822. With wheat prices at half their wartime peak, it was widely believed that the landowner class would be ruined.[23]

As the post-war fall in farm prices brought the cost of living down agricultural labourers in full employment were well placed to see an improvement in the purchasing power of their wages which, in general, were maintained at about twelve shillings a week. But agricultural employment and incomes varied depending on the quality of the farm land and while some labourers in regular employment experienced a rise in living standards, labourers in disadvantaged farming areas suffered the opposite. Furthermore, a three year period of bad weather, between 1826 and 1829, badly damaged harvests throughout the county and seriously reduced wages and demand for labour as farmers sought to cut their costs and minimize their losses.[24]

The rise in social distress amongst the rural working classes of Britain during the 1820s was accompanied by a contagious rise in pauperism and crime throughout the eastern counties. In Lincolnshire, poverty-induced crime, such as the theft of foodstuffs most commonly corn, potatoes, eggs, meat, and dairy produce from fields, game reserves, barns, hen roosts, larders, and outhouses, was endemic and took place almost nightly in and around the villages. Stealing sheep and poultry and poaching of rabbits, hares, and game birds was rife in many areas. As well as the ubiquitous prevalence of petty subsistence crime, sporadic attacks upon property and persons were also increasing.[25]

Notes to Chapter 6

1. SRNSW: NRS 12210; Butts of Certificates of Freedom, [4/4319]; reel 992, certificate 33/1328.
2. AOTAS, Convict Conduct Record, CON 23/1/3. No.803.
3. SRNSW: NRS 12188; Principal Superintendent of Convicts, Bound indents, 1788-1842; [4/4012]; Microfiche: 666. p.227.
4. SRNSW: NRS 12188; Principal Superintendent of Convicts, Bound indents, 1788-1842; [4/4012]; Microfiche: 666, p.224.
5. Bishop's Transcripts, 1562-1833, Church of England, Parish of North Killingholme, LDS FHL British Film 504260 Item 1.

6   Lincolnshire Archives (LA), Calendar of Prisoners: a printed list of all those due to appear at the Quarter Sessions Court at Kirton in Lindsey, Lincolnshire on 20 October 1826, LQS/A/1/500/14.
7   LA, Bonds of Prosecutors and Witnesses, LQS/A/1/500/128.
8   LA, LQS/A/1/500/132.
9   LA, LQS/A/1/500/129.
10 LA, LQS/A/1/500/130.
11 LA, LQS/A/1/500/131.
12 LA, LQS/A/1/500/133.
13 Thomas Allen, *History of the County of Lincolnshire*, Vol. II, p.231, Saunders, London & Lincoln, 1834.
14 Historic Buildings Report: Manor Farm House, North Killingholme.
15 White's History, Gazetteer and Directory of Lincolnshire and Hull 1826, p.67.
16 Allen, op.cit., Vol.II p.234 & Vol. I p.96.
17 White's History, Gazetteer and Directory of Lincolnshire and Hull 1826, p.23.
18 Allan Rogers, *A History of Lincolnshire*, Darwen Finlayson, Henley on Thames, 1970.
19 J.D.Chambers and & G.E.Mingay, *The Agricultural Revolution*, 1750 – 1880, Batsford, London 1966, p.104.
20 Rogers, op. cit., p.65.
21 Hammond, J.L. & B., *The Village Labourer*, Vol. 1, Longmans, Green & Co., London, 1948, pp.20-21.
22 Rogers, op. cit., pp.65 and 68.
23 T.L. Richardson, *The Agricultural Labourers' Standard of Living in Lincolnshire, 1790-1840: Social Protest and Public Order*, The Agriculture History Review, Vol. 41, I, pp.1-19.
24 Ibid. p.8.
25 Ibid. p.9.

Chapter 7

Trial

The Calendar list of Prisoners charged and appearing before the court on October 20th, 1826 at Kirton[1] exemplifies the types of crimes that were being committed 'upon property and persons' at this time.

- Stolen - two flagstones the value of sixpence
- Feloniously stealing - one silver cased watch
- Feloniously stealing, taking and carrying away - a tea caddy
- Stolen - a hat with assault upon a person
- Feloniously stealing, taking and carrying away - one woman's and one child's bonnet
- Feloniously stealing, taking and carrying away – two pairs of braces, nine gross of white moulds, and several other articles.
- Violent assault
- Feloniously stealing, taking and carrying away from a brickworks – three mats for covering bricks and tiles
- Feloniously stealing, taking and carrying away – a pair of jane trousers, a penknife. A pair of striped trousers and other articles
- Disturbance of the peace.
- Forcibly taken away and robbed of – a hat, smock frock and coat and about nine shillings in money
- Feloniously stealing, taking and carrying away – one coloured silk handkerchief
- Feloniously stealing, taking and carrying away – one silver watch
- Stealing and carrying away – two black silk cloaks

- Disturbance of the Peace
- Feloniously stealing, taking and carrying away – one woman's and one child's cap, one child's shirt, one striped muslin binder, and one white muslin binder and also on copper.
- Feloniously stealing, taking and carrying away – one checked apron, one woman's shift and one checked handkerchief

Of the twenty two people charged, one was 66 years old, two were in their forties and three in their early thirties but the rest ranged in age from 16 to 27 years old highlighting the plight of the young. In addition there were five people charged with vagrancy appearing that day. Agricultural labourers were so hard pressed that some found it a relief to be committed to the House of Correction where they could at least obtain food and shelter.

The stolen items in the list above were sold for money or exchanged for food but some may have been kept for personal use. Perhaps the items stolen by our quartet were to be worn by Charlotte Dawson and Mary McQueen and their crime was more one of receiving rather than one of 'feloniously stealing, taking and carrying away'. Perhaps some of the items were stolen as a birthday gift for Charlotte. As we shall see later Charlotte was particularly gullible in that regard and perhaps a bit too trusting.

During the Sessions a further thirty five people previously convicted or committed to the House of Correction were sentenced. Their crimes included misdemeanours at the Lincoln assizes, petty larceny at the Kirton Sessions, assaulting a constable, absconding from a Master's service, theft of potatoes and walnuts, being absent from work, not obeying orders of filiation, having a bastard child, destroying a mare with a potion composed of mercury, poaching using a snare, vagrancy and debt. All of these received sentences of imprisonment with hard labour except for the poacher and two debtors who received only prison sentences of 80 to 100 days duration.

Held at the House of Correction, or Kirton Bridewell as it was known, Charlotte was separated from her family, who, although allowed to visit and provide support, may not have had the means or ability to do so. Kirton in Lindsey was a small market town of about 330 houses and 1,500 people in 1826. Situated on the summit and western side of the Limestone Ridge, 29 kilometres north of Lincoln, the village has a westward outlook towards the Trent River valley. A weekly market was held on Saturdays and two annual fairs for the sale of cattle and pedlary took place on the 18th of July and 11th of December.[2] The village also had seven inns, four of them around the small market square, a Church of England in the western part of the town, a grammar school and a Methodist church. The Quarter Sessions every three months had a major impact on the town socially and commercially. Not only were criminal cases dealt with but also a wide range of administrative matters, and the consequent influx of enormous numbers of people strained the town's capacity to the limit much to the delight of the merchants and innkeepers.

Until 1790 the prison for this area of Lincolnshire had been in Gainsborough. It was over crowded, filthy and disease ridden, conditions typical of all the prisons of the eighteenth century in England. In 1790 it was decided to build a new House of Correction at Kirton in Lindsey, and provide a Court House within the prison in which Quarter Sessions could be held. The house of correction in Kirton was one of three which served the administrative district of the Parts of Lindsey, the others being at Louth dating from the late 17th century, and Spilsby.

Three and a half acres purchased on the north-eastern edge of the village for the sum of £260 became home to the House of Correction, Sessions Court and Governor's quarters. Set on a hill, in a healthy dry position surrounded mostly by open land, it was believed to be a major humanitarian improvement in the confinement of those charged and convicted of criminal offences.

An imposing building, it was constructed using local limestone and finished with stone imported from Yorkshire. Built to house 116 prisoners, its principal design consisted of a ground floor and an upper floor contained in north and south wings for male and female prisoners respectively. Each floor contained 16 cells. Approximately 8 feet wide by 8 feet long, each cell accommodated at least 3 prisoners at a time. The central eastern part of the building contained the Sessions Hall at the end of which was a room for the Clerk of the Peace. The Sessions Hall was also used as a chapel for the prisoners on Sundays. The western part contained the Magistrates room and on the remainder of the ground floor other ancillary facilities included kitchens, bathrooms, a laundry, a bakehouse, work room, a coal house, lumber room and stable. Day yards flanked the central part of the building between the Sessions Hall and the prisoners' cells on the ground floor. On the second story, above the Sessions Hall and the Gaoler's apartment, was a room for the grand jury.

Prison staff included the Governor, a Matron, a Chaplain and a Surgeon plus as many male and female gaolers as were thought necessary at any particular time. John Lee, aged 40, was Governor and Chief Gaoler in 1826. In charge of the day to day running of the prison, he was also required to keep eight different administrative journals which could be referred to by the visiting magistrates. His salary[3] was set at £100 a year from which he paid the Matron's and Turnkey's salaries. The Matron, Lee's mother, carried out similar work to the Governor in relation to the female prisoners. The Surgeon, George Foster of Kirton, examined each prisoner on admission and was on call at all times. Rules required him to visit all sick prisoners and monitor prisoners under any form of disciplinary punishment on a daily basis. He could intervene if he thought a prisoner was being injured in mind or body. He inspected the prison with regard to its cleanliness and ventilation, gave reports and post mortems on deaths and provided a yearly report to the magistrates on the prisoners' health and disorders.

Prisoners were required to attend chapel every day with the Governor and all staff, except the Surgeon, in attendance. The Chaplain, Henry William Richter, in addition to taking these half hour daily divine services, saw and admonished each prisoner on admission and discharge, and counselled each prisoner alone at least once a month. Each day he also visited the sick and those in solitary confinement.[4]

Poverty, resulting from idleness and the unwillingness to work diligently, was regarded as the major inducement to crime. Therefore hard work was considered to be a corrective measure and prisoners were productively employed spinning and weaving wool and picking oakum. In 1822 a treadmill was installed, supposedly for grinding beans or grain. The Stamford Mercury of 13 December 1822 gave the opinion that the device would no doubt 'produce an equally beneficial effect as a preventative of crime in that district as it has done in other places.'[5]

By the 1820s the prison was overcrowded and required extensive alterations. Categorization of prisoners into serious and petty criminals and the requirement to separate them in the prison compounded the problem of lack of space. A new prison and Sessions house built at Louth for the southern division of the parts of Lindsey had by 1826 eased the overcrowding to some extent and minimised travel distances for some of the magistrates. In the late 1860s the decision was taken to reorganise the penal system in the Parts of Lindsey. A new prison for the whole of Lindsey was opened in 1872 in Lincoln, and the three existing houses of correction, including Kirton, were closed.

Subsequent to the committal, Charlotte and her three companions were held in the prison for the three days preceding the trial. Classed as 'committed for trial' they were not required to work. On the day of the trial they were ushered into the courtroom. The trial was brief, perhaps lasting less than fifteen minutes. Sixteen other cases and five vagrants had to be dealt with that day as well as the sentencing of previously convicted offenders. All had to be dealt with quickly to complete the order of the day.

Until 1836, anyone charged with a felony was not allowed to have legal counsel present the case for their defence. Legal representation, if it could be afforded, was allowed only to examine and cross examine witnesses. The accused, in many cases poor and uneducated men and women, were left to speak for themselves. It was argued that to allow persons the aid of counsel in putting forward their statement of fact would make justice slower, more expensive and more theatrical. Furthermore it was contended that the judge represented the interest of the prisoner, a contention which could well be disputed from the evidence of inequality in sentencing.[6]

Charlotte and her companions pleaded not guilty to both charges. The jury, quickly arriving at a verdict, delivered it with equal haste.

LINCOLNSHIRE, LINDSEY.

TO WIT. THE JURORS for our Lord the King upon their Oath, That *James South* late of the parish of *Elsham* in the Parts of Lindsey, in the County of Lincoln, *Laborer, John Grant late of the same place Laborer, Charlotte Dawson late of the same place Spinster and Mary McQueen late of the same place* on the *Twentieth* Day of *October* in the *Seventh* Year of the Reign of our Sovereign Lord George the Fourth, of the united Kingdom of great Britain and Ireland, King, &c., with Force and Arms at the Parish of *Elsham aforesaid* in the Parts and County aforesaid *one checked apron of the value of three pence and one shift* of the value of *three pence* of the Goods and Chattels of one *John Fidell* then and there being found, feloniously did steal, take, and carry away, against the peace of our said Lord the King, his crown and Dignity.[7]

The minute book for the Sessions dryly notes '*Pleas not Guilty – Jury say Guilty*'[8]. Regarding the theft of the checked handkerchief, valued at six pence, belonging to Sarah Fidell, the jury's presentment was the same.[9] Strangely the minute book records that the indictment brought by Sarah Fidell was not heard.[10] This may be in error, but it can be assumed that once they were convicted on the first indictment, it followed that it was of no consequence whether or not they were guilty on the second indictment. To save time there was no need to hear the case and the jury's presentment was drawn up as a matter of course.

Juries were always composed of men aged between twenty-one and sixty who possessed the required property qualification. For Assizes and County Sessions the property qualification was the ownership of freehold land worth £10 per year or leasehold land worth £20 per year, the occupation of a house with fifteen or more windows or the occupation of a dwelling with an annual value for rating of £20.

The work of compiling a jury was left to Sheriff's officers who, for a small sum, would often omit the names of persons best qualified to serve. Payment was no incentive to do jury duty as common jurors received only 8 pence per day in civil cases and nothing at all when sitting on a criminal jury. Therefore, in general, common juries were of poor quality mainly consisting of small farmers and shopkeepers, many of whom were uneducated and had only a narrow horizon of experience.[11] Based on the legal principle that Englishmen should be tried by their peers, jury selection at least provided local geographical representation. As well some jurors served on more than one occasion, which meant that there were at least a few experienced members who were familiar with court procedure, perhaps enhancing the ability for trials to be conducted and concluded quickly.

Sentence was passed immediately once the verdict was received. At the end of the day the list of sentences handed down was officially transcribed.

> Lincolnshire Lindsey To Wit
> At the General Quarter Sessions of the Peace of our Sovereign Lord the King, holden at *Kirton* in and for the Parts of Lindsey, in the County of Lincoln, on *Friday & Saturday* the *Twentieth and Twenty First* Days of *October* in the Seventh Year of the Reign of our Sovereign Lord George the Fourth of the United Kingdom of Great Britain and Ireland, King, &c. and in the Year of our Lord 1826 Before *Sir Robert Sheffield, Baronet, Chairman, Robert Marriott, John Tufnell and John Uppleby Esquires and others*
> Justices of our Lord the King, assigned to keep the Peace of our said Lord the King, in the said Parts of Lindsey, in the said County, and also to hear and determine divers Felonies, Trespasses, and other Misdemeanors, committed within the Parts aforesaid. *James South John Grant Charlotte Dawson and Mary McQueen convicted of Petty Larceny ~ To be*

Remains of a Highland tenant farmer's house, Wester Aberscross, Golspie, Sutherland, Scotland. The rafters were burnt during the clearance and later most of the stone from the walls carted away to be used in constructing other buildings.

A typical Highland "black house" similar to John Campbell's home at Aberscross. *Image courtesy of The Ness Historical Society.*

Wester Aberscross looking towards Loch Fleet. The remains of a kailyard dominate the central portion of the photo.

Elizabeth Gordon Leveson-Gower, (1765 - 1839), 19th Countess of Sutherland and 1st Duchess of Sutherland, *Engraving by S Freeman after T Phillips from the book National Portrait Gallery Volume II ca 1820, Universal Images Group 1899-19342.*

Dunrobin Castle, Golspie, Scotland. Residence of the Earls of Sutherland and home to Countess Elizabeth and her husband Lord Stafford.

View of the Port of Leith, c. 1822. *Francois-Joseph Dupressoir, Scottish National Gallery, D 5511.*

Entrance to Portsmouth, Hampshire, c. 1825, line engraving by E. Finden. from *The Ports, Harbours, Watering-places and Picturesque Scenery of Great Britain Vol. 2,* by William Finden.

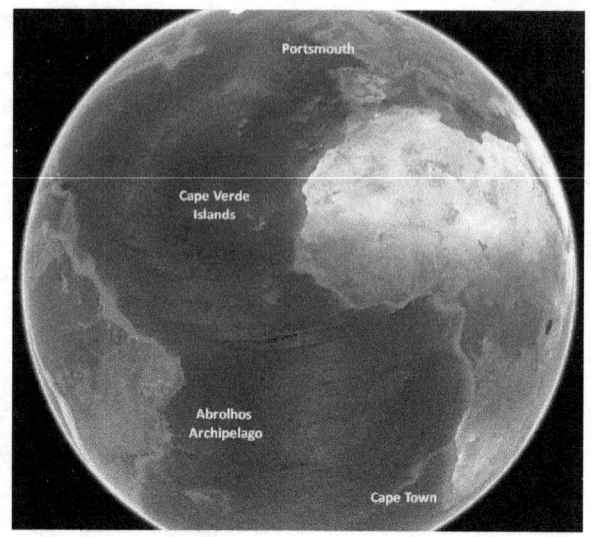

Cape Verde, off the west coast of Africa, and the Abrolhos Archipelago, off the east coast of South America. *Image courtesy of Google Earth.*

View of Cape Town as seen from Oranjezicht farmstead c. 1820. The Government gardens can be seen the middle distance. *Western Cape Archives and Records Service, Photo E9188.*

Hobart Town, Van Diemen's Land, View of the Harbour, c. 1823 when John Campbell first arrived in Australia. *Hand coloured lithograph, Felix Achille Saint Aulaire, 1833. Allport Library and Museum of Fine Arts, Tasmanian Archive and Heritage Office, AUTAS001131821043.*

Hobart Town, Van Diemen's Land, c. 1828. The building at the middle of the left edge of the painting is the warehouse of the Australian Company of Edinburgh and Leith. *Hand coloured lithograph, John Orde Ommanney, 1833. Allport Library and Museum of Fine Arts, Tasmanian Archive and Heritage Office, AUTAS001139593909.*

Thornton Abbey gatehouse c. 1826. From *Thomas Allen, History of the County of Lincolnshire, Vol. II, p.236. Engraving by W. Watkins after a design by J.N. Rhodes.*

St Denys, Church of England, North Killingholme. The building dates from the 12th century.

All Saints Church (C of E), Elsham. The building retains some 12th century Norman features and two 13th century reliefs flanking the arched entrance.

The Stables and courtyard, Elsham Estate.

Village of Elsham nestled below a field of wheat, ripened and ready for harvest.

House of correction and court house, Kirton in Lindsey as it was in 1826. *Image courtesy of the Kirton in Lindsey Society.*

Sir Robert Sheffield (1786-1862), 4th Baronet of Normanby, Lincolnshire, Magistrate. *National Portrait Gallery, London, NPG D40686.*

Changing horses at Spital in the Street. *Image reproduced courtesy of Lincoln Central Library, Lincolnshire County Council, Image LC26095.*

Lincoln Castle – Main east gate.

Inside Lincoln Castle. The red brick building is the gaol. In the foreground is the north end of the County Hall completed in 1826. In the distance, dominating the skyline beyond the gaol is Merryweather's Observatory Tower.

Lincoln Cathedral viewed from the gallows on Cobb Hall Tower.

Inside Lincoln Castle Gaol. The long narrow passageway from the entrance leading to the cells.

Coach and Four driving through the Stonebow, Lincoln, c. 1800. *Image reproduced courtesy of Lincoln Central Library, Lincolnshire County Council, Image LC3638.*

Woolwich Dockyard c. 1790. Oil painting, Nicholas Pocock, *National Maritime Museum, Greenwich, London, BHC1950.*

Prison reformer Elizabeth Fry speaking to prisoners on a convict ship. *English School, The Stapleton Collection, Bridgeman Art Library , STC335883.*

The East India ship *Mellish* entering the harbour of Sydney in 1829. *Edward Duncan. National Library of Australia, nla.pic-an9576808b.* Images of the ships Greenock and Harmony have not been found. The Mellish at 425 tons seen here entering Sydney harbour in 1829 is most likely similar in size and shape to the Greenock and slightly larger than the Harmony.

transported to some place beyond the Seas for the term of seven years ~¹²

The list continued giving the names and sentences handed out to the seventeen other individuals tried, and was signed by Robert Sheffield, Chairman. About a week later, on the 3rd of November, the list was published in the Stamford Mercury newspaper.¹³

The minutes of the Session recorded that Sir Robert Sheffield, Baronet, Richard Ellison and Henry Hutton, Esquires were '*nominated and appointed to contract with any person or persons for the Transportation of the said James South, John Grant, Charlotte Dawson and Mary McQueen as above mentioned and to cause such security to be taken as the Statutes in that case made and provided direct to be taken by order of the Court and also to order the said James South, John Grant, Charlotte Dawson and Mary McQueen to be delivered pursuant to such contract to the person or persons contracting for them or to his or their Assigns.*'¹⁴

Who were these magistrates who passed sentence on those presented before them that day? Sir Robert Sheffield (1786 to 1862) was the 4th Baronet of Normanby in the County of Lincoln and had served as High Sheriff of Lincolnshire. He was married to Julia Brigida Newbolt, daughter of Sir John Henry Newbolt, Chief Justice of Bengal. The Sheffield Baronetcy title was created in 1755 for Charles Herbert Sheffield, the illegitimate son of John Sheffield, 1st Duke of Buckingham and Normanby. John Uppleby Esq was from an established family which had resided in the Barton on Humber area for several centuries. His residence, Wootton Hall, and its associated estate were inherited. He died in 1839. Robert Marriott, Esq. held the estate of Barton and John Tufnell the estate of Horkstow. As well as Commissioners of the Peace, all were Deputy Lieutenants of the Subdivision of Brigg. Other Commissioners of the Peace acting as magistrates, who were referred to in the preamble to the sentence list but not named, were the Reverend Valentine Grantham, D.D of Scawby, Reverend Henry John Wollaston of Scotter, Reverend Frederick Peel of Willingham by Stow, Reverend Richard William Vevers of Marton, Reverend John Robinson of Rasen, Reverend John Nelson of Lincoln, Reverend Sir Charles John

Anderson Baronet of Lea and Reverend John Hildyard of Bonby and Horkstow.[15]

Lord Brownlow, the Lord Lieutenant of Lincolnshire, chose the magistrates for the whole of Lincoln. He insisted on choosing men from the best of landed gentry in the county, but as there were insufficient persons from this class to fill the benches he chose well connected clergymen.[16] No doubt their judgements and the sentences passed were influenced as much by moral concepts as facts under law.

The magistrates rotated throughout the day as each case came before the bench. Charlotte and her companions faced Justices John Uppleby and the Reverend John Hildyard. Uppleby from Wootton, about 5 kilometres west of North Killingholme and Hildyard from Bonby, 5 kilometres north of Elsham may have known them and been aware of any misdemeanours previously committed by any one or all of the four charged. Certainly arresting constable and witness Richard Lawson of North Killingholme would have known Charlotte and been aware of her background. James South in particular had previously been convicted of 'house breaking' in Hull, Yorkshire, a crime for which he had served a lenient sentence of 18 months in the House of Correction at Beverley.[17] Hildyard was 63 years old at the time of the trial and died a year later in November 1827 at the Bonby Vicarage.[18]

Passing sentence was easy once the jury had delivered its verdict. The sentence handed down to Charlotte and her companion petty larcenists was the first to be recorded on the official list of those sentenced that day. Surprisingly none of the other eighteen miscreants was sentenced to transportation. Eleven were sentenced to the Kirton Bridewell for periods varying from 1 to 12 calendar months with or without hard labour, four were acquitted and discharged and the three charged with failing to keep the peace were discharged. Two of the vagrants were discharged, two were recommitted till the next sessions and one was recommitted until the visiting magistrate passed by.

The bonds of the prosecutors and witnesses were discharged,[19] and the expenses associated with the trial paid. It is astounding to see that the costs of the trial were far in excess of the value of the articles stolen. Before the distinction between petty larceny and grand larceny was abolished in 1827, petty larceny was defined as the theft of items valued at less than one shilling (12 pence). The items in this case had a total value of 12 pence, which meant the crime bordered on grand larceny. However, if allocated equally among the four charged each person would have been exposed to a value of only 3 pence. Alternatively, if taken as separate prosecutions the items involved in the theft from John Fidell had a value of 6 pence and the handkerchief stolen from Sarah Fidell had a value of 6 pence which may have influenced the classification of the crime as one of petty larceny. As well, without any aggravating circumstances such as assault or breaking and entering, juries used their discretion to find people accused of thefts of goods valued at one shilling or more, guilty of the lesser crime of petty larceny.

But the classification of the crime is immaterial and the value of the goods stolen insignificant when compared to the bills of expenses relating to the costs of prosecution. Accounts for the two prosecutions amounted to more than 300 times the total value of the items stolen. For the case presented by John Fidell costs were £7 2s 10d in total and for Sarah Fidell £8 3s 10d.[20]

The itemized accounts[21] show that major costs related to the presence of the witnesses at the trial, with horse hire accruing the greatest expense.

For John Fidell
Acc re pros.   *John Fidell vs*
James South John Grant,
Charlotte Dawson and Mary McQueen
For stealing a checked apron

	£	s	d
Instructions for Bench		6	8
Drawing and engrossing same	1	1	0
Fee to W. Hildyard Clerk	1	3	6
Attending him therewith and thereon		4	8
Attending the Trial of this Prosecution 2 days Horsehire etc.	2	2	0

Journey W Thomasin Fidell from Worlaby to Kirton 16 miles		...	8	...
Two days		...	13	...
Sarah Fidell a Witness the like		1	1	0
Wm Thompson a Witness from Brigg 2 days 8 miles		...	7	...
Paid Court fees		...	3	...
		£8	1	10
No.1	debit	1	1	0
Allowed 8 : 1 : 10		7	0	10
			2	
	order	7	2	10

Robt Sheffield   Chairman

For Sarah Fidell

    Acc. re pros.   Sarah Fidell vs
                     James South John Grant,
                     Charlotte Dawson and Mary McQueen
                For stealing an checked Handkerchief

	£	s	d
Instructions for Bench		6	8
Drawing and engrossing same	1	1	0
Fee to W. Hildyard Clerk	1	3	6
Attending him therewith and thereon		6	8
Attending the Trial of this Prosecution			
2 days Horsehire etc.	2	2	0
Prosecutor's Journey from Worlaby to Kirton 16 miles	...	8	...
Two days		13	
Richard Lawson a Witness from East Halton 20 miles	...	10	...
Two days	...	13	...
Wm Thompson journey from Brigg 8 miles 2 days	...	17	...
Paid Court fees	...	3	...
	£8	x3	10

No.3
    Allowed   8 : 3 : 10
        order   4

Robt Sheffield   Chairman

Although the crime was committed at Elsham, John and Sarah Fidell lived at Worlaby about 2 kilometres north of Elsham. Richard Lawson, came from East Halton, 2 kilometres north of North Killingholme, and William Thompson from Brigg, the major market town and administrative centre for the district, located about 7 kilometres southwest of Elsham. Kirton in Lindsey, where the trial took place, was about 20 kilometres southwest of Elsham by road.

It was a major endeavour for the Fidells to undertake a prosecution and tender witnesses at the trial. There was no public prosecution structure. The victim of a crime was expected to carry out investigations, apprehend the suspect with or without the aid of the parish constable, and conduct the actual prosecution in court either personally or by engaging legal counsel. Responsibility for the expenses incurred in the prosecution was also borne by the victim and his or her family.[22] There was therefore a great incentive to recover the goods directly from the defendants outside of court proceedings. If recovery was impossible to achieve, the relatively high individual bond rate of twenty pounds was security that the prosecutors and their witnesses would appear.

Perhaps John Fidell was a member of the 'Associations for Prosecuting of Felons' in Kirton in Lindsey[23] and his expenses defrayed to some extent through membership in this or a similar group. Local traders, landowners and merchants formed such associations to share the costs of criminal investigation and prosecution, in the event that one of their members became a victim of crime.

The legal procedure seems to have been a great waste of time and money and the sentence considered to be very harsh. Today crimes of this sort are usually resolved by fines or repayment, community service work or left unresolved, the victims obliged to seek recompense through insurance claims. But standards were different in the early nineteenth century and concerns over rising levels of property theft meant that as many cases as possible had to be addressed, concluded and exhibited on the presumption that their public display would act as a deterrent to others.

Property was to a large extent considered to be as valuable as human life and until 1827, defendants found guilty of stealing goods worth more than 12 shillings could be sentenced to death. A sentence of death was mandatory if the value of the goods was 40 shillings or more. Transportation was considered to be a more onerous punishment than imprisonment with hard labour, and a growing revulsion towards execution often resulted in the death penalty being commuted to transportation for life.

Transportation, as a penalty, had been around since the 17th century but had commenced to Australia only in 1787 after the American War of Independence and the loss of the American colonies. Removal to such a distant land gave a far greater sense of finality to such a sentence. Furthermore a return from transportation before the period of the sentence had elapsed was a felony punishable by death. Thus, although it was believed that transportation might lead to the reformation of the offender, the primary motivations behind this punishment were a belief in its deterrent effect, and a desire to simply remove criminals from society for lengthy periods of time if not for good. It also seems there was an unstated objective in providing a growing population for the Australian colonies not only as a cheap workforce but also to bolster Britain's claim to the island continent. But by the 1820s, there appears to have been a growing belief in the greater population that transportation was not as bad a form of punishment as it was promoted to be.

Notes to Chapter 7

1   LA, Calendar of Prisoners: a printed list of all those due to appear at the Quarter Sessions Court at Kirton in Lindsey, Lincolnshire on 20 October 1826., LQS/A/1/500/14.
2   Thomas Allen, *History of the County of Lincolnshire*, Vol. II, p.32, Saunders, London & Lincoln, 1834.
3   Accounts & Papers relating to Gaol Commitments; Convict Establishment; Game Laws; the Tread Wheel, Session 3 February to July 1825, Vol XXIII, House of Commons, p. 152.
4   Rosemary Weaver, *Kirton In Lindsey, Historical Aspects, The Life and Times of the House of Correction.*, pp.44-55, Kirton in Lindsey Writers' Group, Belton Ltd., Gainsborough, 1993.
5   The Lincoln, Rutland and Stamford Mercury, Friday, December 13, 1822, p.3, col.3.

6   Hammond, J.L. & B., *The Village Labourer*, Vol. 1, p2.198-200, Longmans, Green & Co., London, 1948.
7   LA, Jurors Presentments (Verdicts) LQS/A/1/500/ 144.
8   LA, Minute Book, Michaelmas 1826 LQS/A/2/40.
9   LA, Jurors Presentments (Verdicts) LQS/A/1/500/ 143.
10   LA, Minute Book, Michaelmas 1826 LQS/A/2/40.
11   David Bentley, English Criminal Justice in the Nineteenth Century, Hambledon, London, 1998, chapter 10, pp.89 – 94.
12   LA, List of Sentences: for those appearing at the Quarter Sessions Court at Kirton in Lindsey, Lincolnshire on 20th and 21st October 1826, LQS/A/1/500/170; Lincolnshire Archives, Minute Book, Michaelmas 1826 LQS/A/2/40.
13   The Lincoln, Rutland and Stamford Mercury (LRSM), Friday, November 3, 1826, p.4. col.1.
14   LA, Sessions Minutes, Michaelmas 1826 LQS/A/2/40.
15   Thomas Allen, op. cit., Vol. I, pp. 96-99.
16   Rosemary Weaver, op. cit., p46.
17   AOTAS, Convict Conduct Record, CON 31/1/38, p270, No.803.
18   The Gentleman's Magazine and Historical Chronicle from July To December 1827, Volume XCVII. *Clergy Deceased* p 570.
19   LA, Sessions Minutes, Michaelmas 1826 LQS/A/2/40.
20   LA, Bills of Expenses, LQS/A/1/500/183 & 184.
21   The Minute Book records that Sarah Fidell was ordered to pay £7.2s.10d and John Fidell to pay £8 3s 10d This is at odds with the itemised accounts in the Bills of Expenses showing total charges of £7.2s.10d to John and £8 3s 10d to Sarah.
22   Douglas Hay and Francis Snyder, (eds) *Policing and Prosecution in Britain 1750-185*, Clarendon, Oxford, 1989.
23   The Lincoln, Rutland and Stamford Mercury, Friday, October 20, 1826, p.2, col.4.

Chapter 8

Gaol

When their trial had finished, the verdict read and sentence passed Charlotte, Mary and the two men were returned to the cells in the Bridewell. It was normal for prisoners under sentence of transportation to spend the first part of their sentence in the prison where they had awaited trial until such time as the secretary of state ordered their removal to a convict facility.

Charlotte and her companions remained only a few days at Kirton. Accompanied by an official from the jail, they were taken out to the turnpike road east of town and put on one of the coach services. Travelling south along the straight turnpike road, they made a brief stop at Spital in the Street for a change of horses and were quickly on their way. They entered Lincoln through the Newport Arch, the ancient Roman portal to the city, and proceeded along Bailgate Road until they were between Lincoln Cathedral to their left and Lincoln Castle to their right. Turning sharply to their right, Lincoln Castle loomed over them, its arched Norman gateway flanked by imposing, dull yellow, drum shaped stone towers. The castle's thick limestone walls extended left and right at a height of 40 feet, the wall to the left terminating at a corner topped with a round turret.

Passing through the gateway they entered the bailey, a spacious area of more than 6 acres, in which, immediately to the left, stood the prison, a brick built Georgian building, elegant in style if not in purpose. Directly in front in the middle of the bailey was the grand, new Gothic Style County Hall with its high battlemented turrets, arcaded facade and lancet arched windows. Against the bailey wall to the right, was a small, rectangular stone built bathhouse. Other than the high stone walls surrounding the bailey, not much more could be taken in before they were deposited in the gaol.

The Lincoln Castle Gaoler simply noted in his journal on the 25th of October 1826 *'No complaints. Four more transports committed this day from Kirton'*.[1] The Matron examined the women and the Surgeon inspected them prior to admission to their proper ward. Once they were settled in, the Matron ordered them to take a warm bath and clean themselves. Although rules for governance of the gaol stated that necessary clothing should be issued on arrival there is no note in the Gaoler's diary that clothing was given to the women and it can be assumed that, initially at least, they wore the clothes they had arrived in and any changes of clothing brought with them.[2]

More was revealed in Surgeon, F.E. Franklyn's notes for the day. South and Grant were medically examined and found to be free from infectious diseases. Mary McQueen was free from sickness, but Charlotte Dawson's condition was described as 'Venereal'. Three days later James South was also determined to have the same infection.[3] Charlotte and other venereal patients, both male and female, were soon separated from the rest of the prisoners.

Lincoln Castle is situated on the summit of a hill along the limestone escarpment, the same geographical feature on which the village of Kirton in Lindsey to the north is located. From the top of its walls and towers, splendid views over the Trent Valley to the west and the surrounding countryside and city in all directions can be obtained. To the east, the magnificent Lincoln Cathedral dominates the view.

Originally a Roman fort occupied the summit. It was further fortified by the Normans in the 11th century and over the ensuing centuries a castle developed. The castle's defences were constantly improved and dungeons for holding prisoners were constructed under Cobb Hall, a 13th century tower guarding the north east sector of the castle. A court house and a county gaol were built within the precincts of the castle about the beginning of the 17th century.[4] The cathedral, opposite the east entrance to the castle, was first consecrated in 1092 by the Norman Bishop, Remigius, a Benedictine monk, and achieved its present form by the end of the 14th century.

Following a scathing report on the county gaol by prison reformer John Howard, a new prison was completed in 1787. The front half of this building survives today and the facade of the building is much as it was in 1826. Howard believed that prisoners could be rehabilitated and would change their ways if they were given a reasonable standard of living, allowed to keep clean, given fresh food and water and kept occupied through useful employment. They should be provided with the opportunity to benefit from regular religious instruction and education. As well, in order for them to repent of their crimes, he believed they should be given privacy in their own cells for quiet contemplation. Howard's reforms meant that in a model prison, the prisoners wore a uniform, were taught to read and write, were reasonably fed, had their health monitored and were productively employed.

Similarly, Elizabeth Fry sought reforms in prison life, particularly for women incarcerated in gaols throughout the country. Initially she organised groups of women to visit the prisons to give female prisoners support and moral, religious and occupational instruction. In 1827 she published 'Observations on the Visiting, Superintendence, and Government of Female Prisoners' promoting the formation of Ladies Committees to visit the gaols, employment of female officers in gaols and employment instruction and education for the prisoners, provision of medical aid and proper food, clothing and bedding and lastly, attention to the care of the women after they were released from prison.

In theory the models proposed by Howard and Fry were a great improvement, but in practice they were rarely achieved in their entirety. At least, the implementation of some reforms ensured that progress was being made towards improvement in prison conditions and in the well being of the prisoners.

The new prison, a T shaped building, was a vast improvement over the previous gaol but by 1826 was overcrowded. It had three stories consisting of a ground floor and a chamber floor covering the whole building and twelve attic rooms above the front part of the edifice. Inside the prison on the left, in proximity to the main entrance, were the Visiting Magistrates room and Keeper's sitting room, and on the right a room for visitors and a solicitor's room. Also in the front part of the building, further to the left of the rooms just described, was the Keeper's private entrance, his office and his dining room, kitchen, pantry and scullery. On the opposite side of the building were day rooms principally for Certified and Master Debtors and a kitchen, hall and room for officers of the prison.

Directly ahead of the entrance and slightly elevated, was a long, narrow passage running the length of the building and bordered by day rooms and night cells. Doorways to these rooms were fitted with metal studded, thick wooden doors. Exterior to the passageway and cells and accessible from the dayrooms were four large separate courtyards, two each side of the building, enclosed by thick walls.

At the end of the passage way, on the left side, were two dayrooms, 13 feet long by 8 feet, 2 inches wide, each with its own smaller courtyard for the female prisoners and females awaiting trial. On the right was a small dayroom or holding cell 9 feet, 6 inches long by 8 feet, 2 inches wide with its own attached small courtyard for convicted females. Also on the right, behind the female cell, was the prisoners' kitchen with an adjacent small courtyard as well.

On the Chamber or first floor, again at the front of the building on the left and accessed by a private staircase, were five lodging rooms for the Keeper. Two softwater cisterns and an officer's room were also located in this area. On the right side of the building were the turnkey's lodging room, an officers' room and debtors sleeping rooms and with separate access to the ground floor. The passage way, repeated on this floor, was flanked by nine sleeping rooms of two different sizes, 10 feet long by 9 feet wide and 12 feet, 6 inches long by 9 feet wide. Further on were two large store rooms, one each side of the passage and at the end of the passage, the chapel, at 28 feet long by 27 feet, 6 inches wide, the largest room in the prison.[5]

Each prisoner was given a mattress and bolster filled with dry, clean rye or wheat straw and as many blankets or rugs as required for warm or cold weather. The straw was changed, at the very least, during April, June August and December and the mattress and bolster covers washed and laid on clean when the straw was changed in April and August. Unless other directions had been given, the four new arrivals settled in to used mattresses and bolsters stuffed with old straw. Clean sheets were put on the women's beds when they arrived and changed on the last Friday of each month. Dirty clothing was washed and returned clean to its owner every Saturday.[6]

The cells were sparsely furnished to provide minimal comfort. As well as bedding, each sleeping room was supplied with a covered soil-pail for a toilet and clothes pegs, the two items listed together in the rules suggesting some sort of useful relationship. A copy of the New Testament was placed in every sleeping room and a copy of the Lord's Prayer hung on the wall. Rooms occupied by sick prisoners were furnished with a hand bell for summoning help. The day rooms were supplied with two ounces of soap per person each week, washing bowls, seats, pegs, mops, brooms, water buckets and coal pans. In each day room was a Bible and Prayer Book.[7]

Two types of prisoners were kept in the gaol: debtors and felons. Debtors, imprisoned for private debt, lived in a sort of limbo between being free men and felons. They formed the largest number of prisoners at any one time and were divided into two groups: Master Debtors who maintained themselves with help from friends and relatives at no less than 5 shillings per week, and Certificated Debtors who, unable to pay 5 shillings, were maintained by the county. Gifts of food were not allowed and if made were sent back to the donor.[8]

Felons, including transports, were maintained by the County and kept in small, cramped day cells and night cells euphemistically referred to as rooms. The sexes occupied separate wards with no fewer than three males and not less than two females in their respective day rooms. Male prisoners, other than debtors, were divided into two classes: convicts and those committed to trial, the latter class subdivided into three classes according to conduct and nature of offence. Similarly female felons were divided into two classes: those convicted and those committed to trial without further division as to character.[9]

The High Sheriff of the County had overall authority in the implementation of rules and regulations legislated by parliament for governing the gaol. At the General and Quarter Sessions of the Peace, Justices of the County were instructed to nominate and appoint those officials required for the governance and administration of the gaol. They also nominated two or more justices from their number to be Visiting Justices who inspected the Gaol on the first Friday of every month.[10]

The prison was administered along the same lines as described for the House of Correction at Kirton In Lindsey, the principal control of the prison being under the command of a Keeper or Gaoler, often endearingly referred to as the 'Governor'. He was assisted by a Matron who superintended the female prisoners, a Chaplain and at least one duty Surgeon plus several other officers including turnkeys. Both the Keeper and the Matron resided within the prison. Their salaries and those of the other officers were fixed by the Justices of the County at the General and Quarter Sessions and paid out of the County rates. Regulations ordered the officers to behave impartially and kindly to all prisoners and prohibited them from making fun of any prisoner, holding unnecessary communication with them or employing any of them in their personal service.[11]

In 1826 the Keeper of the prison was John Merryweather. He was 59 years old. Earlier in his career he had been accused of brutality towards a female prisoner and his fiery, confrontational personality combined with devious business practices connected with his official position won him few friends. He took an interest in astronomy and one of his greatest achievements was the building of a turret, Observatory Tower, on the southeast corner of the castle where he could pursue his hobby. The Tower completed in 1822 became Lincoln's most famous landmark after the castle. But his enemies accused him of spending more time at his telescope studying the activities of the female prisoners than in observing the planets and stars. It was claimed that he and his architect, Sir Robert Smirke made a small fortune using convict labour rather than local contractors for building the new Shire Hall, now the Crown Court, completed in 1826 within the castle grounds. This work led to great controversy and both men, were accused of lining their pockets with public money and criticised for their handling of the matter. In spite of these shortcomings Merryweather often showed compassion and benevolence towards the prisoners in his gaol and the inmates seem to have liked him. A lifelong bachelor, he made no secret of the fact that two daughters living with him were the illegitimate offspring of a female prisoner who had been in his gaol. One of the daughters married a successful lawyer and their son, Frederick Merryweather Burton, became a famous geologist.[12]

Life in the prison followed a set routine. Between 12 October and 10 March, as soon as it was light but never later than half-past seven in the morning or at 6 o'clock during the remainder of the year, a bell was rung and the sleeping rooms' doors opened. Within fifteen minutes the prisoners were counted-off and descended to the days rooms and yards. The turnkey carefully examined the locks, bolts, bars, windows, walls and bedding to ensure all was in order. Hours for meals, instruction, chapel, work and cleaning rooms were appointed to introduce the utmost order system and punctuality in the prison. After the sleeping rooms had been cleaned in the morning, the beds made and soil-pails emptied, the prisoners were denied further access to those rooms until bedtime. A bell summoned inmates to Chapel. Divine Service and Prayers were read daily and the Chaplain preached a sermon every Sunday, on Christmas Day, Good Friday and on the day before an execution. All prisoners were obliged to attend religious services unless they had a legitimate excuse sanctioned by the Keeper or were prevented by conscientious scruple. Provision was made for prisoners of both sexes to be instructed in reading and writing. At sunset a bell was rung, the yards were locked and the prisoners retired to their sleeping rooms. No lights were allowed after dark.[13]

Cleanliness, in its esteemed position next to godliness, was dictated in respect to the prison and its occupants. Each year before the Spring Assizes the gaol was thoroughly cleaned, the walls scraped and whitewashed and paint applied where needed. The prison had been entirely cleaned and the windows washed before the October Gaol Sessions in preparation for inspection by the visiting Justices. It was therefore in good condition when Charlotte and Mary arrived.

Whenever the weather allowed, all sleeping room doors and windows were opened and left open until the yards were locked in the afternoon. Regarding personal hygiene, convenient places for washing and an adequate supply of soap, towels and combs were provided. The women were not required to have their hair cut unless they wished, but were to appear at all times with their faces and hands washed, hair combed and as neat and clean as circumstances would allow.[14]

It was also considered necessary to keep the prisoners as healthy as possible. The day rooms and sleeping rooms were supposed to be kept sufficiently warm in winter and all bedding well aired and kept dry. The surgeon resided near the gaol, visited at least twice a week and when notified of any sick or newly committed prisoners was expected to attend immediately. He was instructed to note in his journal the smallest neglect of cleanliness, or ventilation, any bad quality of provisions and any other mismanagement that may have affected the general health of the prison. He gave directions for isolating prisoners who had or were suspected of having infectious complaints and for cleansing any rooms occupied by such prisoners. Diet, bedding, clothing or other comforts could be given to sick prisoners at his request.[15]

Every prisoner maintained at the expense of the County was allowed a sufficient quantity of plain, wholesome food necessary for the support of their health.[16] In an endeavour to keep costs down and avoid giving prisoners a better life than the poor outside, the prison management purchased low cost provisions and kept the prisoners' food as simple as possible.

Food requirements, established in the 1820s, provided a standard diet, but, although ensuring that the quantity of food was adequate, did not ensure that the quality was of a high standard. Female prisoners, orderly in their conduct and especially if pregnant or suckling a child, could request that all or any part of their diet be converted into money to be spent on 'other proper articles of diet'.[17]

Regulation of daily meals meant the diet was very monotonous. At the very least, every second day, prisoners received a loaf of good wheaton bread weighing three pounds plus two ounces of salt on Saturday and Wednesday.[18] Whatever else supplied was at the direction of the Gaol Sessions and generally consisted of gruel (oatmeal or oatmeal and potatoes) or vegetable soup and, each week, a small ration of meat.

Provision was made for employing all prisoners to the benefit of the County. Tools and materials were supplied pertinent to their various tasks. Males and females under sentence of transportation were kept at hard labour for up to ten hours each day except for Sundays, Christmas Day and Good Friday or any other days appointed for fasting or thanksgiving. They, along with convicted felons at ordinary labour, were deemed to be prisoners at labour, their quantity of work determined and executed in whatsoever part of the prison the Committee of Visiting Justices directed. Time diligently spent in attending infirm prisoners, in cleaning the gaol, or in instruction was considered to be equal to County work and deducted from their daily work requirement. Prisoners who could not be compelled lawfully to work were deemed prisoners at wages and were paid at a rate determined by the Visiting Justices according to the type of work or amount of time during which it was undertaken.[19]

On the fourth day after their arrival, the Gaoler issued clothing, consisting of stockings only, to the two men.[20] But James South and John Grant stayed only briefly in the prison. A letter dated 30th October from George Robert Dawson, Undersecretary for Home Affairs, to the Head Superintendent of the prison ordered their removal, along with ten other male prisoners, to the prison hulk *Leviathon* at Portsmouth. A similar letter was sent to John Henry Capper, Superintendent of the Prison Hulks, instructing him to receive the same.[21]

Ten days later the twelve convicts, accompanied by the Gaoler, set out for Portsmouth[22] and on 12 November 1826 South and Grant were received on board the *Leviathon* as prisoners numbered 7806 and 7807. The Gaoler's report describes John Grant as 'a most daring character and ought never to be at large'.[23] Similarly James South was described as 'a most daring character, has been convicted before, he is never to be at large'.[24]

Both men remained on the hulk for several months under close supervision. They worked on shore; ate and slept in irons. Idleness was punished by the burden of double irons and flogging was common for any misdemeanour or insubordination. Food was often short rationed and at any rate was barely edible at the best of times. Conditions below deck were cramped and squalid and the stench overpowering. At night the hulk was locked down, the prisoners confined below deck left to their own devices. This afforded some relief, rest and recreation, often with women smuggled on board or discretely brought onto the hulk after bribing a prison guard.

South's reputation did not improve during his imprisonment. Initially of orderly character, the overseer's comments during his final 3 months on the hulk were left blank. But his character was later described as 'Bad'.[25] On 21 March 1827, South was sent to the convict transport ship *Governor Ready*[26] (512 tons) which had arrived at Portsmouth from London. The ship sailed for Van Diemen's Land on 5 April under the command of John Young with ship's Surgeon Thomas Braidwood Wilson and arrived in Hobart on 31 July 1827. Out of 192 male convicts 191 were landed in Hobart, one having died from '*Pulmonic Inflammation*' on the voyage.

Wilson seems to have had a penchant for Latin. Whereas most surgeons wrote their journals in English, applying Latin only to medical terms, Wilson's entire journal including his final report to the navy was written in Latin.[27] His brother James was also a surgeon and they, with a third brother, eventually settled in Tasmania. Thomas subsequently moved to New South Wales where he obtained a grant of land which he named Braidwood, the name later given to the town founded there.[28]

John Grant was put on board the *Marquis of Hastings* on 9 April 1827 bound for New South Wales.[29] Charles Stedman, the overseer of the *Leviathon* at Portsmouth gave an account of Grant's bodily state as being good and his behaviour as orderly and good during captivity on the hulk.[30] Perhaps life on the hulk had some reforming effect.

The *Marquis of Hastings* under Master John Jeffrey Drake and Surgeon Gilbert King sailed from Portsmouth on the 14 April 1827 with 168 male convicts on board. At Tenerife the ship stopped briefly for supplies. After a voyage of 104 days the ship arrived in Sydney on 31 July 1827. King was meticulous in his attempts to maintain the health of his passengers and would not allow any prisoners who were diseased or unfit for the voyage on board the ship at Portsmouth. Only three cases of scurvy were reported, attended to and cured during the voyage. Unfortunately there was one death. A child of one of the soldiers had constant diarrhoea. Its mother, thinking it to be a normal condition, neglected to take the child to the surgeon until it was too late. Despite King's efforts to save the child it died.[31]

Meanwhile Charlotte and Mary McQueen, still incarcerated in Lincoln Castle prison, were joined by a third female to be transported to Australia with them. She was Martha Hubbert, convicted and sentenced on 24th October at the Quarter Sessions in Louth to 7 years transportation for stealing a band box, 3 cotton gowns, 2 petticoats, 4 pairs of white cotton stockings, 2 calico shifts, 2 aprons, 3 caps and 3 yards of ribbon from the Greyhound public house. The goods belonged to Bridget Dowey a single woman of Horncastle.[32] Martha, also from Horncastle, was 39 years old and married to Nathaniel Hubbert a labourer. She had been convicted previously in July 1818 and sentenced to seven years transportation. But after spending over a year on the prison hulk *Justitia* waiting to be transported, she had been pardoned on the 23rd of June 1820 and had returned to Lincolnshire.[33] Now she was back in prison. As a repeat offender (having previously been committed to trial on three separate occasions) she had little chance of escaping transportation this time.

Surgeon William Whyers, on duty 28th of October following Martha's arrival the previous day, examined her. He described her as a *'scrofulous subject'* having *'Fluor Albus combined with suppressed menstruation'*.[34] Martha stood five feet and one-half inch tall, had a pale fair complexion, dark brown hair tending to grey in parts and brown eyes. Her face was marked by a mole on the bridge of her nose and a raised mole under her lower lip.

Although regular entries were made in the Gaoler's journal, they were not made every day and usually limited to a brief description of clothing issues, receipt and removal of transports and more commonly about conditions in the prison. From the journal entries one would think it was a model prison with the prisoners looked after in a humane and caring way. The comments rarely varied from: *'no complaints', 'prison clean', 'everything in good order, not any complaints', 'attendance at chapel orderly and good', 'prison is clean and all in good order and free from complaints', 'everything right in the prison and no complaints'*. But the journal entries were more likely an indication of the control exercised over the prisoners, giving the Gaoler nothing to complain about rather than an indication of the prisoners' welfare.

On the night of 16th November, two prisoners in cell block Number 2 pulled up the step under the locked yard door and escaped into the outer yard. One of them succeeded in getting over the bailey wall. The other, perhaps less agile, could not get over the wall and after a considerable search was found hiding in the outer yard. The Gaoler's only comment was that he had '*no other cause of complaint*'.[35]

Wearing apparel was ordered for the three female convicts on 2nd November.[36] The new clothes were of little comfort to Charlotte. Although life in the prison had certain reliable routines, actual living conditions were miserable and, as a result, life was wretched. The small, cramped cell was cold and damp during the winter days and a monotonous menu of gruel with a weekly ration of meat was debilitating. She continued to suffer from venereal disease. To make matters worse just as she seemed to be getting better she spilled a container of boiling water and scalded one of her feet.[37]

Christmas passed by uneventfully, the Gaoler's only comment being '*not any complaints*' as usual. Morning and evening services were held at the chapel on Christmas Day, the Chaplain commenting in his journal that the prisoners were very attentive.[38] A great number of debtors and felons were received the second week in January forcing the Gaoler to procure additional bedding for the increased numbers in the gaol. From time to time, on a specific day, the Gaoler would comment in his journal on the orderly and good behaviour of the prisoners at chapel suggesting that on some occasions this may not have been the case.

In the New Year, daily chapel services were disrupted owing to the construction of iron frames around the felons' seats, perhaps confirming the assumption that order and good behaviour were not usually the norm. After three days the work was still in progress but tools and materials were removed to permit a service to be performed about which the Gaoler commented that '*everyone conducted themselves properly*'. Chapel services were then discontinued for a further week while the workmen completed their task.[39]

Charlotte suffered headaches at the end of December and indigestion early in January. On the 8th of January Mr Franklyn visited the prison, for the second time that day, to examine the venereal patients. He wished to examine Charlotte but was *'peremptorily refused'* and was *'therefore unable to prescribe for her case'*.[40]

In mid January, Mr Whyers treated Charlotte and Mary McQueen for constipation of the bowels. A new diet for the Crown Prisoners had commenced on 27th January but must not have been much better than the one previously dispensed. There were complaints to the Gaoler from some of the prisoners and when the Visiting Magistrate inspected the prison on the 9th of February, the prisoners complained to him about the insufficiency of food. The Gaoler was given orders to give the prisoners an additional half pound of beef on Thursday each week until the situation had been reviewed at the next Sessions.[41] The extra food was of little benefit to Charlotte. On 4th of March she was diagnosed as having scurvy.[42]

Later that month all of the prisoners were exposed to a sobering event. On 23rd March, William Udale, convicted of sheep stealing, was executed by public hanging on the roof of Cobb Hall Tower. The elevated position of the scaffold offered the crowds outside the castle, and the prisoners inside, a good view of the event. It also gave the condemned man a brief opportunity to enjoy a wonderful view of the cathedral. Udale had entered the gaol on 14th of March directly after having received the death penalty at the Lincoln Assizes.[43] A second prisoner Thomas Barnes had also been convicted of sheep stealing, but his sentence of death was recommended for commutation to transportation for life.

William Udale, had stolen eight sheep in the parish of Sutton St Mary's on the 6th or 7th of December 1826. The sheep belonged to Richard Peel of the same Parish. Udale, 31 years old, was a drover, but in December was working as a labourer, getting work when and where he could. William Ward, Mr Peel's shepherd and witness, stated that his master had 50 sheep in a close in Sutton St Mary's on Wednesday the 6th. Eight of them were missing on the following Friday morning. The prisoner lived near the field from which the sheep had been stolen.

Ward saw Udale on the next Sunday morning and asked if he had seen the eight missing sheep, stating that Udale knew their mark very well and 'must have known the sheep if he had met them.' Udale said he should know them well enough, but he had not seen any of them. When Ward asked him where he had been for the last day or two Udale replied that he had been in Wells Fen (10 miles away), where he was keeping some sheep.

On the Monday, Ward had found four live sheep, and the skin of a dead one, at Mr Richardson's of Chatteris in the Isle of Ely, 28 miles from Sutton. The blue, shoulder paint mark, identifying the sheep as Peel's, had been obscured by a broad red ochre mark, but on separating the wool, he discovered the blue mark underneath. An ochre mark had also been put over the tail. He could swear positively to their being his master's sheep.

The second witness John Richardson, a farmer, from Chatteris stated that Udale had come to his house between 8 and 9 in the morning of Friday the 8th of December, and asked to be allowed to put five sheep into his cole-seed. He consented to the request, and in the afternoon he saw the sheep in his field. Udale called again in the evening and Richardson told him that he had seen the sheep and mentioned the marks to him. Udale said he had 'well marked them'. Udale left that night on a coach but before leaving he offered to sell the sheep to Richardson and said if he could not send him the money for the sheep in a few days, he was to forward them to market in Richardson's own name. Richardson also informed the court that Udale was married to his sister and he had never heard anything against his good character. He explained that since Udale was a drover he expected that the sheep belonged to him. On behalf of Udale he had intended to send them to market in his own name.

Two of Mr Richardson's servants stated that they had witnessed Udale deliver the sheep to their master's place. One of the servants had skinned the sheep which had died. Udale in his defence said he had sold scores of sheep for Mr. Peel, and his sheep were not marked as those five were. Mr Peel, called to witness, said the prisoner had not sold any sheep for him since 1822. The Judge, in summing up, instructed the jury to determine whether the prisoner having said he had 'well' marked the sheep did or did not mean that he had put on the ochre to conceal the rightful paint mark.[44]

In contrast, Thomas Barnes, a 30 year old labourer from Alford was tried at the same Assizes for killing a sheep, the property of Mr William Cook of Burgh. The sheep was killed in a field at Croft on the 12th of September and the carcass stolen. The principal witness for the prosecution was Solomon Kelk, an accomplice who stated that he and Barnes had gone with a cart and three asses to Gibralter Point near Wainfleet to gather samphire. As they were going Barnes said they would have some fowls or something before they went home. Kelk replied that he would not do it, implying that if caught they could face transportation. Barnes retorted that he would do it indicating that someone he knew had been transported for such a crime and had liked it so much that he wanted to go back. Therefore he would wish to be transported if caught and convicted.

After gathering a cart load of samphire they set out for home. Between seven and eight-thirty in the evening they had a few drinks in Chequers public-house at Croft before continuing on to Burgh. About a mile from Croft, Barnes asked Kelk to stop for a minute and climbed over the rails into a field saying 'we'll have a sheep'. They had some difficulty catching one, Kelk falling down and pleading with Barnes to give up the pursuit. Barnes was adamant that they continue. One was eventually caught, killed, dressed and the carcass put in a sack and placed in the cart. The cart was taken to Barnes' home at Alford, where they arrived between 2 and 3 o'clock in the morning. Thomas Walter, the landlord of Chequers confirmed that the pair had been drinking at the pub and Joseph Dairs, a labourer of Alford, stated that a cart had disturbed him between two and three in the morning. Looking out of his bed room window he had seen Barnes and Kelk, unloading the cart at Barnes' house.[45]

In both cases the jury returned a verdict of guilty and Chief Justice Best in sentencing the two prisoners to death gave the following address.

> You William Udale and Thomas Barnes, have been convicted by an intelligent jury, upon most clear and satisfactory evidence, of the crime of sheep-

stealing. Another prisoner had been tried at these assizes for a similar offence and others on charges of cattle-stealing. Property kept in the fields is very much exposed to depredation; and the farmer distressed as he is by the state of agriculture, must be brought to ruin, if his property is not protected by the most severe punishment being inflicted on those who commit depredations upon it. I do not mean that in all cases of this nature, it would be proper to carry into execution the extreme punishment of the law; but where this species of crime is shown to be prevalent, and in cases which are marked by aggravating circumstances, it is the undoubted duty of a Judge to endeavour to stop it by inflicting the most severe punishment. With respect to you, Thomas Barnes, I am most happy in saying that I shall be able to recommend you to his Majesty's mercy; you appear to have been impelled to the commission of this crime by hunger and want; but if his majesty should be pleased to attend to my recommendation (of which I entertain no doubt), you will be removed out of this country for the rest of your life. I am afraid that you will find that you are dreadfully mistaken in supposing that the punishment of transportation is now a pleasant thing. I do not wish to aggravate your sufferings, but I wish to deter others from being led to a commission of crime by the idle notion that transportation is a light punishment. You will be sent from this country to a bad and distant clime; you will be compelled to work for the benefit of others, receiving no reward for your labour. I know of no punishment more severe except that to which I am about to sentence you, William Udale, yours is an aggravated case: You stole not to satisfy the cravings of hunger, but for the purpose of sale – to support an idle and profligate life. If ever any one case was more fit than another to make a severe example of, yours is that case. You had been a drover, and therefore well knew the value of the property you stole; you had been employed by the prosecutor; you have made no appeal to anyone for character, except to the brother of your wife; and you acted like an accomplished thief, using the most cunning means to evade detection. Let me, however, tell you, and others implicated in crime, and it is the opinion of one who has had much experience of such matters, that, by the wise dispensations of Providence, the very means used to avoid detection, most frequently lead to a confirmation of guilt. Be assured no cunning of a guilty mind is sufficient to guard against the detection of crime. Let me strongly recommend you to make all the reparation in your power to the country whose laws you have violated, by a discovery of any accomplice you may have had, that they may be arrested in their guilty career. Repent of your crimes, and let the fruit of that repentance be, a full confession for the benefit of society. My fervent prayer is, that you may obtain at the fountain of all grace that mercy which cannot be extended to you on this side of the grave. Employ the little of this life that remains to you, in preparing for another. Put yourself under the guidance and protection of the Rev. Clergyman whose duty it is to attend persons in your unfortunate situation; observe his directions for obtaining forgiveness of your sins, through the mediation of a merciful Redeemer; and may you receive the hands of a heavenly Judge, that mercy which must be denied you here.[46]

Udale was not without some support, seemingly from powerful connections. Three appeals were made for mercy on his behalf. The first petition was from the Reverend Doctor Chatfield, vicar of Chatteris, Cambridgeshire. It was dismissed by Robert Peel, Home Secretary, who saw *'no reason whatever in the circumstances'* inspite of Udale's powerful connections, *'why the Law should not take its Course'*. The letter to Chatfield from Henry Hobson, undersecretary of State for the Home Office, stated that Peel did not perceive any circumstance stated in the petition *'that would justify him consistently with his Public Duty, in recommending the Prisoner to His Majesty as a fit object for an extension of the Royal Mercy.'*[47]

A further appeal came from Lord Charles Manners, member for Cambridgeshire, a General in the British army and second son of Charles Manners the fourth duke of Rutland. Robert Peel's reply from Whitehall on 20th March was brief. *'My Lord, I have the honor to acknowledge the receipt of Your Lordship's letter of yesterdays date in favor of Wm. Udale under Sentence of Death at Lincoln for sheep stealing, and I am sorry to inform Your Lordship that I see no ground for interfering with the discretion of the Judge who tried The Prisoner.'*[48]

With the same words, Peel, on the 21st of March, also dismissed a letter in Udale's favour from the Right Honourable Lord Francis Godolphin Osborne, second member of parliament for Cambridgeshire.[49] Hope of a reprieve for Udale was now exhausted.

In the days leading up to his execution the Gaoler reported Udale to be composed and his conduct described as orderly, becoming and proper. As he could not read, two prisoners who could read were placed with him to assist him in *'his religious exercises'*. His wife and child came from Long Sutton to visit him on the night of the 21st of March. They were admitted again the following morning. Preparations were made for the execution and the sermon for the condemned man was given that afternoon.[50]

Through all this the Chaplain's journal is strangely silent. The Reverend George Davis Kent was a prebendary of the cathedral at St. Martin's church in St Martin's Lane, but as well as his duties there he held daily services in the prison chapel. Except for certain special religious occasions, such as Christmas Day (which in 1826 occurred on a Monday), entries were made in his journal only on Saturdays. Perhaps this routine explains the lack of comment, but one would have thought that he would have at least mentioned the sermon delivered on Thursday. His only comment is on Friday the 23rd of March: *'William Udale executed this day for sheep stealing confessing the justice of his sentence'*. However he felt that the prisoners obtained some reformative effect from Udale's fate stating on Saturday the 24th:

> *Service every day this week as usual. The prisoners appear very seriously affected by the fate of the late unfortunate Wm. Udale. Their behaviour at Chapel was devout and attentive. No complaints.*[51]

The execution, reported in the Stamford Mercury newspaper was very descriptive.

> *Udale*, the wretched convict for sheep-stealing was executed on the 23rd inst. About a quarter before 12, the usual melancholy procession issued from the prison, and crossed the castle-yard to the north-east tower called Cobb's Tower, upon the top of which the platform had been previously erected. In the lower chamber of the building the last services of religion were administered with impressive fervour by the chaplain (the Rev. G.D. Kent), till within a few minutes of 12 o'clock, at which time Udale ascended the steps leading to the scaffold with many penitential exclamations, accompanied only by the executioner (a convicted horse-stealer) and the gaoler. He walked with a firm step; and as soon as the rope was adjusted properly, the executioner hurried below to draw the bolt which supports the flooring: the criminal, dropping through the opening, appeared to die almost instantaneously: he being a light man, a longer rope was allowed than usual in order to produce a fall of sufficient effect; on which account but little of his body was visible to the crowd below. The concourse of spectators was as large perhaps as ever was known: for a quarter of an hour before the execution, they

continued without intermission pressing forward up the hill in one dense unbroken stream, and from their apparent demeanour might as easily have been supposed to be hurrying to a horse-race or a boxing match as to the most awful of all sights which a human creature can witness. It is particularly disgusting on these occasions to observe the number of *females*, and children, the latter perhaps shouting and chasing each other through the crowd, as at any other place of 'public amusement,' and many of them (incredible as it may seem) actually brought by their parents for the express purpose of *taking warning*. Such parents should surely be told, that an education begun at the gallows, is often but too likely to end there; and, with the additional course of instruction to be derived from dog-fights, pugilism and bull-baitings, has but too often, so ended. – One is tempted to wish that the same discretion which excludes children from the fouler details of a court justice, was also exercised in regard to the brutalistic processes of our public executions.[52]

Graphically descriptive as this article may be, the journalist has skilfully led his readers to a conclusion which reflected the feelings of an ever increasing number of people. Attitudes towards suffering and violence were changing. Execution for crimes against property was considered to be an unjust form of punishment which had little effect as a deterrent to crime; public execution was an unjustified gross spectacle. It was felt that a civil society should show a more humanitarian concern for it citizens whether they were good or bad and that convicted felons could be reformed to become useful members of society.

Udale's body was interred in the burial ground at St Nicholas' Church, beyond the Newport gate rather than in the usual place of internment within the castle-yard. No burial service was read. That evening, a sheep belonging to Mr George Bruce, a butcher at The

Stonebow[53] in the city, was slaughtered and the carcass carried away from a field along the road to Greetwell.[54] This event occurred not far from the place where Udale was executed, emphasising the fact that the threat of execution was no deterrent to a person driven by hunger. Fortunately for Thomas Barnes, the King exercised his mercy and he was transported to Van Diemen's Land later that year on the ship *Asia*.[55]

Charlotte and the other prisoners witnessed the execution. No doubt the event would have had a profound effect on them. The Surgeon's Journal makes no mention of Udale or of the execution. A condemned man's physical health was probably of no concern to the medical practitioners even though they may have been dismayed by their inability, in this case, to preserve life. However, they were still concerned for the health and welfare of the other prisoners in their care.

In mid March, Mr Franklyn had ordered that Martha Hubbard was to be given bread and milk for breakfast instead of the usual prison diet. Within two weeks her health was much improved. Prompted by these results, Charlotte and Mary McQueen were also given bread and milk for breakfast commencing on April 1st and within a few days they were much better.[56] Perhaps there was some urgency to improve the health of the three women as much as possible. Soon they were to be removed from the gaol to a ship moored in the River Thames, waiting to transport them to Australia.

As early as the 21st of December, Robert Peel had requested that the Lords of the His Majesty's Treasury give immediate direction to the Commissioners of the Navy for chartering vessels to transport 140 female convicts and 40 of their children and 15 females, wives of convicts and their 23 children, to Hobart Town, Van Diemen's Land and Port Jackson, New South Wales. It was also requested that their Lordships give directions to the Commissioners of Victualling to provide a sufficient quantity of supplies for their subsistence during the voyage and that the usual quantity of clothing, medicines, medical necessaries, hospital furniture and articles of comfort for everyone be provided for the voyage.[57] Sixty of the female convicts and the 15 wives of convicts and their children were to be sent to Hobart Town and eighty female convicts to Sydney.[58]

It took some time to contract the required vessels. It wasn't until the 30th of March 1827, that the Navy informed the Home Office that the ship *Harmony* had been engaged for *'the conveyance of Eighty Female Convicts and thirty of their children to Port Jackson or Hobart Town'* and asked at which place they were to be landed. Hobson replied that it was Mr Peel's wish that all *'of these persons should be landed at Port Jackson'*.[59]

Once the *Harmony* was at Woolwich in the Thames River near London, the Governor of Lincoln Gaol received instructions to remove Charlotte Dawson, Martha Hubbert and Mary McQueen to the convict transport ship. On the 29th of April Merryweather recorded in his journal that he was preparing to leave home for Woolwich the next evening with the three female convicts.[60]

In 1827 there were two regular coach services between Lincoln and London: The Royal Mail and the Express Post. The Royal Mail departed Barton On Humber for London at 9 am each morning. At Lincoln, it picked up passengers daily at the Saracen's Head Inn (the main headquarters for Coaches in Lincoln)[61] near The Stonebow Arch and departed at half past one in the afternoon. On alternate days it stopped for passengers at the Rein Deer Inn about a mile south.

The Express Post Coach departed Barton at 6 pm daily except Sunday. It also departed from the Saracen's Head and Rein Deer Inns, but at the time of half past eleven in the evening. It arrived in London at half past five in the afternoon the next day, the journey from Lincoln taking approximately 18 hours. Both coaches from Barton took the same route along the turnpike road (now principally the A15) through Brigg, Lincoln, Sleaford, Bourne and Market Deeping to Peterborough and then on to London through Baldock via the Great North Road. The average speed of the coaches, including stoppage time, was between 7 and 8 miles per hour. To maintain this pace, fresh horses were supplied every 10 to 15 miles.[62]

Coaching was in its heyday during the first three decades of the 19th century, before the widespread arrival of railways. Coach design had greatly improved by the end of the 18th century with the introduction of sprung axles, lighter body construction, secure luggage boots and more comfortable seats. Improvements in the quality of the turnpike roads using John L. McAdam's principles of elevating and cambering the road surface by employing successive layers of graded stones finished with a top sheeting of crushed stone, provided an almost level, well drained surface for fast coach travel. By 1820 it was quicker to travel by fast coach than on horseback.[63] Still, roads built in this way could be very rough in places. Stiff competition for business made racing a common occurrence and the cause of many fatal coaching accidents.

Charlotte, Mary McQueen and Martha Hubbert accompanied by the Gaoler were taken from the Castle on the evening of 30th April. They proceeded down Steep Hill and along High Street to the Saracen's Head where they caught the Express coach to London at half past eleven. Having entered Lincoln city through Newport gate in the old Roman wall on the north side of the city they now departed Lincoln through the Stonebow Arch on their journey south.

Four inside passengers and up to twelve outside passengers could be carried on the coach. This contrasted with mail coaches which, for safety reasons and to ensure a faster journey, allowed only three or four outside passengers. Stage coach fares were about 2d a mile outside and 4d a mile inside.[64] The faster mail coaches were more expensive, fares averaging about twice those of the stage coaches. As Crown Prisoners the women's journey was authorized by Robert Sheffield and their fares paid by the government accordingly.

Whether they were seated on the inside or outside of the coach is open to speculation but at 59 years of age and in a position of authority, Merryweather probably took an inside seat. In keeping with his character, the three women were likely kept inside with him. The journey to London was uncomfortable enough for passengers on the inside of the coach due to cramped conditions, hard, leather covered wooden seats and the roughness of the road. On the outside, passengers perched on the roof, many with their legs often dangling over the edge, had the added discomfort of being exposed to the elements. To make the journey even more arduous, all passengers were required to descend from the carriage and walk when going up steep hills to spare the horses.

Merryweather and the three women arrived in London late in the afternoon of May 1st. The women were not allowed to rest after the journey from Lincoln and were immediately taken to the *Harmony* anchored in the Thames River at Woolwich.

Notes to Chapter 8

1. LA: CoC 5/1/1, Gaoler's Journal; The Lincoln, Rutland and Stamford Mercury, Friday, October 27, 1826, p.3, col.3.
2. Rules for the Government of the County Gaol and Castle of Lincoln, Court of Gaol Sessions, Lincoln, 5th day of January 1827, p17-18.
3. LA: CoC 5/1/11, Surgeon's Journal.
4. Cries from the past, A History of Lincoln Castle Prison, Lincolnshire County Council, 2005.
5. Rules for the Government of the County Gaol and Castle of Lincoln, op.cit., gaol plans.
6. Ibid., p.17.
7. Ibid pp.16 – 18 and 23.
8. Ibid pp.15-16 and 19-20; Lincolnshire Archives, Gaoler's Journal, CoC 5/1/1.
9. Rules for the Government of the County Gaol and Castle of Lincoln, op.cit., Extracts from Acts of Parliament, p.34.
10. Rules, op. cit., p7.
11. Ibid., p.8-10.
12. Cries from the past, op.cit., p.12.
13. Rules, op. cit., pp.13-16; Extracts p.40.
14. Ibid., pp.16-18.
15. Ibid., pp.18-19.
16. Ibid. p.20.
17. Ibid.
18. Ibid.
19. Ibid., pp.24-25; Extracts p.40-42.
20. LA: CoC 5/1/1, Gaoler's Journal, 29th October (1826).
21. HO13/47 AJCP reel PRO3092 p.316.
22. Gaoler's Journal, op.cit., 10th November (1826).
23. HO9/8, p.150, AJCP reel PRO 4881.
24. HO9/8, p.160, AJCP reel PRO 4881.
25. AOTAS: Convict Conduct Record, CON 31/1/38, p270, No.803.
26. HO8/11, p.200, AJCP reel PRO 5171.
27. Adm101/30 AJCP reel PRO 3196.
28. Charles Bateson, *The Convict Ships 1787-1868*, Reed, Sydney,1974, p.277.
29. HO8/12, p.14, No.7807, AJCP reel PRO 5171.

30	HO8/10, p.120, No.7807 AJCP reel PRO 5170; HO8/11, p.201(left), No.7807 AJCP reel PRO 5171.
31	Adm101/50 AJCP reel PRO 3203.
32	LA: LQS A/1/501/63, 97, 112, 113, 132, 185, 201 and The Lincoln, Rutland and Stamford Mercury, November 3,1826, p.4, col.1.
33	HO27/ 15, Criminal Registers, England and Wales, pp.856-857; HO9/4, Convict Prison Hulks: Registers and Letter Books, Justitia, p.78, No.3746; HO9/5, Convict Prison Hulks: Registers and Letter Books, Justitia, Gaoler's Report, p.16, No.3746.
34	LA: CoC 5/1/11, Surgeon's Journal, 28th October (1826).
35	LA: CoC 5/1/1, Gaoler's Journal.
36	Ibid., 2nd November(1826).
37	Surgeon's Journal, op.cit., 14th December (1826).
38	LA: CoC 5/1/20, Chaplain's Journal.
39	LA: CoC 5/1/1 and CoC 5/1/11.
40	LA: CoC 5/1/11, Surgeon's Journal, 7th & 8th January (1827).
41	LA: CoC 5/1/1, Gaoler's Journal, 9th February (1827).
42	LA: CoC 5/1/11, Surgeon's Journal, 4th March (1827).
43	LA: CoC 5/1/1, Gaoler's Journal, 14th March (1827).
44	LRSM, Friday, March 23, 1827.
45	Ibid.
46	Ibid.
47	HO13/48 AJCP reel PRO3093, p.140.
48	Ibid., p.149.
49	Ibid., pp.150-151.
50	LA: CoC 5/1/1, Gaoler's Journal, 16th -22nd March (1827).
51	LA: CoC 5/1/20,Chaplain's Journal, 23rd-24th March (1827).
52	LRSM, Friday, March 30, 1827.
53	White's History and Directory of Lincolnshire and Hull 1826.
54	LRSM, Friday, 30 March 1827.
55	HO11/6 p.238.
56	LA: CoC 5/1/11, Surgeon's Journal, 13th March – 6th April (1827)
57	HO13/48 AJCP reel PRO 3092, p.2.
58	Ibid., p.15.
59	HO13/48 AJCP reel PRO 3093, p.198.
60	LA: CoC 5/1/1, Gaoler's Journal, 29th April (1827).
61	R.H.R.E.Clapson & M. Stockdale, *Roads Coaches and Carriers in Barton Before 1900*, Fathom Writers, Barton-on-Humber 2009.
62	White's History and Directory of Lincolnshire and Hull 1826.
63	Philip S. Bagwell, *The Transport Revolution from 1770*, Batsford, London, 1974, pp.40, 47-49.
64	Ibid., p.51

Chapter 9

Transportation

Woolwich lies along the River Thames seven and a half miles downstream from London and about 30 miles upstream from where the river mouth meets the North Sea. Along the north shore were marshes, but on the southern shore was the Woolwich Warren, the site of naval shipbuilding since the 16th century and home to The Royal Arsenal since 1805. From the late 18th century, prison hulks were moored off Woolwich and it became a staging area for the transportation of convicts to Australia. The Warren, a maze of workshops, warehouses, wood-yards, barracks and foundries, provided a ready source of employment for the male convicts imprisoned on the hulks.

The *Harmony*, had been receiving female transports since the 16th of April. Under the command of Captain Richard Middleton with Surgeon-Superintendent William McDowell in attendance, the ship was waiting to fulfil her complement of convicts prior to departure for New South Wales. For McDowell, M.R.C.S., R.N., this was the second of six voyages to Australia as a convict ship's Surgeon-Superintendent.[1] The Surgeon was entirely responsible for the health and welfare of the convicts during their time on board. A policy of repeatedly employing the same naval surgeons for the convict service, meant that prisoners benefited greatly from the experienced attention they received, and ensured that conditions under which the vessel was chartered were observed. Regulations regarding conditions on board specifically provided for the supply of bedding, clothing and food rations, regular cleaning, fumigating and ventilation of the convicts' quarters, and medicines, medical supplies and hospital equipment. Conditions were stipulated for allowing prisoners access to the upper deck for fresh air, exercise and to air their bedding.[2] By 1827 medical conditions had improved to the extent that there were few if any deaths during the long voyage, and the prisoners and crew generally arrived at their destination in good condition. Still illnesses during the voyage, either contracted prior to boarding or while at sea, did occur.

On embarking the Surgeon examined the women and issued each of them with clothing, bedding, and utensils for cooking and eating, as prescribed in the regulations. They were divided into mess groups of six people who would eat and sleep together throughout the voyage.[3] Allowed to choose their own messmates it is highly likely that Charlotte, Mary and Martha were in the same mess group.

McDowell's medical and surgical journal for the period from 16th April to 13th October, describes the various illnesses the women suffered and the treatment applied during their time on board the ship.[4] The first entry in his journal is for Martha Hubbert, examined on the day of her arrival, when the ship was still at South Woolwich. Her age is given as 34 and the symptoms of her disease described as follows:

> *Complains of pain and great soreness in her external organs of genitalia, which I found on making particular inquiry into her complaints she had several chancres on the external Labia Pundindi and very much swoolen and inflamed.*[5]

McDowell prescribed and prepared a bolus made from *Pil. Hydrarg.* (a pill composed of mercury, honey of rose and liquorice powder) and *Opii. Colati.* (an opium compound) to lessen the painful diuretic effect of the mercurial ingredient.[6] The resulting tablet was to be taken twice a day. The chancres were dressed, cold plasters applied and the sores occasionally touched with caustic. This treatment was continued until the 15th of May at which point the swelling and inflammation were still present but had gradually subsided. Her mouth was a *'little sore and her bowels were open'*, conditions no doubt due to side effects of the mercury treatment. *Pil. Hydrarg.*, the opium and dressings were continued and she was confined to bed.[7]

By the 12th of May the ship had received its complement of 80 female Convicts. At the direction of the Home Secretary, William Sturges Bourne, the Undersecretary, Spencer Percival, sent the list of women prisoners to R.W. Hay, Private Secretary to The Secretary of State for the Colonies, with a request to *'lay this document before Lord Goderich, and move his Lordship to be pleased to forward the same to the Governor of New South Wales'*.[8]

Arranged in alphabetic order according to the place of each woman's conviction, the transportation list contained the names of the 80 female convicts, the date when they were convicted and the term of their sentences.[9]

Name	Where Convicted	When	Term
Ann Balfour	Berwick Upon Tweed Quarter Sessions	15th January 1827	Seven years
Catherine Smith	Bristol (City) Quarter Sessions	8th January 1827	Seven years
Mary Harris	Bristol (City) Quarter Sessions	8th January 1827	Seven years
Caroline the wife of Abraham Kensey	Essex Assizes	10th July 1826	Life
Naomi Wright	Essex Assizes	10th July 1826	Life
Elizabeth Jones	Gloucester Assizes	3rd August 1826	Life
Susan Parteridge	Gloucester Assizes	3rd August 1826	Fourteen years
Elizabeth Parker	Gloucester Assizes	3rd August 1826	Seven years
Susan Bartrip	Hertford Special Session of Gaol Delivery	6th December 1826	Life
Mary Edwards	Kent Assizes	1st August 1826	Fourteen years
Martha Millington	Kent Special Session of Gaol Delivery	6th January 1827	Life
Margaret Stroud	Kent Special Session of Gaol Delivery	6th January 1827	Seven years
Mary Wickham	Kent Special Session of Gaol Delivery	6th January 1827	Seven years
Mary Hindle	Lancaster Assizes	8th August 1826	Life
Ann Entwisle	Lancaster Assizes	8th August 1826	Life
Isabella Brennett	Lancaster Quarter Sessions	23rd October 1826	Seven years
Ann Butterworth	Lancaster Quarter Sessions	10th January 1827	Seven years
Ellen Pollard	Lancaster Quarter Sessions	10th January 1827	Seven years

Ellen the wife of John Barrett	Lancaster Quarter Sessions	10th January 1827	Seven years
Mary Martin	Lancaster Quarter Sessions	15th January 1827	Life
Elizabeth Hague	Lancaster Quarter Sessions	15th January 1827	Fourteen years
Mary Ann Welsh	Lancaster Quarter Sessions	15th January 1827	Fourteen years
Rosanna Welch	Lancaster Quarter Sessions	15th January 1827	Fourteen years
Margaret the wife of Joseph Ellam	Lancaster Quarter Sessions	15th January 1827	Fourteen years
Susannah Lloyd	Lancaster Quarter Sessions	15th January 1827	Fourteen years
Elizabeth MacMahon	Lancaster Quarter Sessions	15th January 1827	Seven years
Elizabeth Warhurst	Lancaster Quarter Sessions	15th January 1827	Seven years
Elizabeth Davies	Lancaster Quarter Sessions	15th January 1827	Seven years
Ann Woodward	Leicester (Borough) Assizes	19th July 1826	Life
Rebecca Bloxam	Leicester (Borough) Assizes	19th July 1826	Life
Mary Duddell	Leicester (Borough) Assizes	12th October 1826	Seven years
Elizabeth Millwood	Leicester (Borough) Assizes	15th January 1827	Fourteen years
Mary the wife of Francis Lowe	Lincoln (Grantham with the Soke) Sessions of Peace & Gaol Delivery	13th October 1826	Seven years
Mary McQueen	Lincoln (parts of Lindsey) Quarter Sessions	20th October 1826	Seven years
Charlotte Dawson	Lincoln (parts of Lindsey) Quarter Sessions	20th October 1826	Seven years
Martha Hubbert	Lincoln (parts of Lindsey) Quarter Sessions	24th October 1826	Seven years
Mary Mumford	London Gaol Delivery	15th February 1827	Fourteen years
Margaret Murphy	London Gaol Delivery	15th February 1827	Seven years
Eliza Brown	London Gaol Delivery	15th February 1827	Seven years
Susannah Hammond	Middlesex Gaol	11th January 1827	Life

	Delivery		
Mary Cockhead	Middlesex Gaol Delivery	11th January 1827	Fourteen years
Charlotte Harrison	Middlesex Gaol Delivery	11th January 1827	Seven years
Catherine Robinson	Middlesex Gaol Delivery	11th January 1827	Seven years
Hannah West	Middlesex Gaol Delivery	11th January 1827	Seven years
Isabella Kirk	Middlesex Gaol Delivery	11th January 1827	Seven years
Margaret Goulding	Middlesex Gaol Delivery	15th February 1827	Life
Elizabeth Addison	Middlesex Gaol Delivery	15th February 1827	Life
Mary Smith	Middlesex Gaol Delivery	15th February 1827	Life
Margaret Kane	Middlesex Gaol Delivery	15th February 1827	Life
Sarah Chamberlain	Middlesex Gaol Delivery	15th February 1827	Seven years
Ann Gratton	Middlesex Gaol Delivery	15th February 1827	Seven years
Mary Hughes	Middlesex Gaol Delivery	15th February 1827	Seven years
Eleanor Roberts	Middlesex Gaol Delivery	15th February 1827	Seven years
Ann Bennett	Middlesex Gaol Delivery	15th February 1827	Seven years
Sophia Coleman	Middlesex Gaol Delivery	15th February 1827	Seven years
Sarah Upcroft	Norfolk Assizes	24th March 1827	Fourteen years
Mary Ann Doyle	Nottingham (Town) Quarter Sessions	19th October 1826	Seven years
Elizabeth Smith	Nottingham (Town) Assizes	15th March 1827	Fourteen years
Mary Davies	Pembroke Gaol Sessions	15th August 1826	Seven years
Margaret Williams	Salop Assizes	18th July 1826	Fourteen years
Elizabeth Simpson	Salop Quarter Sessions	16th October 1826	Seven years
Mary Moran	Salop (Town and Liberty of Shrewsbury) Quarter Sessions and Gaol Delivery	20th October 1826	Seven years

Hannah Bryant	Somerset Quarter Sessions	8th January 1827	Seven years
Sarah Trout	Somerset Quarter Sessions	8th January 1827	Seven years
Mary Thompson, alias the wife of Robert Lane	Stafford Quarter Sessions	18th October 1826	Seven years
Sabina Hickisson	Stafford Quarter Sessions	18th October 1826	Seven years
Hannah Caffin	Surrey Quarter Sessions	28th August 1826	Fourteen years
Sarah Wood	Surrey Special Sessions of Gaol Delivery	18th December 1826	Life
Elizabeth Taylor	Surrey Special Sessions of Gaol Delivery	18th December 1826	Life
Mary Ann Knott	Surrey Special Sessions of Gaol Delivery	18th December 1826	Life
Esther McDonald	Surrey Special Sessions of Gaol Delivery	18th December 1826	Life
Ann Brown	Surrey Special Sessions of Gaol Delivery	18th December 1826	Life
Mary Oxley	Surrey (Town and Borough of Southwark) Quarter Sessions	2nd April 1827	Life
Ann Coley	Sussex Special Sessions of Gaol Delivery	3rd January 1827	Seven years
Jane Wood	Warwick Quarter Sessions	16th October 1826	Seven years
Ann Gardiner	Warwick Quarter Sessions	16th October 1826	Seven years
Judith Counter	Wilts (City of New Sarum) Quarter Sessions	4th January 1827	Seven years
Sarah Bodenham	Worcester (City) Quarter Sessions	16th October 1826	Seven years
Mary Ann Birchley	Worcester Quarter Sessions	17th October 1826	Seven years
Sarah the wife of John Mills	Worcester Quarter Sessions	17th October 1826	Seven years

On the same day Percival sent a second letter to the Commander of the Navy stating that he had been directed by Sturges Bourne to inform him that the Bonds and Contracts for the Transportation of 80 female convicts embarked on the Ship *Harmony* had been entered into. It was therefore unnecessary, on account of the Home Office, to detain the vessel any longer. He also requested that direction be given to the commander of the ship to proceed to New South Wales and deliver all the convicts to the Governor of that settlement.[10]

Shortly thereafter the ship weighed anchor and headed down the Thames to the North Sea. At last the voyage had begun. The prisoners were filled with a variety of emotions: apprehension as to what lay in store for them; anticipation, considering the opportunities they might have; and sadness for some, joy for others at leaving their homeland.

The voyage was soon interrupted while the ship anchored in the Downs off the town of Deal on Friday 18th of May[11] to wait for favourable easterly winds that would take her into the English Channel. They were not long in the Downs, departing the following Sunday.[12] A few days later they arrived at Portsmouth where the ship remained for some time, taking on supplies and equipment, and making final preparations for the voyage to New South Wales.

Built in New Brunswick about 1818, the *Harmony* was a second class ship of 366 tons (373 tons new measure) and 16 feet draft. She was constructed of first quality materials, black birch and hackmatack (both species of trees native to Canada) and had been sheathed with copper over boards in 1823. Iron standards and knees formed her internal structure and she had one proved iron cable. In 1824 she had received a new deck and upper works and in January of 1827, some repairs had been carried out possibly in the anticipation of securing the contract for a voyage to New South Wales.[13]

The *Harmony* had three decks: lower, middle (or between) and upper. At 100 feet long by 26 feet, 4 inches wide, and 8 feet in height from floor to floor, the lower deck was spacious. It contained two pumps and access to two water tanks under the floor. There was accommodation for some of the crew here as well. Not as much head room was available in the middle deck, the distance from floor to floor being only 6 feet, 10 inches, but the deck floor space was slightly larger at 110 feet long and 27 feet, 8 inches wide. The top deck was 120 feet long and the same width as the lower deck.

Four cabins were located on the upper deck in the aft quarter of the ship. Two of these located at the stern were larger and occupied by the Captain and the Surgeon. A water closet, centrally located at the back of these two cabins, was accessible only along the inside wall of the starboard cabin. Also in the aft quarter of the ship's upper deck, forward of the cabins, was a mess room occupying the width of the ship and containing a large table with two long benches on each side.[14]

The Commissioners of the Navy, collectively referred to as the Navy Board, chartered the ship from the owner John Marshall at a rate of between £4 and £5 per ton or £1400 to £1800 for the voyage. The Navy Board was responsible for making sure that the chartered vessel was sound, adequately equipped and properly fitted for conveying the convicts. The contractor warranted that the ship was tight, strong and substantial above and below water. He was required to fit out the ship with masts, sails, yards, anchors cables, ropes, apparel and other furniture and to provide coal, wood, fire-hearths, furnaces for cooking and bowls, spoons and platters. Water casks and fresh water were to be provided sufficient to supply each person with 1 butt (105 gallons or 477 litres) for the entire voyage. Scrapers, brooms, swabs and other cleaning materials were to be supplied and employed as directed by the surgeon[15].

The contractor was also required to man the ship with qualified seamen consisting of six or seven men and a boy for every hundred tons of the ship's registered measurement. In this regard the *Harmony* carried 24 men. Whether or not the men were all qualified seamen is unknown, but the ship's company would have included at least two or three officers, a carpenter and a boatswain.[16]

The women were accommodated on the lower and middle decks of the ship. A total of 86 beds, each 6 feet long by 2 feet wide, were available; 40 on the lower deck and 46 on the between deck. During the day the central rows of beds were turned into tables. Benches stowed under the beds were brought out for seating. Also on the between deck were two water closets, both located on the starboard side of the ship, one at the bow and the other just astern of amidships. Ladders through the hatchways gave access to the other decks. Wooden stanchions fixed around the hatchways between the decks held doors that could be locked at night and the ladders hauled up to prevent access to other decks. Compared to a male transport which had two rows of sleeping births, 6 feet long and 18 inches wide, one above the other located along each side of the ship, the *Harmony* seemed roomy and well furnished.[17]

As well as the female convicts, there were three of their children (not named in the transportation and muster lists) and passengers Lieutenant Colonel James Thomas Morisset, his wife Emily Louisa Vaux and their daughter Janetta Louisa.[18] Morisset and his family were accommodated in at least one of the two cabins on the upper deck forward of the two larger cabins. At 46 years of age Morisset was to take up a post as Civil and Military Commandant of the penal settlement at Norfolk Island. He had had a distinguished military career entering the army as an ensign in the 80th Regiment at the age of 18 and initially serving in India and Egypt and later with the Duke of Wellington's army in the Peninsular War (1807 to 1814) as a Captain in the 48th regiment. Morisset was wounded at the battle of Albuera in 1811, suffering a sabre cut which badly disfigured his face.

In 1817 he accompanied his regiment to New South Wales where, in 1818, he was appointed Commandant at Newcastle. While at Newcastle he was promoted major. He earned praise for improving the breakwater, building roads and barracks and for his attention to the prisoners. In 1821 Governor Lachlan Macquarie visited Newcastle, admired Morisset's work and named Morisset's Lagoon in his honour. In November 1823 he was appointed Commandant at Bathurst and was instrumental in restoring order after clashes with natives had led to martial law being declared west of Mount York in 1824.

He returned to England on leave in February 1825 and in August applied for the post of Commandant of Norfolk Island. Although Lord Bathurst had recommended Morisset to Governor Darling for the position, it was not confirmed until August 1826. He was promoted lieutenant-colonel on 19 December 1826 and placed on army half-pay.[19]

Where Morisset and his family boarded the ship is conjectural. His wife came from Ryde on the Isle of Wight and it is most likely they embarked at Portsmouth in order to delay the sea voyage as long as possible. But his daughter, although born in Ryde, was baptised at Sevenoaks, Kent on 7th April 1827 and, considering the location of this town and the date of the birth, they may have embarked either at Deal while the ship was in the Downs or less likely at Woolwich before the ship left London.

The *Harmony* departed Portsmouth on the 4th of June 1827.[20] Once at sea a routine schedule of daytime activities was interrupted only by wet or stormy weather or by the working of the ship. A certain number of women were appointed to prepare meals and captains were selected, usually from the more mature and respected women, to superintend behaviour and make sure the prison was kept clean and tidy. At 5 o'clock in the morning the women selected as cooks were admitted to the deck to prepare breakfast. About 6 o'clock, the women selected as mess captains took breakfast, while volunteers swabbed the decks and all bedding was brought on deck to be aired and stowed. Commencing at eight o'clock, the mess captains served breakfast, after which the deck was scrubbed and the prison and hospital cleaned. At 10 am all were mustered on deck for inspection. After muster, those women not attending school or occupied with designated tasks, were kept busy with sewing, quilting, weaving and making straw hats and striped linen shirts. Religious instruction was given daily and prior to their departure, the women had been provided with religious tracts and bibles for their own study and contemplation. The beneficial effect of this was variable, strips of the religious tracts often found to have been used by the women to paper their curls.[21]

Two days each week were designated laundry days when the women washed and ironed their own clothes and possibly the clothes of the crew and passengers as well. Once each week the clothing, beds and blankets supplied from the Government stores were inspected. Dinner was served at noon and supper at 4 o'clock, followed by dancing and singing and occasionally concerts or masquerades. At sunset all were mustered below and the prison locked.[22]

Food rations were adequate comprising a pot of gruel every morning with sugar or butter in it, a daily quota of three quarters of a pound of biscuit and a main meal of beef or pork or plum-pudding.

Pea-soup was served several times a week and vinegar issued to the messes weekly. Once the ship was at sea, one ounce of sugared lime-juice was administered daily to guard against scurvy. Red wine and fresh water were also part of the regular diet. Also, each woman was issued with a tin pot and the mess supplied with tea, sugar and a kettle so she could make tea for herself in the morning and at night.[23]

Peter Cunningham, a surgeon of the Royal Navy who made several voyages to New South Wales during the 1820s transporting both male and female convicts, commented that the women were 'more quarrelsome and more difficult to control than the men'. He attributed this to the more excitable nature of their tempers and the added incentive of the usual leniency shown to their sex. He found they were also more abandoned in their expressions when excited having less control over their passions and their tongues.[24] Fraternisation between the crew and the female convicts was not allowed but was unavoidable and covertly arranged night time assignations were frequent. This often led to serious relationships which survived the voyage, but created problems for the ship's captains and the colonial authorities.

Martha Hubbert was still receiving treatment, but no longer confined to bed, when the ship left Portsmouth. The Surgeon reported:

> *Swelling and inflammation in the parts quite reduced, chancre appears healthy and healing fast, continued Pil Hydrarg et opir ut antea and sores dressed until June the 10th chancres well, mouth sore, bowels regular ---- gargle for mouth and Pil Hydrarg et opir combined with cathartics occasionally as required until the 1st of July when Discharged.*[25]

The second entry in McDowell's journal is more startling:

> *Charlotte Dawson*
> *Atal: 24 first visit June 10th at sea*

Thermometer 80 in shade

This woman came from the same Prison as the woman whose case I have just given and her complaint the same venereal symptoms and general treatment so much alike the case immediately described above that I hope it will be sufficient for me to state that she was continued in the sick list taking Pil Hydrarg etc as directed until July 20th when Discharged.[26]

There is an implication here that both women were infected in prison before they arrived on the *Harmony*, perhaps so-stated to absolve McDowell of any lack of control over sexual relations on board the ship. He may also have been implying that the prison surgeons were not doing enough to prevent or cure the disease prior to the prisoners being dispatched to the transport ships. McDowell probably did not know that Charlotte had the infection when she arrived at the prison. She received no treatment, possibly due to her refusal to submit to an examination and, as a result, had not been cured.

In Martha's case, she had probably contracted the infection while at Lincoln Castle Gaol or she may have had it prior to her arrival there, although there is no specific reference in the prison surgeon's journal. However, it does seem peculiar that Charlotte's condition was not detected until she had been on the ship for 40 days, particularly since Martha Hubert was diagnosed with the disease on the day of their arrival.

Unfortunately no ship's log or Captain's journal of the voyage has been found. Surgeon McDowell restricts his records to medical issues, but does give the temperature on the day a patient first visited him for treatment. Happily for him there were only eight patients who received initial treatment at sea. As an exception, probably because it was one of the few times if not the only time land was sighted during the voyage, he recorded that on June 30th they were off Cape Verde. The temperature that day was 84 degrees Fahrenheit in the shade. From there the temperature gradually decreased; 80° on July 8th, 79° on July 11th, 61° on August 11th, 54° on September 16th and 49° on September 18th virtually charting their course south in the Atlantic Ocean, around Cape of Good Hope and east into the Southern Indian Ocean where the strong westerly winds of the forty degree latitudes drove them towards Australia and the Pacific Ocean.[27]

By the 18th of September they were in the Pacific Ocean at the east end of Bass Strait, the ship rolling heavily in huge seas. In the unstable conditions, while getting into her berth, Elizabeth Addison badly bruised her knee. It became very swollen and inflamed, compelling McDowell to tie a cold compress around her knee and confine her to bed. She was given a low regimen of cathartics occasionally *'as the state of her bowels required'*.[28]

As the *Harmony* approached her destination, the high, yellow-brown layered sandstone cliffs, capped in dark green shrubs, gliding by off her port side presented a refreshing view after the prolonged period on the boundless ocean. At last on the 27th of September, after 115 days at sea, the ship was spotted entering Port Jackson about 4 o'clock in the afternoon.[29]

She passed between North and South Head, the two high sandstone cliffs which bracket the entrance to Port Jackson, and proceeded southwest and then west towards Sydney. It was a clear, sunny day. The sky was bright blue and the temperature a mild 66° F.[30] After so many days at sea, the view was both welcome and pleasant. Along both sides of the harbour the precipitous cliffs gave way to a more undulating landscape covered in evergreen native shrubs and small trees. Romantic little bays with white sandy beaches intermittently broke the rocky shoreline[31] and a few rocky islands, lightly covered with scrub, lay scattered along the course of the harbour. Here and there were glimpses of slender streams gurgling down narrow rock sided valleys towards the rocky shore. To the left, as they proceeded up the harbour, whitewashed pilot-houses with their small fairy gardens were perched at the bottom of a snug little sandy bay, then a pretty cottage and further on a beautiful twin domed sandstone mansion with a manicured lawn and gardens situated on a rocky point.[32] Passing by the rocky islet of Pinchgut they rounded into Sydney Cove and dropped anchor about 5 o'clock in the afternoon.[33] Ahead on the south shore of the cove was the

Government Wharf and, in the distance, they could see the slender conical spire of St James church.

Notes to Chapter 9

1. Charles Bateson, *The Convict Ships 1787-1868*, Reed, Sydney,1974, p. 227.
2. Ibid., pp.12, 19 and 277.
3. Babette Smith, *A Cargo of Women*, Allen & Unwin, 2nd edition, 2008, p.47.
4. William McDowell, Surgeon, Journal of His Majesty's Convict Ship Harmony, Adm 101/32 AJCP reel PRO 3197.
5. Ibid, May 1st.
6. J. Wilson, *Pharmacopoeia Chirugica*, Cox, London, 1811, pp.181-183.
7. McDowell, op. cit.
8. HO13/48 AJCP reel PRO 3093, p.355.
9. Transportation Register, Harmony, HO11/6 AJCP reel PRO 88, pp.175-179; SRNSW NRS 1155, Musters and other papers relating to convict ships, Harmony, 1827, [2/8262, p.13], Reel 2422.
10. HO13/48 AJCP reel PRO 3093 p.355.
11. The Morning Post, (London) Monday, May 21, 1827, p.2, col.3.
12. The Standard, (London) May 21, 1827, p.1, col.3.
13. Lloyd's Register 1827, No.162; Lloyd's Register 1828, No.184; Lloyd's Register 1829, No.179.
14. SRNSW: NRS 906,Colonial Secretary, Special Bundles, Prison Discipline, Letter No 62/762, [4/740.1], Harmony as an emigrant vessel 1862.
15. Bateson, op.cit., pp10, 13 & 85; Lloyd's Register 1828.
16. Bateson, op.cit., p.13; Report of Arrivals at Sydney, SRNSW AO Reel 1263, Vol.4/5198, 1827.
17. Harmony op. cit.; Peter Cunningham, *Two Years in New South Wales, A Series of Letters, Comprising Sketches of the Actual State of Society in that Colony; of its Peculiar Advantages to Emigrants; of its Topography, Natural History, &c. &c.* Henry Colbourn, London, 1827, Vol.2. p.215.
18. SRNSW: NRS 1291, Colonial Secretary, Shipping Reports, Unassisted Passengers 1826 – 1900, [4/5198], Reel 1263.
19. Vivienne Parsons, *Morisset, James Thomas (1780–1852)*, Australian Dictionary of Biography, (ADB), Melbourne Universtity Press (MUP), 1967, Vol. 2, pp.260-261.
20. The Morning Post, (London) June 6, 1827, p.4, col.1.
21. Peter Cunningham, op.cit., p.280-281; Thomas Bigge, *Report of the Commissioner of Inquiry into the state of the Colony of New South Wales*, House of Commons, 1822, p.11.
22. Bateson, op. cit., p.80; Babette Smith, op.cit., p.51; William Rae, Surgeon and Superintendant, Ship Eliza 1822 Regs_PRO 3194 Adm 101-23.
23. Peter Cunningham, op.cit., pp216 & 217.
24. Ibid., pp271 & 272.
25. McDowell, op.cit.

26 Ibid., June 10th.
27 McDowell, op. cit.
28 Ibid., Sept. 18th.
29 The Monitor, Thursday Evening, September 27, 1827, *Shipping Intelligence*, p.7, col.2.
30 Surgeon's Log of the Prince Regent, Adm101/61 AJCP reel PRO3207.
31 Cunningham, op.cit., Vol 1, p37.
32 Captain Piper's home on Eliza Point.
33 The Monitor, Thursday Evening, September 27, 1827, *'5 o'clock pm- We stop the press"*, p.7, col.2.

Chapter 10

Sydney

Sydney Cove provided an ideal anchorage, its expanse of water protected by two ridges protruding into the harbour at a separation of about 550 yards. At the end of each ridge were fortifications; Fort Macquarie with its four Martello towers and 15 guns located on Bennelong Point on the left and to the right, the Battery on Dawes Point. Fort Phillip with its signal post occupied higher ground uphill from the battery. Inland, the town filled the depression between the ridges, its main street extending from opposite a row of store houses on the west side of the cove for about a mile and a half to the south. A stream trickled onto the mudflats at the head of the cove. Upstream tanks were cut into its sandstone bed for holding water and two arched stone bridges spanned the stream connecting the east and west sides of the town. To the east at the head of the cove was the Government Wharf, a short, narrow stone jetty only large enough to accommodate punts and ship's boats; to the west, King's Wharf, a stone quay with a wooden jetty.

It was as if they had returned to civilization after a long forced sojourn in a watery wilderness. Small boats scurried from the shore and soon surrounded the ship, offering fruit and other refreshments. In the harbour was a plethora of vessels and small craft: cutters *Regent Bird, Currency Lass, Sally, Lord Liverpool, Speedwell and Dart*; schooners *Darling, Madeira Packet, Brisbane, Elisabeth, and Henry*; brigs *Industry, Fame, Wellington, Amity, and Lord Rodney*; barques *Leda, Rolla, Pocklington, Lucy Ann and Prince Regent*; and ships *Governor Ready, Alligator, Triton, Governor Philip, the Emma Kemp, H.M.S. Pandora-Hervey, Elizabeth* (Capt. Athernden), *Elizabeth* (Capt. Powditch), *Alfred, and Cambridge*.[1]

The barque *Prince Regent* (Captain William Richards and Surgeon Superintendent William Rae, Esq., R.N.) had arrived earlier that afternoon having left Deal on the 11th of June, stopping at Teneriffe for supplies and departing that port on the 2nd of July. She carried 108 male prisoners and passengers Ensign Darling of the 57th regiment (nephew of Governor Darling), Major Mitchell with his wife and family, Lieutenant Hughe R.S.C and Mr P. Elliot Assistant Surveyor. The Guard consisted of Lieutenant Campbell and 29 men of the 47th Regiment. She also brought mail including the London newspapers.[2]

At 5 o'clock pm The Monitor stopped press to announce the arrival of the ship *Harmony* under the command of Captain Middleton with 80 female prisoners and passengers Colonel Morisset, lady and family. The announcement mistakenly included Major Mitchell, Assistant Surveyor General as a passenger, the stop press action befuddling the journalist charged with reporting the Shipping News.[3]

The next day the Sydney Gazette and New South Wales Advertiser reported in its Shipping Intelligence column that the ship *Harmony* had arrived the previous day under Captain Middleton:

> with 180 female prisoners, and 3 children. Surgeon Superintendent, Dr. McDowell. Passengers, Colonel Morisset, wife, and family[4]

And in its Postcript column declared enthusiastically that:

> The metropolis was thrown into a bustle the whole of yesterday, by the arrivals of the Harmony and Prince Regent from London. .... We perceive that Colonel Morisset returns to the Colony, an event we long since mentioned as likely to occur, it having been rumoured that this Gentleman had received the appointment of perpetual Commandant of Norfolk Island.[5]

The arrival was also reported in the Australian, correctly stating 80 female prisoners.[6]

Morisset and his family disembarked almost immediately on arrival in Sydney Cove in order to make arrangements for taking up his post at Norfolk Island. However, Governor Darling objected to a married man being stationed at a penal settlement where only males were allowed and quickly appointed him to act as a magistrate and Superintendent of Police. Morisset bitterly resented this arrangement and Darling was eventually forced by extenuating circumstances to appoint Morisset, Commandant of Norfolk Island, in February 1829 as originally planned.[7]

The town was well and truly in a state of excitement and activity, with the arrival of a cargo of women and the prospect of news from home. Since the arrival of the First Fleet in 1788 with over one thousand settlers including 586 male and 192 female convicts, the colony had grown to more than more than 40,000 people. The male to female ratio stood at more than three to one[8] and there were many bachelors eager to progress their search for a wife.

From 10 am to 4 pm, hopeful people anxious for news from friends and relatives in England besieged the post office. Unfortunately, the mail had not been delivered as a first priority when the *Prince Regent* and *Harmony* had arrived and the disappointed populace had to keep their hopes alive for another day. The newspaper was apologetic for printing the news from the English papers a day late. It claimed that owing to the delay in delivery of the mail the day the ship arrived, there had not been enough time to read the papers in preparation for printing. The fact that the English papers were almost 4 months old and one extra day was of no material consequence, demonstrates how starved people were for news from the mother country.

By 1827 Sydney was a well established and thriving community having survived the early years when drought, lack of food and disease had threatened its survival. Conflict between the governors and the military were in the past. Social and economic development over the 39 years of its existence had seen Sydney transformed from a penal colony to a budding free society populated by a growing proportion of free settlers, freed convicts and their children.

George Street, the main north-south thoroughfare, formed a baseline for a grid of wide but unlighted streets, paved with stone and gravel, running parallel and at right angles through the town. Near the head of the cove and along its west side the topography dictated a less orderly arrangement of streets running off at angles or curving along the contour of the land. Extending south from Fort Macquarie, the Government Domain, a large tract of land surrounded the neighbouring cove to the east. It contained the Botanic Gardens, and Government House (a large white plastered farmhouse and its adjoining brick guard house), surrounded by fields, gardens and groves of trees. The house, situated a few hundred yards from Sydney Cove in a slightly elevated position, had a commanding view of the harbour and surrounds. Between the Domain and the Cove was a footpath built mainly in solid rock. The path was popular for evening walks when Sydney's population could enjoy the cool sea breeze and beautiful views of the harbour.

On the southwest side of the domain, Macquarie Street accommodated the substantial buildings of the light horse barracks, the colonial hospital, the convict barracks and the recently completed Saint James Church. Macquarie Street gave way to a central promenade through Hyde Park, an open area used for recreation, sports and the exercise of troops. At the park's northeast corner stood a Gothic style Catholic Chapel.

The hospital (two storeys high) and its exterior buildings, contained sufficient accommodation for 300 patients and all the required offices and quarters for six medical officers. Verandas surrounded all the buildings. The hospital grounds included garden areas both for medical officers and the sick and yards for exercise and air, the entire premises enclosed with a brick wall nine feet high.[9]

Near the centre of town was an allotment of 2 acres planted with shrubbery and enclosed with a low wall and wooden railing named 'Macquarie Place'. In the centre of the grounds, stood a stone obelisk from which the distances in miles to the different settlements in the colony were measured. Macquarie Place also contained a stone fountain, erected over a spring, for supplying water to that part of town and the only street light in Sydney.

On the west side of the cove was the busy commercial docks area with its wharfs and store houses. The Government or Commissariat Store, one of the largest buildings in the port, was located there. It had its own stone quay and timber wharf. To the North of the wharf, an area set aside as a Naval Dockyard contained wharfs, quays, repairing docks and boat houses. A stone wall 12 feet high, enclosed its store houses, sail rooms, workshops, and offices for the Master Builder and Master Attendant of the Colonial Marine. Beyond the dockyard, towards Dawes Point, the extensive wharf, store houses and mansion of Robert Campbell, a prominent, local merchant, crowded the shore line. To the south on the heights, Fort Phillip, The Royal Military Hospital, The Military Windmill, St Phillips Church and Scots Church on Church Hill dominated the topography. And conveniently located on opposite sides of York Street were the Military Barracks and Barracks Square parade ground (12 acres). The Military Barracks, built of brick, stood two stories high. It could accommodate 1000 soldiers and the full proportion of commissioned officers. Office facilities for the latter were located in the building.

Below Fort Phillip, but on the more elevated portion of this precinct, sat the most densely populated part of the town. In this area known as The Rocks, a respectable population employed in the maritime industry occupied rows of neat white houses and sandstone buildings. In sharp contrast, the lower part and rugged face of the promontory was covered in a ramshackle assortment of cottages, row houses and hovels, reported to be inhabited by whalers and sailors and the most profligate and depraved part of the population. Nearby, on George Street, south of King's Wharf, perhaps conveniently located to both the harbour and The Rocks, stood the gaol, a strong stone wall 14 feet high enclosing its yard. Within the gaol separate rooms for male and female prisoners, debtors and the gaol gang provided suitable if not comfortable accommodation.[10]

Nestled between these outstretched eastern and western arms and spreading over a mile from north to south and for more than a quarter mile east to west, was the central part of the town filled with dwellings and business premises. The buildings, mainly detached, single or double storied were built of local sandstone or of plastered and whitewashed brick. Nearer the harbour, where the land was more valuable, the houses adjoined each other. Most of the cottage style dwelling houses had front verandas and the grounds, enclosed with wooden paling fences, often contained a large garden. In 1827 there were about 1053[11] private houses in the town of Sydney and these buildings, in the words of Peter Cunningham, gave the town a 'light, airy and exhilarating appearance'.[12]

Commercial and industrial enterprises flourished. The Bank of New South Wales located on George Street had opened in 1817. Four years later, the Chief cashier stole half of the bank's subscribed capital, but although none of the money was ever recovered, the bank had survived.[13] There was a public market place in the centre of the town with all the necessary booths, shops, pens and stores, where grain, livestock and other commodities could be bought and sold. On Cockle Bay, at the south end of Darling Harbour on the west side of Sydney, were two stone built wharfs. Here vessels and boats could unload their supplies which could then be carried a short distance along a good road to the market place.[14]

Located on the west side of the Tank Stream, at the head of the cove and proximal to the arched stone bridges, the lumber yard contained an extensive area for timber storage and saw pits. The yard, enclosed in a 12 foot high stone wall, accommodated workshops where carpenters, blacksmiths and other tradesmen were employed by the government. It also contained brick built offices for the Acting Chief Engineer and Principal Superintendant of Convicts.[15] Scattered about the town and its surroundings were two steam flour mills, three water mills, four windmills, two distilleries and a number of breweries. A great variety of sly grog shops and taverns operated covertly and several licensed public hotels were open for business, The Australian and The Sydney on George Street, and The Fortune of War opposite the Government Wharf being the most notable.

There were general stores where merchandise of every description could generally be bought and specialty shops were starting to appear. On sale at T. Ferris', George Street were Cape Madeira Wine in quarter pipes, superior claret, Saint Estephe, Sauterne, and white Champagne in cases of one dozen each, new raisins for deserts or puddings by the box or lb., patent double refined loaf sugar of very fine quality, butter in tubs, plums, almonds and walnuts, mustard and preserved ginger, gentlemen's, youth's, and boy's black and drab hats, horse hair seating, and ladies' boots and shoes. Parasols, elastic garters and black silk stockings, double barrelled fowling pieces, gunpowder and shot, perfumery and scented soaps, oil and paint, and anti-corrosion paint, Nankeens, Witney blankets, snuffs of different kinds, cigars, and tobacco, maps of New South Wales in sheets, rollers and cases, brandy, rum, and Holland gin in quantities not less than five gallons, London particular Madeira wine in wood and bottle, port wine in bodies, cherry and raspberry brandy, raspberry vinegar, and preserves of all kinds, pickles and sauces of every variety, and capers, hyson, hyson skin, black tea by the chest, half chest, or pound, Isle of France-sugar, and white moist sugar, coffee, raw or roasted, and rice, black pepper by the bag or pound, rein deer tongues, hams and cheese, prime English vinegar and salt petre, real anchovies and essence of anchovies, Embden groats and pearl barley, white and yellow soap, and candles, English salt, starch and stone blue, gentlemen's shaving and toilet glasses and braces, assorted crockery ware, decanters, tumblers and wine glasses, stationery and cutlery, Drill trowsers, and white drill by the yard, check shirts, white cotton shirts and stockings, light summer hats, in imitation of Leghorn, brooms and brushes of every description, maize and Dement potatoes in any quantities, private and cabin stores of every description for gentlemen of the army and Captains of vessels.[16]

M. Mahony offered a similar but less extensive selection of goods at his newly established wine, grocery and drapery warehouse at 104 Pitt Street as did Matthew Hindson at his ladies and gentlemen's furnishings' store at No. 7, Macquarie Place.[17]

For the ladies J. Melville at 39 Pitt Street had silks and shawls, cotton night caps, silk dresses, pelisses, and tippets, fancy straw and leghorn bonnets, Thread and Urling's lace, Cap net, figured and plain, best London stays and Scotch striped shirts, table cloths and covers, baby linen and a great variety of children's dresses, lace caps, gloves, shoes, gingham, Book, mull, and jaconet muslin Scotch cambric, cotton stockings. And Mr John Paul had silks for ladies dresses, Norwich crapes and Bombazines of various colours, waist and bonnet ribbons of the most fashionable patterns, ladies' kid black and white silk gloves, plaids, stuffs and bombazetts, thread net, gauze handkerchiefs, lawn and cambrics, crape and silk shawls, black and white silk hose, mull and book muslins, beautifully fine shirting, parasols, threads, tapes, bobbins, and other articles too numerous to mention.[18]

In its drive to be self sufficient, the colony was expanding its agricultural potential in all possible directions. To the west, Parramatta, the furthest navigable point inland on the Parramatta River and the first inland farming settlement in Australia, was connected to the south end of George Street, Sydney with a paved gravel road. Businesses were springing up along this thoroughfare. Windsor, an agricultural centre on the Hawkesbury River, had been connected with Sydney by road in 1814. Prior to that, Windsor had been accessible only by coastal shipping. In 1815 convict labour had completed a road across the Blue Mountains opening up agricultural land further west. Construction of The Great North Road linking Sydney to the Hunter River region 260 kilometres to the north had commenced in 1826. The Hunter region was rapidly developing as an agricultural district principally accessed by vessel to Morpeth, the furthest inland port on the river. To the southwest of Sydney, Liverpool, at the head of navigation of the Georges River, had developed into another agricultural centre.

Food staples were readily available at average prices of 13s sterling per 100 lb for fine flour, for second flour 10s, bread 4d per loaf, beef by the carcase, 3d per lb and by the joint, 6d to 7d per lb, mutton 4d to7d, pork 5½d to 8d, butter 2s 0d to 3s 6d per lb, cheese 1s 3d, eggs 1s 0d to 1s 6d per dozen, fowls, 3s to 4s 6d per couple, ducks 4s to 5s, geese 11s to 13s, turkeys 14s to 18s, potatoes 6s 0d to 8s per cwt., peas 1s 0d to 1s 3d per peck. Grains and fodder were marketed, wheat being sold at 4s to 5s per bushel, maize 6s to 7s, barley 6s 6d, oats 3s 4d to 3s 9d, hay (middling quality) £9 to £11 per ton and straw 25s per load.[19]

Two daily coach services ran between Sydney and Parramatta and there were plans to begin services to Windsor and Liverpool. Cuthbert's Royal Mail post coach departed from Cuthbert's residence in York Street at 8 o'clock, and stopped ten minutes at the London Tavern, opposite the Police office. It also stopped for two minutes at the Spinning Wheel and arrived at Walker's in Parramatta at a quarter past 10 am. Departing Parramatta at 4 in the afternoon, it arrived back in Sydney about a quarter past six in the afternoon. Passenger fares were 3s outside and 5s inside. The Currency Lass departed at seven thirty in the morning from the Rose and Crown Inn calling at the Dove and Talbot Inns to take on additional passengers. The return journey left Parramatta at 4 o'clock in the afternoon.[20] Fares were the same as those for The Royal Mail, however due to competition between the two services, fares were reduced in October 1827 to 6d for outside and 1s for inside passengers.[21]

On the occasion of the Parramatta Races 3rd and 5th October 1827, The Currency Lass was reported to have carried 22 passengers outside and six passengers inside on its outward journey and 22 passengers outside and 9 passengers inside on its return in contravention of the Act which allowed only a total of 18 outside and inside passengers.[22]

Whether or not all of this was what the women of the *Harmony* expected is difficult to ascertain. They were most likely pleasantly surprised and their spirits elevated by the prospects the bourgeoning community offered them in spite of their bondage. On the 29th of September the Colonial Secretary's Office issued the following:

> NOTICE is hereby given, that Families who are in Want of FEMALE SERVANTS, may be supplied from the Prisoners arrived in the Ship Harmony, from London, provided they apply, according to the established Form, to the Principal Superintendent of Convicts, before Tuesday the 9th of October next. Printed Forms, for this Purpose, may be obtained by applying at this Office, or at the Office of the Principal Superintendent of Convicts. By Command of His Excellency the Governor, ALEXANDER McLEAY.[23]

By the end of the next week applications for servants far exceeded the number of women on the ship and the application process was closed.[24] On the 8th of October the Colonial Secretary, Alexander McLeay and the Superintendant of Convicts Frederick

Augustus Hely came on board to conduct a detailed muster of the convicts. The examination of the prisoners was made on the quarter deck in the presence of Surgeon Superintendent McDowell, Captain Middleton and the ship's company.

Each prisoner was asked her name, age, whether she could read or write, her religion, marital status and if married the number of children, her native place, and trade or calling. She was questioned about her offence, where and when she had been tried, her sentence and any previous sentence. The answers were compared with the transportation list transmitted to the Governor and corrected if necessary. Then the height of each woman was measured, her complexion and the colour of her hair and eyes and any distinguishing marks or features recorded. How each woman was to be 'disposed of' and any other remarks were entered in the last column of the record. As there was no shortage of applications for female servants each woman had the name of the person or persons with whom she was to be indentured recorded in the last column.

There was one exception. Elizabeth Addison, who had injured her knee during the rolling of the ship in rough seas off Van Diemen's Land, did not receive employment having been sent to the hospital in Sydney on 29th September.[25] All of the columns in her record were filled in, the last column only containing the remark that she had a *'thick nose'*.[26]

An enquiry was made about the treatment each person had received during the voyage; whether she had received the full ration of provisions prescribed or whether she had any complaints against the captain, his officers or crew. Each woman was asked if she had any ailment or infirmity and Surgeon McDowell was asked about the conduct of each convict during the passage.[27] The muster took about 3 to 4 hours to complete, its duration drawn out by twelve women who lodged complaints against some of the ship's officers.[28]

On Saturday, 13th of October, after almost 6 months confined on the ship, the women of the *Harmony* disembarked. All were immediately distributed to their respective masters and mistresses whose applications had been successful, except for the twelve women who had lodged complaints. They were retained to give evidence concerning their accusations against some of the officers.[29]

The three women from Lincolnshire, who had been companions for almost a whole year, were now separated.

Although her trade or calling was described as a *'farm servant indoors'*, Charlotte Dawson did not go to a country position. Instead she went into the service of Margaret Delaney at 39 York Street.[30] In fact all three women from Lincolnshire remained in Sydney and were able to stay in contact. Mary McQueen, whose trade was listed as housemaid, was assigned to James Bloodsworth in the town and Martha Hubbert, a needlewoman, went to Robert Campbell, Junior of Bligh Street.[31]

Assignment was a relatively cheap method of convict management for the government. The private employers bore the cost of food, clothing, bedding, medical care and accommodation for the assigned convicts, leaving only the administrative costs to the government. It was equally of benefit to the colonists. Placed entirely in the hands of their masters, the convicts provided them with a low-cost labour force. There was no requirement for wages to be paid to the men and women assigned to them. While many convicts were exploited or harshly dealt with, equally as many were well treated, or even indulged, by their masters. Stories of convict successes filtered back to Britain more often than stories of misfortune, creating the impression that transportation was an ineffective form of punishment and lacked the deterrent value it was supposed to have.[32]

In spite of the name of the ship, the voyage had not been harmonious. Governor, Sir Ralph Darling was obliged to appoint a board of inquiry to examine various charges brought by Dr. McDowell against the Commander of the *Harmony*. The board, consisting of Lieutenant Governor, Colonel William Stewart, William Carter, Esq. and Edward Wollstonecraft, Esq., was convened on 13th October at the residence of Mr Wollstonecraft in George Street. Mr Williams attended as counsel for McDowell and several women were called as witnesses.[33] The members of the board were unable to agree in their opinion but Darling seems to have accepted the opinion of William Stewart, and in a letter to the Commissioners of the Navy dated 4th November, stated:

I am strongly disposed to concur with Colonel Stewart that, even admitting the Surgeon's Conduct to have been irritating, the proceedings of the Master was most unbecoming and improper; and I have no doubt that due Notice will accordingly be taken of it.[34]

The matter however did not end there, McDowell eventually bringing a civil action of assault and false imprisonment against Middleton.

The case was heard in the Supreme Civil Court of New South Wales before Mr Justice John Stephen on Friday 21 December 1827. McDowell was represented by Doctor Robert Wardell and Middleton by William Charles Wentworth. From Dr Wardell the court heard that the vessel had not been long at sea before a misunderstanding arose between McDowell and Middleton resulting from Middleton and his crew's improper interference with the prisoners, contrary to the express instructions from the Admiralty board. McDowell had tried every means in his power to prevent such conduct but without effect. He alleged that Middleton developed a dislike of him and looked for every opportunity to annoy him.

Shortly after the vessel had been at sea, and after McDowell had taken possession of his birth, he appropriated a particular water closet for his exclusive use. Divided from his cabin by only a thin and carelessly erected partition, the closet disturbed him with its emissions of light and sound. On the 14th of July, Middleton sent an insulting message to McDowell ordering him to give up the key to this convenience that it might be appropriated for the use of Colonel Morisset's family. McDowell disputed Middleton's right to appropriate what he understood to be part of his accommodation, and refused to comply. Consequently Middleton immediately directed the carpenter to knock off the lock. The carpenter proceeded to comply with his orders. McDowell trying to protect what he considered his own apartment attempted to restrain him from doing so. Middleton joined the ensuing struggle and knocked down McDowell.

The second assault took place on the 19th of August. It arose from McDowell remonstrating with some of the sailors for interfering with the prisoners. Middleton, who overheard what was said, called one of the men aft and told him he was to take no notice of McDowell. He had the crew drag McDowell off the quarter deck and confined him to his cabin. He was refused permission to take his meals at the cuddy table and threatened to be put in irons. The boatswain warned McDowell that if the crew were allowed to have their way, they would throw him overboard.

Two witnesses were called to support McDowell's case. Their testimony went no farther than to say that they saw Middleton on two occasions 'collar the plaintiff' but they could not state anything as to the origin of the dispute.

In Middleton's defence, Mr Wentworth detailed a variety of circumstances to show that McDowell had exercised an assumption of undue authority from the very first hour he embarked on the ship. He stated that Middleton, in order to maintain his own authority as well as proper discipline on board, was obliged to take measures to repress McDowell. Wentworth called witnesses to prove, that the measures Middleton was obliged to resort to arose out of the absolutely mutinous and abusive conduct of McDowell. He asserted that in all the disputes which took place Middleton behaved with the utmost coolness while McDowell's conduct was marked by the utmost degree of violence.

The learned Judge summed up the evidence, and the Jury found a verdict for the defendant, stating they were satisfied that neither Middleton nor his officers had exercised improper conduct towards the prisoners on board.[35] However the Commissioners of the Navy, on Darling's advice, promised to take notice of the less than satisfactory conduct of the master. As Middleton subsequently did not command a convict ship, it can be presumed that he was banned from further service.[36]

Charlotte's position with Mrs Delaney did not last very long. By 31st of December she was in Sydney gaol for having run away from her service. She was sentenced to 3 months 3rd class in the Female Factory at Parramatta and sent there on the 7th of January 1828.[37]

Charlotte no doubt had good reason to abscond from Delaney's service. Margaret had a convict past and she was violent. As Margaret Corcoran, 20 years old, she had been convicted of shoplifting in County Longford, Ireland in March 1818. Shortly thereafter she was transported to New South Wales for seven years arriving in November of the same year on the ship *Elizabeth*.[38] By 1827 she had become free by servitude and in light of her freedom may have taken on a superior air giving her the inclination to treat those in her service less than kindly. A stout, formidable woman, 5 feet, ¼ inches tall, of fair complexion, with red hair and blue eyes, she had a disposition towards violence. Settler and Convict lists for the years 1818, 1820 and 1821 show that she was in the government factory each time the data was collected.[39] On 13 April, 1819 she was sentenced by D'Arcy Wentworth and transported to Newcastle for one year.[40] On the 4th of May 1822 she was committed to Sydney gaol by Wentworth and sentenced to 30 days at the Female Factory.[41] Unfortunately none of these records states the reason for her sentence and therefore they do not prove that she was violent. But later reports show a number of incidents where she was brought to court on charges of assault, raising the implication that her earlier stints in the gaol and factory resulted from violent incidents.

Margaret married Lawrence Delaney in Sydney on 12th June 1822[42]. Lawrence had also arrived in the colony as a convict under a life sentence for highway robbery.[43] In March 1818 at the age of 22 he had been convicted in the city of Cork, Ireland and transported on the ship Earl St Vincent later that year. He was an imposing figure over 6 feet tall with a fair to ruddy complexion, brown hair and hazel eyes. A small scar marked his left cheek bone.[44] At the time of Charlotte's indenture to Margaret, Lawrence Delaney, a clerk by trade, was an Overseer at the Commissariat Stores, a position he had held since 1820.[45]

Lawrence's record as a convict was not without blemish but instances of misconduct appear to have been minor and to some extent comical. In October 1819, he was charged with disorderly conduct and sent to the barracks.[46] On Saturday 17th December 1825, Lawrence and Martin Smith, a tailor, were brought before the Police. They were charged with creating a riot and disturbing the peace in King Street on the previous evening. It appeared that in the past they had been good friends and meeting by chance, Smith proposed that they adjourn to a nearby public house to talk about old times over a 'friendly glass'. Delaney agreed and they retired to a snug little room where Smith called for a supply of 'blue ruin', water, lemons, and sugar.

Their glasses emptied, Delaney, not wanting to be indebted to his friend, ordered another round. Subsequently Smith, similarly motivated, called for a third. And so they went on endeavouring to outdo each other's friendship until they were pretty well saturated. When the bill was presented, Delaney insisted that Smith had invited him and therefore he was not obliged to pay. Smith by no means relished this point of view no matter how much he might have relished the constant supply of gin.

Unable to resolve the dispute sensibly, Delaney proposed that they should try a friendly hit at each other. Whoever got the worst of it should pay the 'shot'. Smith had no objection to this means of settlement and accordingly they stood up to spar. Delaney was knocked down immediately. Getting up he cried out 'enough', but his cruel adversary, determining his friend should have the worst of it, knocked him down again, punched him and 'fibbed' him, until some constables arrived. Happily for poor Lawrence the constables relieved him from any further violence. Both men were secured separately in a watch-house.

In the eyes of the court it was simply a matter concerning Lawrence Delaney, holding a ticket of leave, and Martin Smith, prisoner of the crown, who had been apprehended in the act of fighting together in a public house, to the annoyance of the landlord, and to the peril of his decanters and glasses. The men put in a general plea of guilt by intoxication and promised never to be 'guilty of the like again'. The chief constable testified as to Delaney's, peaceable conduct when sober and he was given a light sentence of four days on the tread mill. Smith, who the evidence strongly suggested was the first aggressor, was treated more harshly and received 25 lashes.[47]

Although Lawrence seems to have been a reasonably steady fellow, Margaret was not easy to live with and the Delaneys no doubt had a turbulent marriage. The Sydney Gazette and New South Wales Advertiser reported on 27th May 1826 that Margaret Delaney, free, was charged with a violent assault on Mrs Cullen, the wife of Mr. John Cullen, publican in York Street. Mrs. Delaney was stated to have thrown a glass tumbler at Mrs. Cullen who received cuts from the broken glass. The evidence in the case was so conflicting that it was impossible for the Bench to ascertain which woman was the first aggressor and the complaint was dismissed.[48]

On the 8th of March 1827 the same newspaper reported:

> A man named Delaney, who happens to be blessed with a most incorrigible *rib*, appeared before their Worships at the Police office on Monday, looking very like the Knight of the Woeful Countenance, and beseeching aid in pursuit of the aforesaid rib, who had not only taken herself off that morning, but had also made £200 in hard dollars, the companions of her flight. Their Worships appeared very doubtful how far they could interfere, it being a pretty well settled point of law that a wife cannot rob her husband. They, however, instructed a constable to accompany the complainant, and assist, if possible, in discovering the retreat of the fugitive and inducing her in the best manner he could, and without using force, to reimburse the dollars; and Chapman, having taken upon himself the duty, very soon returned, bending under the weight of the spoil, which be traced to a house where it bad been deposited, and carried it off in triumph, in the absence of Mrs. Delaney. Upon counting over his recovered treasure, the owner found it was £16 minus, since it had left his superintending care, but he, notwithstanding, retired highly satisfied that it was no worse.[49]

In July 1829 she was charged with assaulting Margaret Macarthy. On 31st August the crown prosecutor, Alexander MacDuff Baxter, submitted an affidavit concerning The King against Margaret Delaney. Baxter stated that on the 28th of July, Margaret Delaney, wife of Lawrence Delaney labourer of Sydney, assaulted Margaret McCarthy. Delaney beat, bruised, wounded and ill treated her to the extent that her life was in danger and inflicted 'great damage' to her 'and against the Peace of Our said Lord the King, his Crown and Dignity'.[50]

At the trial held on 3rd September, Delaney pleaded not guilty. Witnesses to the assault, David Hennessy, Mary Arnett, John Murray and Margaret Macarthy the victim, appeared for the Crown. The results of the case are unknown but Delaney was probably released on bail.[51]

The situation did not improve. In fact it got worse. On the 23rd September 1830, she was in gaol on a charge of assault but was released on bail two days later.[52] She wasted little time and less than two months later she was back in gaol once more on a charge of assault. At the Quarter Session in Sydney she was found guilty and released on bail on the 14th of November.[53] The Sydney Monitor reported the facts:

> Mistress Delaney made her twentieth appearance before the bench, charged with not only breaking the peace, but six squares of glass at the same time, in evidence of which a quantity of large stones were produced, which had been picked up in the house directly, after the smashing in of the windows. Having been frequently bound over to keep the peace, she was ordered to find securities, herself in £60 and two sureties in £30 to keep the peace for twelve months.[54]

After this episode Mr Delaney appears to have had enough. He placed a notice in the Sydney Monitor dated 16th November advising:

> The public are hereby cautioned against giving Trust or Credit to my Wife Margaret, as I will not

be responsible for any debts she may contract after this notice.⁵⁵

Although Lawrence's action seems to have brought a hiatus in her rude behaviour, it did not stop her forever. Toward the end of April 1833 she appeared before the Bench to answer a charge of striking Sophia Hamilton who lived on the opposite side of York Street. According to Mrs Hamilton and a witness, William Barrett who lived with her, Mrs Delaney had verbally abused her as she passed by Delaney's door on Wednesday evening. Delaney had called her a 'damned whore'. Mrs Hamilton, who had a child in her arms, turned to Mrs Delaney and said that it was a shame for her to use such language in the street. Delaney then had thrown several stones at Mrs Hamilton, one of which struck her on the chin and knocked her down. She still had the bruise caused by the blow. Mrs Hamilton explained that she had given the defendant no provocation, but had been abused by Delaney previously on several occasions since coming to the neighbourhood.⁵⁶

When the magistrate, Charles Windeyer, asked her what she had to say regarding the matter, Margaret's words, apparently affected by alcohol, were to the effect that she did not have the eloquence of Mrs Hamilton and there was no use in putting questions to the 'likes of her'. Understanding from the magistrate that she was not allowed to call any witnesses on her behalf, Margaret refused to say anything in her defence. She was accordingly committed to bail in the amount of £20 and the provision of two sureties at £10 each.⁵⁷

Margaret Delaney's conduct over the years suggests that Charlotte had been mistreated while in service eventually prompting her to run away. But it may not have been the only reason why she had run off. John Grant, who had been convicted with Charlotte at Kirton in Lindsey in October 1826, had arrived in Sydney at the end of July 1827. As a stonemason and cutter, Grant was very useful in the colony and was immediately put to work in the Engineers' Department. He was relatively quiet until January 11, 1828 when he entered gaol for having run away from the Hyde Park Barracks.

While on the run Grant most likely met up with Charlotte. He definitely was an inducement for her to run away from the implied brutality of her employer. Both are mentioned in the list of prisoners absent from their employment as of 11 January 1828 published in the Sydney Gazette and NSW Advertsier on the 14th of that month. Obviously both had been captured by the time the list was published. This was the second time Grant had run and they may have met previously, following Charlotte's arrival in the Colony. For his second absence, Grant was sentenced to 3 months on an iron gang.[58]

Notes to Chapter 10

1. The Monitor, Thursday Evening, September 27, 1827, *Shipping Intelligence*, p.7, col.2.; The Australian, Friday, September 28, 1827, p., col.1.
2. Ibid.
3. The Monitor, op.cit.
4. The Sydney Gazette and New South Wales Advertiser, Friday, September 28, 1827, *Shipping Intelligence*, p.2., col.1.
5. Ibid., *Postscript*, p.2., col.1.
6. The Australian, Friday, September 28, 1827, p.3., col.1.
7. Vivienne Parsons, *Morisset, James Thomas (1780–1852)*, ADB, MUP 1967, Vol. 2, pp.260-261.
8. Louis de Freycinet, *Reflections on New South Wales 1788-1839*, Translated for Freycinet's *'Voyage autour du monde* (Paris 1824 – 1844)" by Thomas Cullity, Hordern house, 2001, pp260-264.
9. HRA Series I Vol.10, p.685.
10. Ibid.
11. HRA Series I Vol.13, p.367-368, Mssrs Oxley, Dumaresq and Busby to Governor Darling, Sydney 18th May 1827.
12. Peter Cunningham, *Two Years in New South Wales*, Vol 1, p47.
13. http://www.westpac.com.au/about-westpac/westpac-group/company-overview/our-history/. Accessed 19 September 2013.
14. HRA Series I Vol.10, p. 686.
15. Ibid., p.685.
16. The Australian, Friday, September 28, 1827, p.4, col.1.
17. Sydney Gazette and New South Wales Advertiser (SG&NSWA), Friday, October 5, 1827 p., col.4; The Australian, October 12, 1827, p.1., col.4.
18. The Australian, Friday, September 28, 1827, p.4, col.1.
19. The Monitor,Thursday Evening, October 4, 1827 p.3, col.3.
20. The Monitor,Thursday Evening, September 27, 1827, p1, col.3.
21. The Monitor, Monday Evening, October 8, 1827, p.3, col.1.
22. Ibid., p.6, col.2.
23. SG&NSWA, Wednesday, October 3, 1827, p.1, col.1.
24. SG&NSWA, Wednesday, October 17, 1827 p.2, col.6.

25 Journal of His Majesty's Convict Ship Harmony, William McDowell Surgeon, Adm 101/32 AJCP reel PRO 3197.
26 SRNSW: NRS 12188 Principal Superintendent of Convicts, Bound manuscript indents, [4/4012, pp. 222 - 231], Fiche No.666.
27 Thomas Bigge, *Report of the Commissioner of Inquiry into the state of the Colony of New South Wales,* House of Commons, 1822, pp. 13-16.
28 SG&NSWA, Wednesday, October 17, 1827 p.2, col.6.
29 Ibid.
30 SRNSW: Fiche No.666, op.cit.
31 Ibid.
32 Ian Brand, *The Convict Probation System, Van Diemen's Land 1839 to 1854,* Blubber Head Press, Hobart 1990 p.6.
33 SG&NSWA Monday 15 October 1827 p.2, col.2.
34 HRA Series I, Vol.13, p.593.
35 SG&NSWA, Wednesday, December 26, 1827, p.3, col.2.
36 Charles Bateson, *The Convict Ships 1787-1868,* Reed, Sydney, 1974, p.227.
37 SRNSW: NRS2514, Sydney Gaol Entrance Books, [4/6430, December 31, 1827] Reel 851.
38 SRNSW: NRS 1155, Colonial Secretary, Musters and other papers relating to convict ships 1790-1849, [2/8257, p.217] Reel 2421.
39 HO10/2, AJCP Reel PRO 60; HO10/14 AJCP Reel PRO 64; HO10/ 17 AJCP Reel PRO 65.
40 SRNSW: NRS 937, Colonial Secretary, Copies of letters sent within the Colony1814-1825, [4/3500, p.80], Reel 6006.
41 SRNSW: NRS 2514, Sydney Gaol Entrance Books, [4/6360 May 4, 1822], Reel 850.
42 SRNSW: NRS 937, Colonial Secretary, Copies of letters sent within the Colony, 1814-1825, [4/3505, p.381], Reel 6009.
43 SRNSW: NRS 1155, Colonial Secretary, Musters and other papers relating to convict ships 1790-1849, [2/8256, p.114], Reel 2420.
44 SRNSW: NRS 12202, Principal Superintendent of Convicts, Ticket of leave butts, 31 March 1827-31 December 1875, [4/4081, No.31/898], Reel 916.
45 SRNSW: NRS 897, Colonial Secretary, Main series of letters received, 1788-1825, [4/1771 p. 229f], Reel 6058.
46 SRNSW: NRS 900, Colonial Secretary, Petitions to the Governor from convicts for mitigation of sentences, 1810-26. [4/1873 1b], Fiche 3244-47.
47 The Australian, Sydney, Thursday, 22 December 1825, p.4, col.1-2.; The Sydney Gazette and New South Wales Advertiser, Thursday, 22 December 1825, p3, col.2.
48 SG&NSWA, Saturday 27 May 1826 p.2, col.5.
49 SG&NSWA, Thursday 8 March 1827 p.2, col.6.
50 SRNSW: NRS 13477, Criminal Jurisdiction, Letter 29/251, [T29A].
51 Ibid.; SRNSW: NRS 880 [T141] 28 may shed some light on the witnesses' statements and the results of the trial but the document could

not be found in the New South Wales Archives at Kingswood when visited on 15 October 2013.
52 SRNSW: NRS 2514, Sydney Gaol Entrance Books, [4/6431, September 23, 1830], Reel 851.
53 Ibid., November 12,1830.
54 The Sydney Monitor, Saturday, November 13, 1830, p.2, col.6.
55 The Sydney Monitor, Wednesday, November 17, 1830, p.3, col.3.
56 SRNSW: NRS 845, Depositions and other papers, Quarter Sessions cases, 1824-37, April 1833, Sydney, No.94 [4/8457].
57 SG&NSWA, Saturday, April 27, 1833 p.2, col.5.
58 SRNSW, NRS2514 Sydney Gaol Entrance Books, [4/6429 January 11, 1828], Reel 850.

Chapter 11

John Grant, James South and Mary McQueen

As principal characters in Charlotte's story up to this point, it is worthwhile diverging here to examine the lives of John Grant, James South and Mary McQueen as convicts in the Australian colonies.

On the 9th of April 1828 Grant was back in Sydney gaol having runaway from his gang again. At the General Session, later that month, he was ordered to the Lower Branch of the Hawkesbury River[1] where, as a stonemason, he was put to good use building side walls and stone bridges along the Great North Road.

His wanderlust was not deterred. On September 29th, at the General Session, Portland Head, having absconded from his gang eleven times in total several times in possession of government property, Grant was described as *'an incorrigible runaway'*,[2] and sentenced to the penal settlement at Moreton Bay for four years. Sent to the *Phoenix Hulk* anchored at Lavender Bay in Sydney Harbour on the 1st of October to await transportation,[3] he was still there in November at the time of the 1828 census.[4]

The *Phoenix*, a ship of 589 tons, was built on the Thames River, England, in 1798. Under the command of Robert White she arrived at Hobart on the morning of 22 July 1824, after a voyage of 114 days, discharged her cargo of convicts and continued on to Sydney. While entering Port Jackson under the guidance of pilot John M. Gray, she ran aground on the Sow and Pigs reef, a group of rocks a short distance from the harbour entrance.[5] Refloated and towed to Campbell's Downs (Darling Harbour), the ship was determined to be so damaged that it could not be repaired in the Colony. Unfortunately Captain White, owing to the mishap, sustained a private loss of £1000 in this his first trip as Commander of the Phoenix.[6]

In January 1825 the ship's rigging, masts and other fittings were auctioned. The Colonial government purchased the hulk for £1000 converting it to a prison for convicts awaiting transportation to Moreton Bay, Norfolk Island and other penal settlements. Initially moored in Sydney Cove the *Phoenix* was later moved to Hulk Bay, now named Lavender Bay after George Lavender, the hulk's boatswain. The *Phoenix* became the only prison hulk to operate in New South Wales,[7] although later in 1862, plans were drafted for at least one other prison hulk, the *Harmony*.[8]

A report to the Governor on the state of the *Phoenix Hulk*, consequent to a letter from the Superintendent of the hulk to the Chief Magistrate regarding complaints from the prisoners, was published in The Sydney Gazette and NSW Advertiser on 17 November 1825. The magistrates inspecting the prison reported:

> The hulk is a very comfortable gaol. We conclude our Report with again respectfully drawing Your Excellency's attention to the necessity of an improved allowance of food and clothing to the prisoners, and the absolute necessity of the hulk being visited every other day, at least, by one or more Magistrates, until a legal authority is derogated to the Superintendent to punish minor offences.[9]

Evidently the complaints of the prisoners were not directed at the superintendent and his officers or the labour they were obliged to perform but directed towards the provision of food and clothing. With the small amount of 'food (one pound and a half of very course bread), allowed to each individual, they were unable to perform the labour allotted to them'. Many of them insisted they needed clothing and blankets, and 'the appearance of too many of them confirmed the assertion'.

On Friday 19th July 1827, the Grand Jury again visited the *Phoenix* Hulk, and reported, 'with pleasure, that nothing can be more cleanly, wholesome, and complete than the interior arrangements of this spacious vessel. The accommodations are now sufficient for 200 prisoners, in a state of comfort and custody, far superior to the gaol on shore. The Grand Jury have only to recommend, that the room appropriated to the use of the military guard, should be furnished with glazed windows, to exclude the cold, at this season of the year.'[10]

However by 1837 the hulk was described as being in a 'sinking state' and the Government ordered her sent on shore and sold at auction. Advertised as one of the fastest sailing frigates that had ever sailed from England, it was suggested that 'colonial ship builders would do well to examine this vessel and take a model of her'.[11] The hulk was hauled on to the beach at Waterview on 9 November in preparation for her to be sold at auction. There was no intention to replace her and the prisoners were temporarily kept on Goat Island.[12] Purchased by Mr. Thomas Hyndes for the bargain price of £145, the *Phoenix* was finally broken up in December, except for her keel, which Hyndes kept at his yard in Cockle Bay.[13]

After about fifteen weeks on the hulk, John Grant was put on board the *City of Edinburgh* lying in Sydney Cove and set out for Morton Bay on Monday 12 January 1829. The day before the ship's departure the prisoners attempted to cut through the scuttles of the prison and escape. When the sentinel on duty detected their activity the prisoners became so riotous that the Captain found it necessary to exercise his utmost authority to suppress the uprising. He informed them that in case of a second attempt the guards had been given orders to fire amongst them as a last resort. Everything appeared quiet on board until about 3 o'clock in the morning when an alarm announced that the attempt to escape had been renewed.

As the guard descended the stairs to the prison to prevent the escape, the prisoners charged. In the confusion, two prisoners, jumped overboard and swam towards the North Shore. The soldiers found it absolutely necessary to fire on the rioters and eight of them were wounded. A boat arrived containing a party of marines from H.M.S. Satellite, who with the crew and guard of the prison ship, succeeded in restoring order on board. Both men, who jumped overboard, were pursued and one was captured and brought back in the ship's boat.

The other escapee, known as Scotch Jack, was not found and was presumed drowned considering his heavy irons and the distance between the ship and the shore. However he was known to be a good swimmer. A few days previously, heavily ironed, he had gone over the side of the ship with a rope fastened to his body and retrieved a musket which had accidently fallen over the side into 9 fathoms of water. Fortunately his aquatic ability did not fail him in his bid to escape and he reached shore, but was apprehended the next day at Lane Cove.

Six of the wounded men were taken to the General Hospital. On Sunday morning, George Bunn and Thomas Raine, Esqs., Justices of the Peace, arrived on board and instituted an inquiry into the proceedings of the previous night. Nine of the ringleaders were sentenced to corporal punishment, six receiving fifty lashes each, and the remaining three, thirty-six lashes each. In addition to the usual irons, the prisoners were hand-cuffed. James Kelly, who was convicted of receiving stolen notes of the Bank of Australia, was one of the principal mutineers. John Grant, with his record of absconding, would have been prominent in the attempted escape.[14]

One of the wounded prisoners, John Jackson, died and an inquest into his death was held on the 23rd of January in the Rose and Crown Tavern, Castlereagh Street. The inquest found that the deceased, although not immediately connected with the tumult arising from the attempted escape, 'was indiscriminately shot by one of the soldiers in the execution of his duty in order to subdue the serious and alarming tumult that then existed on board.' The Coroner and Jury concluded 'that the deceased died in consequence of a wound inflicted by a musket shot from one of the soldiers on duty, after a mutiny had actually existed for some length of time amongst the prisoners, and which they (the Jury), consider to be justifiable homicide.'[15]

The ship's quota of 137 prisoners arrived at Moreton Bay on 24th January 1829. The Moreton Bay Penal Settlement had been established in 1824 as a place of punishment for convicts who committed a secondary offence while already serving a sentence of transportation in Australia. Originally located on the Redcliffe Peninsula in Moreton Bay, the site was found to be unsuitable for long term residence and in early 1825 it was moved up-river to the present site of Brisbane. Part of New South Wales until 1859 the region was administered by the Colonial Secretary in Sydney who dealt with all the matters pertinent to convicts soldiers and free persons in a remote penal settlement.[16]

The number of convicts in the settlement was comparatively small ranging from an original 75 in 1825 to a peak of 1020 in 1831. The total number for the period from 1824 to 1839 was 2259 male convicts and 144 female convicts with most of the females arriving after 1829. Female convicts were kept at a Female Factory in the settlement.

Convict work included splitting rails and posts, putting up fencing, gardening, digging wells, dairying and tending the sheep, pigs, cows, goats and cattle of the settlement. They were employed as water carriers, bakers, cooks, wardsmen, hospital attendants, personal servants, clerks and overseers, members of boats' crews and mechanics. Agricultural labourers at Eagle Farm tended staple food crops of maize and potatoes.

Free people comprised government administrative officials, storekeepers, the settlement doctor, superintendent of works, a few tradesmen and officers, soldiers and their families. A parochial school was provided for the education of their children and later on the children of convict women were also admitted.[17]

On arrival, John Grant was processed as prisoner number 1595, his original conviction and colonial conviction recorded and his trade as a stonemason and cutter noted. At some point in time his sentence of 4 years' transportation to Moreton Bay was commuted to three years commencing 23 September 1828.[18]

His time at Moreton Bay was not pleasant. He soon contracted dysentery and was treated at the Hospital with '*pil hydrarg. cum cret & acirc.*' a bluish grey pill consisting of mercury and powdered chalk, used in small quantities as a purgative[19].

The Moreton Bay Hospital, in which convicts and soldiers and their families were treated, was established in 1826 with Henry Cowper appointed as the first doctor.[20] A great variety of illnesses and injuries were treated at the hospital, the most common including *febris* (fevers possibly related to a variety of diseases and conditions), dysentery, ulcers *ophthalmia* (inflammation of the eye, conjunctivitis), *cynanche* (severe sore throat and other throat infections including tonsillitis and pharyngitis), *colica* (colic), *psora* (psoriasis or fungal infection including scabies), diarrhoea, nausea, *vermes* (worms), *obstipatio* (intractable constipation), *phlegmon* (phlebitis or inflammation of soft or connecting tissue due to streptococcal infection), *paronychia* (nail infection), *cephalalgia* (headache), *eruptio* (skin lesions) rheumatism, *pleuritis* (pleurisy), *syphilis*, *debilitas* (weakness, lack of strength) contusions (bruises) and *vulnus* (a wound).[21]

Until the middle of the 19th century most symptoms associated with illness were believed to come from an imbalance in the 'humours' or fluids—bile, phlegm and blood. Consequently, remedial practices focussed on purging the body of humours. Dosing patients with powerful purgatives and cathartics was considered to be best practice. Most maladies were treated with mineral compounds composed of mercury, antimony, silver and sulphur or with a combination of minerals and dried, powdered herbs and plants both toxic and edible. The use of compounds containing mercury was favoured particularly as a laxative, diuretic, and antiseptic. Calomel (a mixture of mercury sulphate and sodium chloride), which could have a violent laxative effect, was one of the most drastic purgatives known to the nineteenth century doctors. The poisonous properties of many of the substances used were well known and the amounts of toxic material in each medicine was minimised to produce the desired beneficial effect without being fatal. However, the remedy applied was, all too often, worse than the disease.

On 16 September 1829 Grant was returned to the penal settlement again having absconded.[22] On the same day he was treated with 4 ounces (124.4 grams) of '*Mist. Cath.*' (*Mistura Cathartica*), a purgative mixture prepared by soaking dried mint in boiling water for a quarter of an hour, and dissolving crystals of tartar, sulphate of soda and tartarised antimony in the strained mint liquor.[23] Subsequently he was treated in the hospital a total of 16 days during 1829 and 8 days in 1830. In most cases he was treated for unspecified ailments with the cathartic mixture mentioned above or with extract of Henbane, a substitute for opium. In one instance he was given a combination of Henbane and powdered antimony; on another a mixture of extract of rhubarb and opium, suggesting he suffered from stomach or bowel problems. More specifically he was treated for worms with Jalapa and Henbane and for colic and constipation with '*Pulvis Jalapa Compositus*', a mixture of powdered

Jalap, tartrate of potash and powdered ginger. Jalap, was a well known and often used purgative made from the tuberous roots of Ipomoea Jalapa, a climbing, vine like plant from Mexico.[24]

Hospital records show that Grant and eight other convicts received treatment for wounds from being flogged on 24 November 1829 and again, with five other men, on 10th December.[25] The reason for the floggings is unstated, but was most likely punishment for absconding. Fifty lashes were usually given for such trivial things as refusing to work and stealing food, but up to 300 lashes could be received for more serious offences such as absconding. The flogging was no deterrent. He absconded again, was returned on the 19th of March 1830[26] and on the 21st received 4 ounces of cathartic mixture. Two days later he was given extract of Henbane, to relieve the pain produced by the purgative or the punishment inflicted, or probably both. His last hospital entry was on the 19th of May 1830 when he was given *Pulvis Jalapa* for constipation.[27]

By the end of September 1831 Grant was due to be released having served the three year commuted sentence, but his misdemeanours while at the settlement must have reversed the commutation. In frustration he absconded again and was returned on 14th April 1832.[28] Later that year his sentence was completed and on 23rd November he left the settlement for Sydney.[29] He obtained Certificate of Freedom No. 33/1328 on 16th December 1833[30] and married 33 year old convict Mary Kean (or Taylor) at Windsor on 16th March 1835.[31]

...

James South arrived in Hobart on 31 July 1827 on board the *Governor Ready*. Obviously the sea voyage had a beneficial effect on South as his character was described as '*Good*' during the voyage.[32] But after a year on dry land he returned to his old ways. His conduct record during his seven year sentence in Tasmania is a litany of misdemeanours.

Starting on the 20th October 1828, he was sentenced to 7 days on the tread wheel for being '*drunk at muster for church*' the previous morning. After that, offences were committed and punishment served every few months. On 4 February 1829 he was absent from work in the Governor's garden from 12 o'clock until 7 o'clock in the evening and received another 7 days on the tread wheel.

Indentured to a survey party, he was out of his hut at 2 am on 13th of August but was absolved of any wrong doing as he had gone to see the doctor. Work on the survey party did not seem to suit him - on 8 December he was insolent to the sentry at Waterloo Point and received 25 lashes. And on the 16th for *'using exasperating language to the military and various other misdemeanours'* he was put on a chain gang at Oatlands for 6 months.

This kept him quiet until 9th of August 1830 when he allowed 5 prisoners under his charge on public works to get drunk and found himself back on the chain gang for one month. Released from the chain gang he celebrated a little too much, got drunk on the Sabbath and struck a constable named Ansley. For this assault he received 30 lashes. Two and a half months later he had his original sentence extended by 18 months for neglecting his duty and grossly abusing and insulting Mr Kenworthy Esq. in the execution of his duty. The extended sentence seemed to have no deterring effect for on 27th December 1832 he was served 30 lashes for being absent from work for two days.

He had a particularly bad time during February and March 1833: 1 February, for being absent from Barracks, 25 lashes; 11 February, absent from Barracks, 25 lashes; the 25th absent from Barracks, 6 weeks imprisonment with hard labour on the chain gang; 9 March, disobeying orders, an additional month on the chain gang. He did not allow himself any reprieve and on 23rd May was back in prison for two months with hard labour for being absent without leave.

A month after this sentence ended he went absent from the barracks at night and was imprisoned with hard labour on the Launceston Gang for one month. However, he could not keep his mouth shut and on 13th September for *'making use of improper Language'* an additional 6 weeks on the Launceston Gang was recommended followed by a further one month recommended on 14 October for neglect of work.

In complete contrast to the punishment he had received over the previous 5 years, a memo dated 19th October 1833 from the Colonial Secretary's Office declared that the extension of sentence in

December 1832 was illegal. As a finale, perhaps in response to this decision, he was charged with insubordination on 22nd October for refusing to work and was put in solitary confinement on bread and water for 14 days. A week after his release on 12 November 1833, James South was given a certificate of emancipation and was free from bondage having served his entire sentence.[33] Five years later he married Isabella Dewar at St John's Church in Launceston.[34]

...

On disembarking from the *Harmony*, Mary McQueen spent nine months as a housemaid to James Bloodsworth in Sydney. Continuously besieged by ill health she was *'useless in her service'* and returned to 1st Class in the factory on 28 July 1828.[35] Three days later she was assigned to Captain Steel. But he soon discharged her and she was back in the Factory on 27th October.[36] She was still there in November 1828. Fortunately life took a different turn for Mary. Early in 1829 she met Joseph Low and they were married on 16th April 1829 in Newcastle.[37] She was 21 and he was 32.

Joseph was a groom, from Nottingham, England, employed to clean and look after horses. In January 1818, at 22 years of age, he had been court-martialled in the colony of Demerara, West Indies[38]. Sentenced to transportation for life, he arrived in New South Wales in March 1819 on the *Lord Sidmouth*. He was initially indentured to a Mr Williams, but on 29 March 1820 received 100 lashes[39] and a two year sentence to Newcastle. Transported to Newcastle two weeks later on the *Elizabeth Henrietta*,[40] he entered government employment as a labourer[41]. By 1825 he was employed in government service to Edward Close[42].

Mary and Joseph settled in the lower Hunter River area of New South Wales and raised a family. Mary received her certificate of freedom on 31 May 1834[43] and Joseph was conditionally pardoned on 1August 1839.[44]

...

Woven into the fabric of Australian life, concealed among the masses, Charlotte's three companions in crime faded from view. Perhaps it was youthful exuberance or ambition, but Grant and South certainly paid dearly for their inability to cooperate within the colonial penal system. However, both men having paid the penalty for their crime in England were released after serving their seven year sentences. Mary McQueen, owing to her delicate health appears to have had a comparatively easy time. Within two years of her arrival in New South Wales she settled into a relatively stable, secure marriage in the Hunter River valley. Whether or not Charlotte met her three friends again has not been discovered, but it is highly likely she became reacquainted with Mary McQueen later in life.

Notes to Chapter 11

1. SRNSW: NRS 2514, Sydney Gaol Entrance Books, [4/6430] Reel 851.
2. Ibid., September 29, 1828.
3. Ibid.
4. 1828 Census NSW.
5. Charles Bateson, *The Convict Ships 1787-1868*, Reed, Sydney,1974, pp. 230-231.
6. SG&NSWA, Thursday, September 16, 1824, p.2, col.5.
7. Charles Bateson, (1972). *Australian Shipwrecks - vol 1 1622-1850*. Sydney, AH & AW Reed, 1971, p.66.
8. SRNSW: NRS 910 [4/1079, 62/762], *Memorandum respecting the fitting up of the 'Harmony' as a Prison Hulk, 14 February 1862*. Reel 2726.
9. SG&NSWA, Friday, November 17, 1825 , p.2, col.5.
10. SG&NSWA, Friday, July 20,1827, p.2, col.5.
11. SG&NSWA, Tuesday, November 7, 1837, p.2 col.6.
12. The Sydney Herald, Ship News, Thursday, November 9, 1837, p.3, col.2.
13. SG&NSWA, Thursday, December 21,1837, p.2, col.4.
14. SG&NSWA, Tuesday, January 13, 1829, p.2, col.3.and col.5.
15. SG&NSWA, Saturday, January 24,1829, p.2, col.6.
16. M. Eastgate, A Guide to the pre-Separation Population Index, Moreton Bay Region 1824 to 1859, Queensland Family History Society 1990.
17. Ibid., p.32.
18. Queensland State Archives (QSA): Chronological register of Convicts at Moreton Bay, Queensland State Archives, Item ID869689, Register – prisoners, Microfilm Z7857 p.36.
19. QSA: Item ID2858, Register – Hospital out-patients, Microfilm Z4226.
20. Eastgate, op. cit.
21. QSA: Item ID2858, op.cit.

22 QSA: Item ID869688, Returns – prisoners, Microfilm Z7858, Vol.2, p2.
23 J. Wilson, Pharmacopoeia Chirugica, Cox, London, 1811 p.164.
24 QSA: Item ID2858, op.cit.
25 Ibid.
26 QSA: Item ID869688, Returns – prisoners, Microfilm Z7858, Vol.2, p.64.
27 QSA: Item ID2858, op. cit.
28 QSA: Item ID869688, Returns – prisoners, Microfilm Z7858, Vol.2, p.66.
29 QSA: Item ID869689, Register – prisoners, Microfilm Z7857, p.36.
30 SRNSW: NRS 12210, Butts of certificates of freedom, 1827-67, No.33/1328, [4/4319], Reel 992.
31 SRNSW: NRS 12212, Registers of convicts' applications to marry, 1825-51, [4/4512 p.166], Fiche 792.
32 AOTAS: Convict Conduct Record, CON 31/1/38, No.803.
33 AOTAS: Convict Conduct Record, CON 23/1/3, No.803.
34 Thelma McKay (comp.), Van Diemen's Land, Early Marriages, Vol.2 1831 -1840.
35 SRNSW: NRS 2514; Sydney Gaol Entrance Books, [4/6430] Reel 851.
36 Ibid.
37 NRS 12212, Registers of convicts' applications to marry, 1825-5, [4/4511, No. 683]; [4/4508], Fiche 780.
38 SRNSW: NRS 12188, Bound manuscript indents, 1788-1842, [4/4006, p.288], Microfiche 641.
39 SRNSW: NRS 2514; Sydney Gaol Entrance Books, [4/6360], Reel 850.
40 SRNSW: NRS 937, Colonial Secretary, Copies of letters sent within the Colony1814-1825, [4/3501, p.342], Reel 6007.
41 NAUK Microfilm Publication, HO10/36, p.192.
42 NAUK Microfilm Publication, HO10/19, p.348.
43 SRNSW; NRS 12210 Certificate of Freedom, , [4/4322, No.34/668], Reel 993.
44 SRNSW: NRS 1172 Copies of Conditional Pardons Registered, [4-4438, No.40/137] Reel 778, p219-220.

Chapter 12

Service and the Factory

When Charlotte arrived at the Female Factory in Parramatta, a number of women from the *Harmony* had already been sent to the establishment.[1] Some of them were still there. These women had either been rejected immediately by their masters or mistresses when distributed from the ship or later sent to the Factory because they were no longer needed, were unsatisfactory or had committed some misdemeanour.

Mary Martin, Susan Bartrip, Elizabeth Warhurst, and Mary Mumford were given up before leaving the ship. Superintendant of Convicts, Frederick Hely, sent them directly to the Factory with the instruction that they were to be reassigned.[2] Elizabeth Hague was given up by her master on the day of distribution stating there was no further occasion for her service.[3] Similarly Martha Hubbert was given up by her master on the 17th.[4] Mary Anne Smith, who had been *'found in a house of ill fame in bed with a man'*, was sentenced to two months 3rd Class in the Factory on the 22nd October.[5] Ann Butterworth, who had run away from Parramatta, was returned on the 24th.[6] On the same day Margaret Kane was given up by her master and sent to 1st Class in the Factory[7] and Ann Gratton was charged with drunkenness on and sent to the 3rd Class in the Factory for 3 months.[8] Elizabeth Brown was sent to the Factory on the 30th for making a frivolous charge against her master[9] and on November 14, Mary Harris was charged with being absent from her service and sentenced to 3rd class in the Factory for 1 month.[10] Hannah West was returned to the government on November 19 by her master who claimed she was *'useless in her service'*[11] Three days later Hannah Bryant was returned to the Government by her master.[12] Ann Woodward was delivered to the Factory on 3rd of December for being *'useless in her service'*[13] and the next day Ellen (Robinson) Roberts was charged with drunkenness and absence from her master's service and sent to the 3rd Class for 1 month on 7th December.[14] Margaret Murphy entered the Factory for 1 month in the 3rd Class on 13th December for being absent and neglecting her work[15] and Mary Hughes who was drunk, insolent and suspected of robbery was sentenced on 26th December to 6 months in the 3rd Class entering the Factory on 1st of January 1828.[16]

Conversely, Sarah Upcroft, convicted of drunkenness and neglect of duty on 30 October 1827, was imprisoned in solitary confinement for 7 days instead of being sent to the Factory.[17] Some of the women from the *Harmony* were obviously not coping very well with their new environment.

The Australian newspaper of Wednesday, 31 October 1827 reported:

> A "cauty queen," one of the lately arrived by the Harmony, was charged by the master to whom she had been given up but a week or two before as a bond woman, with conducting herself whilst in service, the better portion of her time in one even tenor of wilful negligence and irregularity. For a few fleeting days, her services were valuable, and she worked and sung most lustily, but her passion for working soon gave way to *la belle passion*, for a strangerman who, without a vast deal of labor, gained access to the casket of her affections —
>
> Built him a willow cabin at her gate,
> And called upon his love within the house,
> Making the babbling gossip of the air cry" -
> Molly come down to me.
>
> The maid, as may be inferred, was not naturally hard-hearted, so she did not fail to go down to him, and to attend his walks more closely than her kitchen, which lay neglected and all forlorn; but stolen visits were not all the maid was charged with — the master found his wine cellar daily

diminishing, and this, he inclined to give the maid and her sweetheart the credit of, 'for not even love can live on air,' so finding his bond woman's services scarce 'worthy a straw' he determined on pruning the evil to the root,. and destroying the unworthy attachment which was the main source of nought but loss of rest and loss of property to himself, by representing to the Bench how matters stood; and the latter considering that the adventure of the wine bottles rested a good deal on suspicion, for unseemly conduct alone, condemned the bond woman to a three month's abode in the Factory, and when that term of probation should have expired, her late master and mistress might have the benefit of her services, if necessary, a second time.[18]

The journalist made no apology to William Shakespeare for corrupting Cesario's love message from Orsino to Olivia in Twelfth Night and since there was no one named Molly on the *Harmony*, the identity of the woman in the newspaper article is unknown. Journalistic license may have combined a number of incidents to create the story, convict women often the butt of amusement for the local newspapers. Alternatively the likely candidates can be narrowed down to Mary Anne Smith, Ann Gratton or Elizabeth Brown.

By the beginning of 1828, the Female Factory was overcrowded. Completed in 1821[19] at a cost of £4778, it replaced an earlier, smaller factory located above the local gaol on the other side of the Parramatta River. The new factory was supposed to accommodate 300 women but had dormitory space for only 172, suggesting that some of the women would take lodgings outside yet work in the factory as had been the situation in the old factory.[20] Women in the third (or penitentiary) class had to eat, sleep and work in the same room, but Governor Darling rectified this by erecting workshops and a dining hall in 1825 as a precaution against the spread of disease.[21] At the end of 1827 there were at least 396 female prisoners and 35 children already in the establishment. Three hundred and sixty six of these women were transported convicts and thirty were free but convicted in the Colony.[22] Another 9 women arrived on the 1st of January 1828 and a further 7 were received on the 7th of January including Charlotte and Mary Wickham from the *Harmony*.[23] Some women may have been distributed into service, but it can be assumed that about 412 women occupied the Factory at that time.

As well as a convict institution, the Female Factory also played an important role in the provision of medical care for the wider female population. As a means of regulating, controlling, distributing, employing and punishing convict women, the female factory became a workhouse and labour bureau, a marriage bureau, gaol, hospital and in some cases a place of refuge.[24]

The whole complex, covering about four acres was enclosed with a 16 foot high stone wall, the perimeter encircled with a moat or wet ditch. A large kitchen garden in the complex was available for the female convicts to grow vegetables for their own consumption. The barrack and factory, a large, stately building built of stone, was three storeys high and had wings of one story each. Designed by Francis Greenway along the lines of a woollen manufactory in Yorkshire, it contained quarters for the Superintendant, rooms for carding and weaving on looms, workshops, stores for wool and flax and an area with facilities for bleaching the cloth and linen manufactured. The roof was oak shingled and the floors paved with 6 inch stones or one inch stringy bark planks. Leadlight windows on the basement level were barred, but windows on all other floors were lead glazed and open. Cell doors were secured by trow-plate or were nailed.[25]

After only eleven days at the Female Factory, Charlotte was returned to Sydney Gaol to give evidence at the Sydney Quarter Sessions against a man named Davis. James Davis was employed as a Clerk in the gaol while serving a colonial sentence of twelve months. Prior to leaving the gaol for Parramatta, Charlotte had sworn an affidavit before her former fellow passenger on the *Harmony*, James Morisset, magistrate and current Superintendent of Police. In the deposition she claimed that while she was in gaol, Davis had offered to change her sentence from 3rd Class to 1st Class in the Factory if she would give him some money. Sarah Jervoise, in the gaol at the same time, witnessed the exchange and also swore an affidavit to that effect. Both affidavits give an account of the incident.[26]

> *James Davis under Colonial Sentence 12 Months*
> *Sydney to wit. Charlotte Dawson being duly sworn deposeth that on Monday last she was sent to the Gaol in Sydney to be forwarded to the 3rd Class in the Factory for three months and on that Evening the Prisoner came into the women's ward in the Gaol and told deponent if she would give him a Pound he would alter her Warrant of Committal so that she should go into the first class for three months instead of the 3rd class and be returned to Govt. deponent required to see the warrant which he refused to exhibit unless she gave him money deponent therefore gave him four ring Dollars and promised him a Spanish Dollar besides the Prisoner then handed the warrant to deponent which warrant was altered from 3 months in 3rd Class Factory to 3 months in 1st Class deponent wanted to keep the Warrant but the Prisoner said she must not and she therefore gave it up to him and he took it away.*
>
> *Sworn before us the 5th January 1828*
>   *Charlotte Dawson her **x** mark*
> *J.T. Morisset J.P. Prinp. Supt. of Police*
> *Alexr Berry J.P.*
>
> *Sarah Jervoise being duly sworn saith that she was present in the Gaol on Monday Evening last the 31st, ultimo when Charlotte Dawson was brought there to be forwarded to 3rd Class Factory for three months the prisoner James Davis whom deponent understands is a Clerk in the Gaol came into the Yard where the women were and told Charlotte Dawson that if she would give him some money he would take her out of the 3rd Class factory and put her into the 1st he required a Pound to do so deponent saw her give him four pierced Dollars and was to give him a Spanish Dollar beside the Prisoner Davis then handed her a Warrant so deponent understood*

and which was altered as deponent was informed for her to be sent into the 1st Class instead of the 3rd Class.
Sworn before us the 5th January 1828
       Sarah Jervoise her **x** *mark*
J.T. Morisset J.P. Prinp. Supt. of Police
Alexr Berry J.P.

In a letter to the Colonial Secretary on 9th January 1828, Morisset pointed out that the case against Davis had been made in full and that he had been committed to trial for obtaining money under false pretences.[27] It was not the first time that Davis had been suspected of committing this offence. However in this instance the case was proved beyond doubt by Charlotte's testimony at the trial and the evidence of the warrant which clearly showed the word *'third'* substituted by the word *'first'*. Davis imprisoned in the gaol was accordingly convicted at the Quarter Sessions on Saturday 19th January and sentenced to seven years transportation.[28]

Charlotte returned to Parramatta on 21 January to complete the remainder of her three month sentence in the 3rd Class at the Factory. On release, she may have been returned to Margaret and Lawrence Delaney, but no record has been found to give evidence to that assumption. However on the 20th of September she was back in Sydney Gaol, the record stating she was *'absent from her service ----'*, the column too narrow to record the offence in its entirety. [29]

But the dashes at the end of the statement and the serious penalty of six months in 3rd Class at the Female Factory implied there was more to the offense than recorded. The misdemeanor occurred about the time John Grant absconded from his gang at Portland Head for the eleventh time. It can be presumed that they met at least once more before Grant was sent to the penal settlement at Moreton Bay. A report from Charlotte's former acquaintance Police Superintendent Morisset to the Governor containing a list of prisoners on 20th September 1828 revealed that not only had she been absent from service but she had also been found in bed with a man.[30]

Charlotte was sent to Parramatta on the 24th of September for 6 months after which time she was to be returned to the government.[31]

Overseeing the Factory was a Board or Committee of Management, consisting of government officials not resident in Paramatta and prominent local residents. Routine supervision of the Factory fell to three of these local people: the police magistrate for Parramatta, Edward Lockyer, a local doctor, Mathew Anderson, and local magistrate and clergyman, the Reverend Samuel Marsden.[32] The day to day management of the Factory was under the control of Matron Ann Gordon assisted by three monitresses, one portress, a male clerk and a male storekeeper.[33]

Gordon's employment at the Factory began with a riot in October 1827 and finished in 1836 with allegations that her husband's conduct with the factory women had been inappropriate. Despite these problems, during her time as Matron of the factory she maintained relative stability. Whether her ability to maintain order resulted from an authoritarian approach or an ability to understand women is unclear.

Certainly some of the women from the *Harmony* were subjected to Gordon's strict control. Martha Hubbert had her evening ration of tea stopped for neglecting her work (Oct 22, 1827); Margaret Murphy, who was in the 2nd Class, spent 24 hours in the cells for buying shoes from a woman in the 3rd Class (5 Feb 1828); Rebecca Bloxam disobeyed orders and spent 16 hours in a cell (8 Feb 1828); Elizabeth McMahon was found sleeping during divine service and passed another probably restful 24 hours in a cell (24 Feb 1828); Mary Ann Welsh in the 1st Class was given 24 hours for insolence to her monitress (27 Mar 1828); also in 1st Class, Elizabeth Hague received 24 hours for disobedient conduct (28 Mar 1828); Ann Entwistle, in the 1st Class, took a loaf of bread out of the mess hall resulting in 24 hours in a cell and demotion to 2nd Class (7 April 1828); Charlotte Harrison in the 3rd Class was abusive to her matron and was punished with 24 hours spent in a cell (25 April 1818); Mary Ann Welsh, demoted to the 2nd Class, was given 20 hours for disobedience (7 May 1828); Margaret Kane quarrelled with Catherine Kelly of the *Princess Charlotte* and each cooled off in the cells for 24 hours (13 May 1828); Elizabeth Warhurst's mutinous conduct in the penitentiary resulted in 4 days in a cell (13 May 1828 - three other women convicted with her spent 24, 48 and 72 hours respectively); a disobedient Charlotte Harrison was back in a cell for 24 hours (3 June 1828); Ann Woodward, from the 1st Class, who was insolent to the matron and drunk on return from a pass, had 4 days in a cell to consider the error of her ways (14 June 1828); and Catherine Robinson, 3rd Class, disobedient, 24 hours (19 June 1828).[34] Any misconduct by Charlotte Dawson during her initial three month sojourn in the Factory went undetected.

If the authoritarian approach was the means of Matron Gordon's control, she would have been ably assisted by the Reverend Marsden, a fundamentalist who regarded any variation from his views as full of vice and corruption. Although Marsden fought for improvements to the Factory and was intent on reforming the women, his character as a magistrate and chaplain was marked with severity. He described the Factory as 'a grand source of moral corruption, insubordination, and disease' spreading 'its pestilential influence throughout the most remote part of the colony'. The conduct of the women was specified as 'destructive of all religion, morality and good order' destroying 'the most distant hope of any reformation'. He declared that nothing could be 'more distressing to the serious, reflecting mind, than to see the vices and miseries of these abandoned females'. Marsden was probably right to some extent, but his views, from an upper-middle class vantage point, were likely biased against the lower or poorer classes and broad in their application tarring all with the same brush. In contrast to Marsden, others in the community commented that the convict women from the Factory assigned to them were essentially good and steady in their conduct. If there was a failing on the part of the women it was that they suffered mainly from their impoverished upbringing and lack of education.[35] Unfortunately, the prevalent view was that the female convicts, particularly those from the lower classes in society with few exploitable skills, were a definite burden and in most cases unable to be reformed.[36]

Under Governor Darling the system of classification and separation in the Factory was restructured along more rigid lines than previously. In 1826 Darling instituted three classes, distinct not only by the status of the women in each class but also by work, clothing and food rations.[37] The First Class (non-penitentiary) was occupied by women employed at the factory or waiting to be assigned. It included those who having been returned from assignment without complaint were eligible for immediate reassignment. It also extended asylum to those who were homeless or destitute. The Second Class or Probationary Class contained women returned from assignment because of bad behaviour and women demoted or promoted from the First or Third class respectively. Females who became pregnant while in service were included in the Second Class. In the Third Class were those who had committed some crime in the Colony or transgression against the rules of the Factory and consequently sentenced to a period of time in that class. Women in the Third Class suffered a number of deprivations indicating that in itself the third class represented punishment. [38] It can be easily understood why Charlotte would have been enticed into accepting the proposition that for a small sum her sentence could be changed from Third to First Class.

Upon admission, all women were required to bathe, were inspected by the matron and issued with clothing or 'slops'. Any money they had was confiscated and women destined for the Third Class had their hair close cropped. Clothing issued varied from class to class. First class women were issued two calico caps, a drab serge petticoat, a drab serge jacket and one apron for weekdays and special clothes for Sunday comprising one white cap, a long dress with a muslin frill, one red calico jacket, two cotton check handkerchiefs, one blue gurrah (plain coarse India muslin) petticoat, one under petticoat of factory flannel, one white calico apron, two shifts, one pair of grey stockings, one pair of shoes, one straw bonnet, and a clothes bag to hold all. Each woman in the Second Class received one blue gurrah jacket, one blue gurrah petticoat, one under petticoat of factory flannel, two calico caps, two shifts, one neck handkerchief and one pair of shoes. The women of the Third Class were clearly distinguished by a jacket of striped linsey-woolsey. To complete their attire they received a petticoat of linsey-woolsey, two caps, two shifts and a leather apron of dressed sheepskin.[39]

Government rations of food also varied according to class. Women in the First Class were given the best diet. For breakfast they received ½ pound wheaten bread, ⅛ ounce tea, ¾ ounce sugar and $1/12$ pint of milk. For dinner ½ pound of fresh meat, 1 pound green vegetables or ½ pound potatoes, and ¼ pound of bread was provided. Additionally 1 ounce of wheaten flour to thicken soup or stew made from these ingredients and 1 ounce of salt was available. Supper was a smaller meal of ½ pound wheaten bread, ⅛ ounce tea, ¾ ounce sugar and $1/12$ pint milk. The only difference in diet for the second class women was the absence of milk and the use of Indian cornmeal for thickening soup. As a punitive measure tea rations were often restricted or withdrawn entirely.

Daily diet in the third class was inferior to the other two classes and tea was notably absent. Breakfast consisted of 4 ounces of Indian corn meal, 1 ounce of sugar, and ½ pound of bread made from equal portions of wheat and Indian corn meal; Dinner - ½ pound of fresh meat, 1 pound of green vegetables or ½ pound potatoes, 1 ounce cornmeal to thicken soup and 1 ounce of salt; Supper - ¼ pound of bread (ingredients as above), 4 ounces of Indian corn meal, ½ ounce of sugar.[40]

As indicated earlier, the Factory was set up as a manufactory for a variety of cloth products. First Class women were employed in making shirts, frocks and trousers for inmates and male convicts. They were required to produce nine articles each week and for each article produced above the requisite number they were paid 9d. Laundry, cooking, cleaning, baking and other household chores were also carried out daily, principally by women of the First Class. Second Class women worked at preparing flax and wool for weavers. Their tasks were wool picking, spinning, carding, and winding. They were paid ½ pence for seven cuts of yarn per day and could receive up to 3 pence for eleven cuts. The women of the third class were engaged in similar occupations as the second class with the distinction that they received no remuneration. The more onerous and laborious tasks of earth moving and stone breaking were generally reserved for women who had received hard labour as a specification in their sentence to the third class[41].

Work was undertaken only during daylight hours. In summer the women were employed in their compulsory work between 6 and 8 in the morning, 9 am and 1p.m., and 2pm and 6 pm. In winter the schedule was altered to the hours between 8 in the morning and midday and from 1 o'clock to 5 o'clock in the afternoon.[42] Time for leisure activities was limited with Sunday being the only day of rest.

At daily prayers and Sunday services the women were separated according to religion and class, Roman Catholics and Protestants in separate mess rooms and First and Second class women on opposite sides of the room.[43] Third class women took their religious duties in the penitentiary.[44]

All inmates were required to bath weekly and were inspected each morning for general cleanliness. A force pump installed in the factory circumvented a prior need to go outside the complex for water, therefore adding to the security and cleanliness of the establishment. But the only facility for washing themselves was a trough in the yard and they do not appear to have been provided with any towels, combs or brushes.[45]

Charlotte was released from the factory at the end of March 1829. Her assignment is unknown but on 31st July she was back in gaol on a charge of being absent without leave, sentenced to 3 months 3rd Class in the Factory and sent to Parramatta on the 4th of August.[46] She was by this time well acquainted with the establishment and may have found it a refuge from the trials, tribulations and uncertainty of life outside particularly if she still had been assigned to Margaret Delaney.

Sometime after she had served her third sentence in the factory, Charlotte was assigned to James Norris, Storekeeper at the His Majesty's Dockyard. Norris had arrived in Sydney with his wife Elizabeth on the ship *Minstrel* on 11 January 1822[47] and taken up residence at No. 26 Pitt Street.[48]

The *Minstrel* had departed London the end of July 1821[49] under the command of Captain William Barns with a cargo of valuable merchandise and passengers Mr and Mrs Hawkins and family, two daughters of Edward Foord Bromley, Naval Officer of the settlement, Mr and Mrs Duncombe and Family, Mr J. Webber, Mr George Cobb, Mr and Mrs Bailey, Mrs Mary Lilly, Mr and Mrs Metcalf and family, Mr and Mrs Norris, Mr Waddingham, Mr Salmon, Mr Paul and Mr Clift.[50] It reached Hobart on the 17th of December where the Bromley daughters, and several other passengers, were landed. The ship continued on to Sydney departing

James Thomas Morisset (1780 – 1852). Morisset arrived in Sydney in the *Harmony* in September 1827 with his wife and child and was appointed acting superintendent of police. *Image courtesy of Ron and Margaret Thompson, Albany Creek, Queensland.*

A ring dollar or holey dollar, with a value of 5 shillings, produced from a Spanish dollar in 1813 to combat the scarcity of coinage. The central plug removed from the Spanish dollar, known as the dump, was stamped with a value of 15 pence. Collections of *State Library of New South Wales, a128577 R277a (ob).*

A rosy view of the Female factory across the Parramatta River in 1826. *Augustus Earle, watercolour, National Library of Australia.nla.pic-an2818460-v.*

Ann Gordon, Matron of the Parramatta Female Factory, October 1827 to 1836. *Photograph courtesy of the Cumberlamd Hospital Museum, Parramatta.*

Original entrance to the Parramatta Female Factory. *Photograph reproduced courtesy of The Society of Australian Genealogists.*

Sleeping quarters for the 3rd Class inmates at the Female Factory. The ground floor is the original building. One of the few original structures on the site, it is of great historical and heritage value.

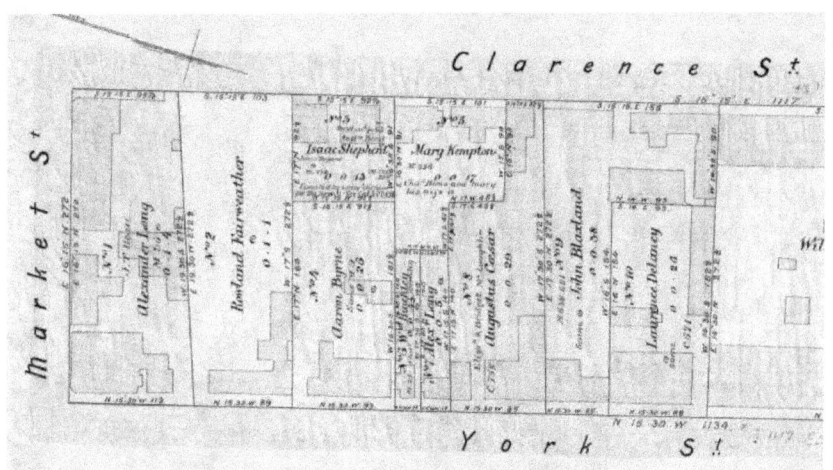

Lawrence Delaney's premises on York Street, coloured red, lower central right on the plan. *City of Sydney Archives - Historical Atlas of Sydney, City Section Survey Plans, 1833: Section 27.*

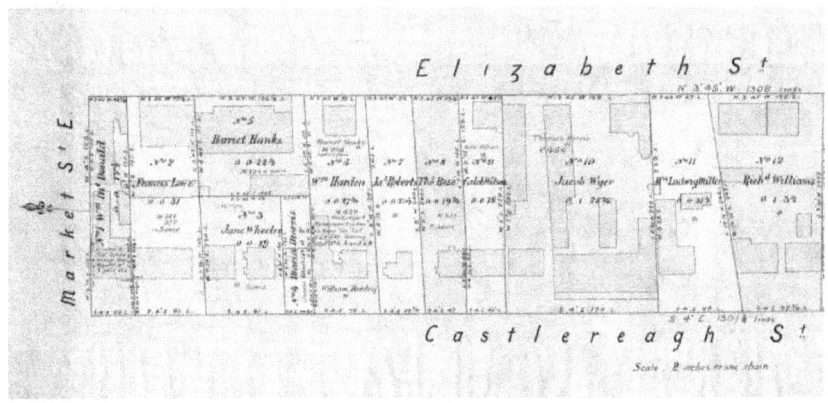

Jacob Wyer's ropeworks between Elizabeth and Castlereagh Streets (coloured blue in the central right of the plan). Wyer also occupied premises on Elizabeth Street between Bathurst and Liverpool Streets and on Bathurst Street between George and Pitt Streets. *City of Sydney Archives - Historical Atlas of Sydney, City Section Survey Plans, 1833: Section 33.*

Morpeth in the mid 1830s. *Watercolour attributed to E.C. Close. National Library of Australia, nla.pic-an4563834-s17.*

Sir George Gipps (1791 – 1847), *Oil painting by Henry William Pickersgill, State Library of New South Wales. GPO 1 - 03763.*
Appointed governor of New South Wales on 5 October 1837, he arrived in Sydney with his wife and son on 24 February 1838. His eight years as governor were very significant and demanded all his administrative skill. The issue of abolition of convict transportation confronted Gipps from the moment he landed in Sydney.

Prisoners' Barracks, Hyde Park. *Drawing by Robert Russell, 1836, hand coloured lithograph. National Library of Australia, nla.pic-an5924561.*

Hobart-Town, Ile Van Diemen. (c.1840). *Lithograph, Auguste Etienne Francois Mayer, National Library of Australia, nla.pic-an20826318-v.*

Group of convicts in a clearing. *Hand coloured engraving, Victor Marie-Felix Danvin. Allport Library and Museum of Fine Arts, Tasmanian Archive and Heritage Office, AUTAS001131820888.*

Location of 'Frogmore' homestead, Penna, Tasmania, marked by a ubiquitous lilac bush.

Frogmore Estate looking towards Pittwater, Tasmania.

New Norfolk Van Diemen's Land (1841). The topography is somewhat exaggerated but the circular road, now in the centre of the village, still exists. *Drawing by L. Le Breton, lithograph by Leon Jean Baptiste Sabatier, National Library of Australia, nla.pic-an20826611.*

The derelict Colonial Hospital, New Norfolk, Tasmania, currently in restoration.

Dr Cornelius Gavin Casey, Superintendent, Colonial Hospital, New Norfolk, 1838 – 1846. A courageous, persistent and responsible man of irascible temperament but kindly, conscientious and humane. He was one of the first in Australia to use surgical anaesthetics. *From R.W. Gowlland, Troubled Asylum Asylum, c. 1981, p.30.*

The new wharf, Hobart Town (c. 1844). *Hand coloured lithograph,. H.G. Eaton, National Library of Australia, nla.pic-an6016168.*

Edward Denny Day, Police Magistrate, Maitland, New South Wales. *Courtesy of the Athel D'Ombrain Collection, University of Newcastle (Australia) image 6320881282 aa8c0c1810.*

Convict built wall, Parramatta Female Factory. Each pecked pattern is specific to the individual male convict who cut the stone block, in effect his signature.

Scotch Creek, Lidney, Miller's Forest, New South Wales.

Lidney, New South Wales.

John Campbell (1798 – 1870). *Photograph courtesy of Graham Campbell, Yamba, New South Wales.*

John Norris Campbell (1839 – 1899), son of John Campbell and Charlotte Dawson. *Photograph courtesy of Fiona Campbell, Sydney, New South Wales.*

Sarah Elizabeth Campbell (1841 - 1903), daughter of John Campbell and Charlotte Dawson. *Photograph courtesy of Graham Campbell, Yamba, New South Wales.*

Hobart on the 1st of January 1822 with Mr and Mrs Norris, Mr and Mrs Hawkins and family, and Captain Smith and servant from Hobart, as passengers.[51]

During the voyage from England, three crewmen, Jacob Evans, Thomas Smith and John Gilmore had used abusive language continually toward Captain Barns and his officers in order to excite mutinous acts.[52] On the morning of making the South West Cape of Van Diemen's Land, Captain Barns had ordered the Chief Officer to have the cables bent. After the usual time allowed for breakfast, the men were summoned to the task. However, none turned out. When the Chief Officer went to the hatchway to determine the reason for their behavior Jacob Evans confronted him and told him he was '*making his pudding*' and if he couldn't have time to do that the officer could be damned for he would not work. The officer insisted that he '*get about his work*' but Evans and Gilmore struck him. Informed of the commotion, the Captain quickly came on deck and confined Evans in irons.

On arrival at the Derwent, Gilmore set a bull terrier on a spaniel dog. The boatswain attempted to separate the dogs, but Gilmore struck him several times threatening to kill him. One of the passengers, Mr Webber, witnessing the assault called the Chief Officer who found Gilmore repeatedly striking the Boatswain with a handspike exclaiming that he would murder the '*old bugger*'.

Thomas Smith had been a constant source of irritation during the voyage, regularly using insulting language to the officers and trying to incite the rest of the ship's company to do the same. It appears he was trying to force the officers to retaliate and strike the men, thereby provoking the men to mutiny.

Barns took Smith and Gilmore before the Police Magistrate in Hobartown, who ruled that given the evidence a sufficient punishment could not be inflicted on them in Van Diemen's Land. He committed the men to New South Wales for trial. The men were sent on board the ship the evening before it sailed for Sydney, the magistrate promising that the necessary papers would be forwarded upon Barns' arrival up there.

The day before they left the Derwent, the crew were ordered to clear the ship and unmoor. The Third Mate went forward to discharge the order, but was struck by one of the crew so violently that he almost lost one of his eyes. Other officers, called to their mate's assistance, ordered the crewman down below. Thomas Smith then became abusive and swore '*he would not get the bloody ship under weigh*'. The Second Mate went ashore and brought the captain back on board where he found the ship in a complete state of mutiny. Considering Smith to be the ringleader, Barns confined him in irons and the ship made for Sydney.

Captain Barns was frustrated in his attempt to have the men punished in New South Wales. In a letter to the Governor, Sir Thomas Brisbane, he stated his case but concluded that since he could '*do nothing with them at this place*', he hoped his Excellency would permit him to '*retain them in jail*' until he left and furthermore allow him to leave Evans and Smith behind considering the dangerous nature of his onward voyage.[53]

Barns was granted permission to do as he had requested, provided the men's gaol expenses were defrayed. Costs for Evans including gaol fees at the Derwent and Sydney, amounted to £14 14s 6d. His wages from 30 July 1821 to 11 February 1822 (6 months and 13 days) at £2 per month amounted to £12 15s 0d leaving the ship to pay a balance of £1 19s 6d. Although Smith had not been detained at the Derwent he had more gaol expenses resulting from cash advances amounting to £4 5s 0d, two issues of tobacco, a clothing issue comprising 1 blue jacket, 1 pair of trousers, 1 pair of shoes, and Greenwich dues of 6s. Total gaol costs amounted to £15 0s 0d His wages were the same as they were for Evans, the ship paying the balance of £2 5s 0d. [54] Gaol expenses and the men's wages paid, Barns and the *Minstrel* departed Sydney on the 15th of February leaving Evans and Smith behind.

On 25th July 1822, James Norris petitioned the Governor for the position of Boatswain at the Naval Dockyards, a position which was currently vacant.[55] He felt well qualified having served for over 20 years in the Navy. Beginning his service in January 1796 on the *Penguin* as a boy, he advanced to ordinary seaman while on that ship and was transferred as an able seaman to the *Royal Sovereign* in May 1803. He served on the *Royal Sovereign* until January 1806 when he was transferred to the *Hibernia* as an able seaman and remained in that position until March 1812. More pertinent to his application was the fact that his final four years in the navy were served on board the *Berwick* as able seaman and purser steward until October 1816.[56]

In his petition, James went on to say that as a consequence of his naval service he had no other trade and desired to continue in His Majesty's Service having expended nearly all his money in order to defray the expenses[57] of his voyage to the Colony. He felt he was fully competent to discharge the duty of Boatswain of the Dockyard.

On 26th August 1822, Colonial Secretary, Frederick Goulburn wrote to James informing him that the Governor, Sir Thomas Brisbane, had directed that he offer him the newly created position of Storekeeper at His Majesty's Dockyard. His salary would be 7s 6d per day. Except for fuel, he would receive no other perquisites and would have to provide his own accommodation and provisions for himself and his family. Neither would he be entitled to a 'Government Man'.[58]

Norris replied the next day. Accepting the position he expressed his gratitude to the Governor, vowing to pay strict attention to his duty and to faithfully discharge his commission in such a way as to show he was worthy of the confidence placed in him.[59] The appointment was gazetted on the 29th of August but back dated to 22nd July on account of the dismissal of Mr. Milton[60] the former Boatswain.

As a landholder[61] and government employee in an important position, Norris became a well respected individual in the community. By the time Charlotte came into their service, James was 46 years old and Elizabeth was 33. They had no children.[62] In her occupation as a servant Charlotte's duties mainly consisted of housekeeping chores, cleaning, cooking, laundry and sewing. This was a good position. The work although constant and laborious was not overtaxing. She had some time to herself and both James and Elizabeth treated her with kindness and respect. It was a welcome change from the regimented labour in the factory and the cantankerous nature of Margaret Delaney. As a result Charlotte disappears from the records for a period of time.

Unfortunately the position did not last. On 20th September 1830 James Norris gave his consent to an application for her transfer to the service of Jacob Wyer.⁶³ Four days later Frederick Hely, on behalf of the office of Superintendent of Convicts, allowed the transfer on the condition that Wyer's wife was free.⁶⁴

Just why Charlotte was transferred is unknown. There is no record that she committed an offence during the intervening period since her last release from the factory in November 1829. Perhaps Norris had started to feel the pinch of poorer economic circumstances. Reductions in staff at the Dockyard were occurring frequently and Norris finally lost his job as Storekeeper in 1831.⁶⁵

With the intention of establishing himself as a farmer, James sought a land grant in November of 1831. But mistakenly he sent his request directly to the Secretary of State for War and the Colonies in London, Viscount Goderich, rather than through Governor Bourke in New South Wales. This error in protocol resulted in a refusal to consider the request. Furthermore Goderich stated in his letter of refusal, dated 19th June 1832, that he had no way of knowing the merits Norris proclaimed in his memorial without a previous report from Bourke. Therefore he did not feel at liberty to grant Norris any land except by purchase at the going rate.⁶⁶

Charlotte's new employer, Jacob Wyer, was a ropemaker from Wiltshire. Jacob and his brother Joseph had been convicted of felony at the Surrey Assizes on 11th August 1814 and sentenced to 7 years transportation.⁶⁷ Departing England on the Ship *Baring* in April 1815, they arrived in Sydney on the 7th of September. Jacob was 38 years old. He was tall (5 feet 11 ½ inches), of fair, pale complexion and had dark brown hair and grey eyes.⁶⁸

On arrival Jacob was put into government labour in the city, his ropemaking skills obviously an advantage.⁶⁹ He remained in this position until 1818 when he was assigned as a servant to William Singleton in the city⁷⁰ but was back in government service in 1820⁷¹ where he remained until 1822. He had then served his seven years and was due to receive his certificate of freedom. But in May 1822 he appeared before the Judge Advocate at the Criminal Court in Sydney charged with '*burglariously breaking and entering the dwelling house of Richard Archibald*'. Although the jury returned a verdict of not guilty he was sentenced to 4 years at the Port Macquarie penal settlement 'for receiving goods stolen by persons unknown'. Mary Black, accused of receiving stolen goods, presumably from Wyer, was also judged not guilty. But on a second charge of knowingly receiving goods from persons unknown, she was convicted and sentenced to 4 years also at Port Macquarie and transported with Wyer on the *Lady Nelson*[72].

By 1825 Mary was Jacob's wife, defacto if not dejure, and they had one son George, two years old.[73] At the age of twenty, Mary had been convicted of wilful and corrupt perjury at the Gaol Sessions, Old Bailey, London on the 28th of October 1812.[74] She arrived in Sydney on the *Wanstead* on 9 January 1814 to serve out a sentence of 7 years.[75] Five days after arrival she and all the other women of the *Wanstead* were sent to the Female Factory at Parramatta.[76]

From the Factory Mary was initially indentured as a servant to Mr H McArthur, Esquire[77] and remained with him until 1819 when she obtained a ticket of leave and recorded as '*wife to T. Moore*' in 1820.[78] Strangely she was noted as the wife of George Tubb in 1821, whose wife in 1820 was Mary Bourke. Bourke's name appears one above Mary Black in the list of convicts for 1820, so there is most likely an error in one or both of the 1820 and 1821 lists. Since no marriage record has been found it is difficult to say exactly what her status was at this time.

The Wyer family remained at Port Macquarie until at least May 1826 when their four year sentences ended. By November 1828, they were living in Market Street, Sydney. Joseph, Jacob's brother was living with them and George, Mary's son was 8 years old.[79] Jacob and Joseph established a ropemaking business and by 1830 Jacob was also the licensee of the Rope Maker's Arms at the corner of Market Street and York Street selling wines, malt and spirituous liquors to thirsty customers.[80]

The rope making business flourished and by July 1831 Jacob was advertising for 20 to 30 rope makers and 20 good flax dressers offering constant employment and liberal wages.[81] When he died on 25 November 1835, his death notice read: '--- in Castlereagh Street, Mr Jacob Wyer, for many years the principal ropemaker, of Sydney'.[82]

Charlotte possibly worked as a servant in the public house (not the best venue for her employment considering her past record) and assisted Mary Wyer with household chores. However, after only two months she was transferred from Jacob Wyer to William Wynne.[83] She had either proved unsuitable or had been required only briefly. The definitive two month period hopefully suggests the latter of the two possibilities.

William Wynne had arrived in Sydney on the 6th of March 1814 as a convict under a seven year sentence. He had been convicted in Dundalk, County Louth, Ireland in July 1812 and transported on the *Three Bees* in 1813. Twenty eight years old, he stood 5 feet 5 ¾ inches tall, had a pale, sallow complexion, black hair and hazel eyes.[84]

Initially assigned as a servant to William Wilson, he was freed by servitude in 1819 and worked as a labourer in Sydney for several years.[85] A charge of assault found him committed to court by D'Arcy Wentworth on the 22nd of October 1822, placed on a surety, and discharged to the police office the next day.[86] His labouring jobs most likely involved some form of woodworking. Records for 1825 show that he was employed as a mill right and similarly in the census of 1828 as a carpenter residing in York Street with his wife Ellen Hickey.

Wynne had married Ellen Hickey in May of 1828.[87] She was a convict who had arrived on the ship *Brothers*, 4 February 1827. Although they were Roman Catholics, William and Ellen were married by Reverend Richard Hill in Sydney who, in his capacity as a Church of England clergyman, seems to have catered to all denominations without discrimination.

Hill had been ordained in London in 1813 at the age of 31. After serving several curacies, he was appointed to a chaplaincy in New South Wales on 1 January 1818. He arrived in Sydney with his wife Phoebe Sapphira in the male convict transport ship *Hibernia* on 18 June 1819 and was initially appointed as assistant to Reverend William Cowper at St Philip's, the only church in Sydney at that time. In 1821 he was given charge of the new district of St James, and when the new church was consecrated in February 1824 Hill became its regular minister.[88]

Ellen Hickey was from Killarney, Ireland and had been convicted on 6th August 1826 at Cork for stealing money. She was 30 years old, a diminutive 5 feet ½ inches tall, of ruddy complexion with blonde hair and hazel eyes and had an angular scar on the outside of her right arm. A widow with no family she had two previous convictions against her. There was no chance of escaping a seven year term of transportation.[89]

On arrival in Sydney Ellen had immediately been sent to the Female Factory. There is no record of her assignment and she may have remained in the factory until she was married. William probably wished he had left her there. On 16th September 1828 she was charged with drunkenness and sent to the 3rd Class in the factory for one month.[90] A little more than three months after her release she was in trouble again and sentenced on 21st of January 1829 to 3 months in the third class for *'exposing her person ---'*. She was sent to Parramatta the next day.[91] After these expressions of individuality, Ellen disappears from the records. She had either reformed after the last escapade or had died.

Whatever the case might have been with Ellen, in September 1830 Charlotte came into Wynne's employ, her duties principally concerned with household chores. At some time during her various assigned positions, most likely during her assignment to William Wynne, she met John Campbell, a carpenter, who may have known Wynne through the carpentry trade. Charlotte's service to Wynne ended on 27th June 1831 when there was no further use for her service and she was returned to 1st class in the Factory for re-assignment.[92]

Notes to Chapter 12

1. HRA Series 1 Vol.14 p.186.
2. SRNSW: NRS 2514, Sydney Gaol Entrance Books, [4/6429] Reel 850; [4/6430] Reel 851.
3. Ibid.
4. Ibid., October 17, 1827.
5. Ibid., October 22, 1827.
6. Ibid., October 23, 1827.

7   Ibid., October 24, 1827.
8   Ibid.
9   Ibid., October 27, 1827.
10 Ibid., November 14, 1827.
11 Ibid., November 19, 1827.
12 Ibid., November 22, 1827.
13 Ibid., November 29, 1827.
14 Ibid., December 4, 1827.
15 Ibid., December 10, 1827.
16 Ibid., December 26, 1827.
17 Ibid., October 30, 1827.
18 The Australian, Wednesday, October 31, 1827, p.3, col.3.
19 Thomas Bigge, *Report of the Commissioner of Inquiry into the state of the Colony of New South Wales,* House of Commons, 1822, p.73.
20 Carol Liston, *Convict Women in the Female Factories of New South Wales,* in Women Transported, Life in Australia's Convict Female Factories, p35; Bigge op.cit., p.72.
21 HRA Series 1 Vol.14, p.185.
22 Ibid., p.186.
23 SRNSW: NRS 2514, Sydney Gaol Entrance Books, [4/6430] Reel 851, December 6 and 31, 1827. Mary Edwards was also charged on 31 December with being 'out after hours" and sentenced to 3rd Class 6 months and may have gone to the female factory on or before 7 January 1828.
24 Annette Salt, *These Outcast Women – The Parramatta Female Factory 1821 – 1848,* , Hale & Ironmonger 1984, p.44.
25 HRA Series 1 Vol. 10, pp.689-690; HRA Series 1 Vol. 14, p.185 HRA Series 1 Vol. 15, p.272-273; Salt, op.cit., p.9.
26 SRNSW: NRS 905, Colonial Secretary's Correspondence 1826 – 1831, Letter 28/262 [4/1962]. The affidavit has been transcribed lacking punctuation as written.
27 Ibid.
28 SG&NSWA, Wednesday, January 23, 1828, p.2, col.6.
29 SRNSW: NRS2514, Sydney Gaol Entrance Books, [4/6430] Reel 851, September 20, 1828.
30 SRNSW: NRS 906, Colonial Secretary, Special Bundles, Police reports of persons tried and summonses issued, Sydney, Jul - Sep 1828, [X821 p.95], Reel 660.
31 Ibid.; SRNSW, NRS 2514, [4/6430], op.cit.
32 Carol Liston, *Convict Women in the Female Factories of New South Wales,* in Women Transported, Life in Australia's Convict Female Factories, p37-38.
33 HRA Series I Vol.14, p.184.
34 SRNSW: NRS906, Colonial Secretary's Correspondence - Special Bundles, 1826-1832, Female Factory, Parramatta: Returns of Punishments, 1 Jul 1827 - 30 Jun 1828 [2/8211], Reel 2278.

35 Gay Hendrikson, *Myth and Reality*, in Women Transported, Life in Australia's Convict Female Factories, p12, 15-16.
36 Salt, op.cit., p.44.
37 Governor Ralph Darling, Rules and Regulations of the Female Factory Parramatta, Governor's Minutes, Minute 130, SAO Ref 4/990.
38 Salt, op.cit., pp.72-78.
39 Ibid., pp.72-76; 92-93.
40 Darling, op.cit.
41 Hendrikson, op.cit., p.9 and 24; Salt, op.cit., pp.104-107.
42 Rules and Regulations for the management of Female Convicts in the new factory at Parramatta 1821, State Library of new South Wales [MLN365/N] p.4.
43 Salt, op.cit., pp.76-78.
44 Darling, op.cit.
45 Salt, op.cit., p.77.
46 SRNSW: NRS 2514, Sydney Gaol Entrance Books, [4/6431], Reel 851.
47 J.S. Cumpston, Shipping Arrivals and Departures, Sydney 1788-1825, Roebuck, Canberra, 1977, p.130.
48 SRNSW: NRS 897 Colonial Secretary, Main series of letters received, 1788-1826 [4/1756, p.139] Reel 6053.
49 The Morning Post (London), Thursday , August 2, 1821, p.4, col.2, Ship News.
50 Hobart Town Gazette &Van Diemen's Land Advertiser, Saturday, 22 December 1821, p.2, col.1.
51 I.H. Nicholson, *Shipping Arrivals & Departures, Tasmania, 1803 – 1833*, Roebuck 1983, p.76.
52 SRNSW: NRS 897, Colonial Secretary, Main series of letters received, 1788-1826, [4/1759], pp.95, 137-139, Reel 6054.
53 Ibid.
54 Ibid.
55 SRNSW: NRS 897 Colonial Secretary, Main series of letters received, 1788-1826 [4/1756, p.139] Reel 6053.
56 Ibid.
57 Crewman's Exeter Flying Post of Thursday, June 7, 1821 (p.1 col.4) advertised passage on the *Minstrel* 'at or less than 30 Guineas in the Cabin and 20 Guineas in the Steerage per Head". Therefore it can be estimated that the voyage cost Norris at least £42 and possibly more than £63 for his and his wife's passage. This was an enormous sum considering the wages he would have received in the Navy.
58 SRNSW: NRS 937, Colonial Secretary, Copies of letters sent within the Colony, 1814-1825, [4/3506, pp.207-8], Reel 6009.
59 SRNSW: NRS 897 Colonial Secretary, Main series of letters received, 1788-1826 [4/1756, p.144], Reel 6053.
60 SG&NSWA, Friday, August 30, 1822, p.1, col.2.
61 HO 10/20, New South Wales, General muster 1825, p.80.

62　Malcolm R. Sainty & Keith A. Johnson (eds.), *Census of New South Wales, November 1828*, Sydney : Library of Australian History, 1980, p.287.
63　SRNSW: NRS 905, Colonial Secretary's Correspondence, 1826-1831, Letter 30/7129, [4/2082].
64　SRNSW: NRS 962, Colonial Secretary's Correspondence, Letters sent re. convicts, 6 October 1826 to 27 November 1832, No. 30/781 [4/3667 p.314] Reel 1043.
65　HRA Series I Vol. 16, p.670.
66　Ibid.
67　SRNSW: NRS 12188, Bound manuscript indents, 1788-1842, [4/4005], Microfiche 635.
68　Ibid.
69　HO10/3 AJCP Reel PRO60, p.283.
70　HO10/10 AJCP reel PRO63, p.355.
71　HO10/13 AJCP Reel PRO64, p.254.
72　SRNSW: NRS 2514 Sydney Gaol Entrance Books, [4/6360], Reel 850; NRS 898 Colonial Secretary's Papers, 1788-1825, Special bundles, 1794-1825, "Baring", [X820 p.49].
73　HO 10/20 AJCP Reel PRO 66, New South Wales, General muster1825, p.285.
74　Old Bailey Proceedings Online, October 1812, trial of MARY BLACK (t18121028-129), www.oldbaileyonline.org, version 7.0, accessed 25 February 2013.
75　HO 11/2 AJCP Reel PRO 87, p.55 (107), Convict Transportation Registers; SRNSW NRS 12188, Bound manuscript indents, 1788-1842, [4/4004], Microfiche 634.
76　SRNSW: NRS 937, Colonial Secretary's Papers, 1788-1825 Copies of letters sent within the Colony, 1814-1825, [4/3493] Reel 6004, p.12.
77　HO10/2 AJCP Reel PRO 60, p.16 ; HO10/9 AJCP Reel PRO 62, p.12; HO10/11 AJCP Reel PRO 63, p.13.
78　HO10/14 AJCP Reel 64, p.11.
79　HO10/27 AJCP Reel PRO 69 p.127; Sainty & Johnson, op.cit., p.393.
80　SRNSW: NRS 14401, Butts of publicans' licences, 1830-1849, [4/61] Reel 5049, Licence No.91.
81　SG&NSWA Tuesday, July 26, 1831 p.3, col.5.
82　The Sydney Herald, Thursday November 26, 1835 p.3, col.1.
83　SRNSW: NRS 962, Colonial Secretary's Copies of letters sent re convict No. 30/978 [4/3667 p.512] Reel 1043.
84　SRNSW: NRS 12188, Bound manuscript indents 1788-1842, [4/4004] Microfiche 634; HO 10/27 AJCP reel PRO 69, Census 1828, p.128.
85　HO 10/1/2 AJCP reel PRO 60 p.202 ; HO10/3 AJCP reel PRO 60, 1816 p.279; HO 10/10 AJCP Reel PRO 63, 1818 p.352; HO 10/13 AJCP reel PRO 64, 1820 p.251; HO 10/16 AJCP reel PRO 65, 1822 p.190.
86　SRNSW: NRS 2514, Sydney gaol Entrance Books, [4/6360] Reel 850; [4/6428], Reel 850.

87 SRNSW: NRS 12212, Applications to Marry, No.511, [4/4508] Fiche 780.
88 K. J. Cable, *Hill, Richard (1782–1836)*, ADB, MUP 1966, Vol.1, p.537.
89 SRNSW NRS 12188, Principal Superintendent of Convicts, Bound manuscript indents [4/4012, p.19], Fiche 663.
90 SRNSW: NRS 2514 Sydney Gaol Entrance Books, [4/6430], Reel 851.
91 Ibid., [4/6431], Reel 851.
92 Ibid., [4/6432], Reel 851.

Chapter 13

Marriage

After what seems to have been only a brief spell at the factory, Charlotte's next assignment was with Mrs Raymond. The Raymonds had recently lost a female servant who had been found in a disorderly house in Castlereagh Street between four and five o'clock in the morning on 20th of June 1831. She had been brought before the magistrate and, acknowledging that the fault was entirely her own, she was sentenced to six weeks' factory discipline. On receiving her sentence she replied to the bench that she would be free in a month. The magistrate replied that it was no concern of his and she should inform them at the Factory.[1]

James Raymond was the postmaster for the Colony. He had been a landowner and magistrate in County Limerick, Ireland, but became involved in disturbances there and was forced to abandon his property when his life was threatened. He decided to emigrate, and with his wife Aphrasia and nine children, arrived in Sydney on the ship *Thames* in April 1826. Initially appointed to the position of coroner in Parramatta, he became searcher and surveyor of customs in 1827. In April 1829 he was appointed postmaster becoming postmaster-General in 1835, a position he held until his death in 1851.[2]

With a large family and an important position in the community, Raymond required the services of several servants. Charlotte was fully occupied with housework and care of the younger children in the household. She was in her late twenties and her relationship with John Campbell had strengthened to the point where they sought permission to marry.

Mrs Raymond gave her consent to the marriage and the Reverend Richard Hill registered their application for publication of Banns at St James Church, Sydney on 21st September 1831. Charlotte's three misdemeanours and respective sojourns in 3rd Class

Factory were noted on the application, although in addition to absence from service, '*drunkenness*' replaced the lovers' tryst as the other reason for her return to the Factory in September 1828[3]. The notification was merely a formality presenting no impediment and permission to marry was granted on the 30th of September.[4]

On 7th October 1831, John Campbell, a bachelor and carpenter, and Charlotte Dawson, a spinster, were married in St James Church with the consent of the Governor. The marriage was solemnized before Reverend Richard Hill in the presence of William and Lydia Gooden of Goulburn Street. The married couple signed the register, Charlotte making her mark with an X.[5]

William and Lydia Gooden were friends of the newly married couple. William had arrived as a convict on the *Shipley* in March 1822 and Lydia had come as a free immigrant to join her husband arriving in Sydney on the *Medway*, 5th December 1829.[6] After she arrived William applied for a Ticket of 'Exemption from Government Labor' which was granted on 30 March 1830.[7] The Ticket allowed him to reside with his wife in Sydney rather than in the Hyde Park Barracks. He received the same exemption again in January 1831.[8]

A woollen draper by profession from Lancashire,[9] William had been convicted of embezzlement at the Middlesex Gaol Delivery June Sessions, Old Bailey in 1821 and sentenced to 14 years' transportation.[10] In Sydney he served as a clerk to Robert Campbell, Junior a wealthy merchant and pastoralist,[11] but was convicted of embezzlement again in January 1824 and sent on the colonial cutter *Sally* to Port Macquarie penal settlement for 3 years.[12] During his three year sentence he also spent some time at Moreton Bay returning to Sydney from there in January 1827.[13] By November 1828 he was once again a clerk for Robert Campbell, Junior.[14]

William appears next as a clerk for Jacob Wyer in his ropemaking business until July 1832 when, without a reason being given, he was discharged from Wyer's service.[15] He was considered to be a valuable employee when sober but had a fondness for drink, which may have been the reason for his dismissal. Or perhaps once again he had been found with his hand in the till.

Charlotte knew William from the time she spent with Wyer in 1830 and most likely met Lydia at that time as well. Sometime after his discharge in 1832, and possibly after Jacob's death in 1835, William was re-employed by Mrs Mary Wyer as a clerk and superintendant at the ropeworks. He received a Ticket of Leave on 10th September 1833,[16] which allowed him to live freely with his wife without the requirement of a Ticket of 'Exemption from Government Labor', and on 13 November 1835, having served his fourteen year sentence, he was granted a Certificate of Freedom.[17]

Unfortunately he met an untimely death at the age of 45 while working for Mrs Wyer. On Monday 8 January 1838 he was taking a load of flax in a one horse dray from the Wyer ropemaking establishment on Castlereagh Street to Wyer's business premises in Surry Hills when the horse bolted in a rutted section of the road between the Roman Catholic burial ground and Smith's farm. Gooden was thrown from the dray. Attempting to stop the horse, the shaft of the dray struck him in the chest. He was knocked down and a wheel of the dray passed over his left foot and leg lacerating them severely. Brought to the medical hall on Brickfield Hill in Sydney, his injuries were operated on, but he died early on Wednesday morning.[18] He was buried the next day.

At the inquest the jury returned a verdict of accidental death with a deodand[19] of one shilling on the wheel that had passed over Gooden. The horse, considered to be a perfectly safe animal when driven with care, escaped any responsibility for the death.[20]

The newly titled Mr and Mrs Campbell remained in Sydney, John continuing to work as a carpenter and Charlotte as a laundress. Charlotte was now free from the revolving door spinning her in an out of service and the Female Factory. Her life became more secure in her attachment to a husband and she disappeared from the court records suggesting that her life had also become more stable and comfortable. By mid 1833 she had an assigned servant, Elizabeth Watson, to assist her with her work as a laundress.

Elizabeth had arrived from England in November 1829 on the *Lucy Davidson* to serve a sentence of seven years for receiving stolen goods. Initially she was indentured to Mr. William Small at 2 Kent Street[21] but as with most female convict assignees she was in and out of service and the Female Factory several times finally ending up with Mrs Campbell's about August 1833. This was indeed her final assignment as she drowned herself on the 14 October 1834.

Mr Hutton, a labourer employed by Robert Campbell Junior of Bligh Street, found her body close to the water's edge, near Mrs. Bigges' bathing house in the Government Domain. Hutton who resided at the bathing-house, was at home having his dinner when his son, a boy of about twelve years of age, informed him that he had seen something in the water which resembled a human body. Armed with a pole Hutton went into the water, retrieved the body, and informed the proper authorities. With the assistance of the constabulary, the body was taken from the shore and placed under a rock ledge. Surgeon Band examined the body, but discerning no marks of external violence, he was of the opinion that suffocation from drowning had caused her death.

The following morning an inquest was held at Mr. Joseph Jennings' public house,[22] the Bricklayer's Arms, in Market Street. The deceased proved to be a female about 32 years of age. She was not wearing a bonnet and did not appear to have been in the water for any length of time when her body was recovered. Hutton testified that he did not recognise her but stated that his wife had seen a woman without a bonnet walking in the neighbourhood.

A sodden, barely legible note found in her pocket contained the following words which apparently she had written: 'Oh, George! and can you say what you did of me? and did I ever give you any reason for it in a foreign land? but never mind now, and I'll put you to your oath as a dying woman, if I have not been a wife, and a mother, and a father to you, why should you say what you did of me?'

Mrs. Campbell, residing in Elizabeth Street, said she had been to view the body of the deceased, which she identified as that of Elizabeth Watson, her assigned servant. Elizabeth had been with her for the previous fifteen months. She was a good worker but attached to the bottle. Before coming to her service, Elizabeth had been living for some years with a prisoner of the crown, named George Turner who was assigned to a Mr. Wilson, a gentleman residing about 20 miles out of Sydney. She desired to join him and although Mrs Campbell (being a laundress) could not spare her services, she had consented to let her go. To facilitate the transfer Mrs Campbell had waited upon Mrs. Wilson, at Mrs. Dixon's place, in Park Street. Unfortunately Mrs. Wilson informed her that she had received a note from Turner stating that Elizabeth was so unsteady that he did not wish to have anything further to do with her. He had requested that she not be transferred to the Wilson family.

Mrs. Campbell returned, home between 1 and 2 o'clock in the afternoon that day, and informed Elizabeth what Mrs. Wilson had said. Elizabeth, visibly distraught, replied in words similar to those contained in the note found in her pocket. Shortly afterwards she went out of the house, saying she would be off and Mrs Campbell had not seen her again until viewing the body near Mrs. Bigges' bathing house.

The Coroner summed up the evidence in a 'perspicuous manner'. He suggested that Mrs Campbell, whose husband was a carpenter, should see that the deceased was decently interred, to which she readily agreed, stating that she regretted the fate of her servant 'who was a most attentive workwoman, except when she had a glass in her head, which she would always take when she could get it.' The Jury returned a verdict that the deceased had drowned herself while under temporary mental derangement.[23] Elizabeth was buried the next day in the parish of St Phillips. Reverend William Cowper performed the ceremony.[24]

Notes to Chapter 13

1. SG&NSWA, Thursday 23 June 1831, p2., col.6.
2. Vivienne Parsons, *Raymond, James (1786–1851)*, ADB, MUP 1927, Vol.2, p.365.
3. SRNSW: NRS 905 Colonial Secretary's Correspondence, [4/2126.7], Reel 719.
4. SRNSW: NRS 12212, [4/4512], p.23, No.273; NRS 12212,[4/4508], No.273.
5. SRNSW: NRS 12937 Reel 5003, Vol.15, Entry No. 1085, Saint James, Cumberland 1831: p. 81, Sheet 135, Entry No. 322.
6. SRNSW: Colonial Secretary: Reports of Vessels Arrived, Reel 1263 Vessels Arrived 1829.

7 SRNSW: NRS 12196 and 12197, Registers and Butts of tickets of exemption from Government Labour 1827-32, No.30/115, [4/4284, 4/4061], Fiche 1004, 1006.
8 SRNSW: NRS 12196 and 12197, Registers and Butts of tickets of exemption from Government Labour 1827-32,No. 31/66, [4/4284, 4/4062], Fiche 1004, 1006.
9 SRNSW: NRS 12188; Title: Bound manuscript indents, 1788-1842; Item: [4/4008]; Microfiche: 647, p.88.
10 HO 26/27AJCP reel PRO2738, p. 68.
11 HO 10/36 AJCP reel PRO72, p.124.
12 SRNSW: NRS 939, Colonial Secretary's Papers, [4/3864], Reel 6019, p.103.
13 Ibid., pp. 460-461; QSA Item ID1700775, Register - prisoners (SRS5653/1/1) Chronological register of convicts at Moreton Bay1824-183 , p.3.
14 Malcolm R. Sainty & Keith A. Johnson (eds.), *Census of New South Wales, November 1828*, Sydney : Library of Australian History, 1980, p.165.
15 SG&NSWA, Thursday July 19,1832 p.4, col.1.
16 SRNSW: NRS 12202 Principal Superintendent of Convicts, Ticket of leave butts, 1 May 1833-1 Oct 1833, No. 33/596 [4/4089], Reel 919.
17 SRNSW: NRS 12210, Certificate of Freedom, No.35/1218, [4/4331], Reel 996.
18 SG&NSWA, Saturday, January 13, 1838, p.2, col.7; The Sydney Monitor Friday 12 January 1838. P.2, col.3.
19 deodand – a thing forfeited or a payment to the crown to be used as alms having caused a human death.
20 SG&NSWA, Saturday, January 13, 1838, p.2, col.7.
21 SRNSW: NRS 12188, [4/4014], Microfiche: 67, pp257 & 262.
22 The Australian, Friday, August 5, 1831 *Licensed Publicans,* p.4, col.3.
23 The Australian, Friday, October 17, 1834, p2, col.4; SG&NSWA, Thursday , October 16, 1834 p.2, col.5; The Sydney Herald, Thursday October 16, 1834, p.3, col.2.
24 Register of Burials in the parish of St Phillips Vol.18, No. 1770, Reel 5004.

Chapter 14

Morpeth

Although the town of Sydney offered John and Charlotte employment they were aware most likely that they had limited opportunities for advancement. Perhaps to relieve themselves of the convict stigma in Sydney or compelled to further improve their situation through a life on the land, John and Charlotte moved to the Green Hills (Morpeth) on the Hunter River, about 100 miles north of Sydney. There John took up farming.

The exact date of their departure from Sydney is unknown but it most likely occurred in 1835. Their names appear in a list of unclaimed letters at the General Post Office published in the Sydney Gazette and New South Wales Advertiser on 28 February 1835. Later documents indicate that they arrived in the Morpeth area about 1835.

Although a system of roads connected Sydney to the Hunter River area and Newcastle, overland travel was slow, hazardous and difficult. The advent of steam powered vessels plying the coast in the 1830s made travel from Sydney to Newcastle easier and the duration of the journey was reduced to about 8 hours.

It was this form of transport that John and Charlotte took to their new home. The journey could be made overnight, the steamer leaving from the wharf below the Rocks in the evening and rounding Nobby's head early the next day to dock shortly thereafter at the Newcastle wharf. Newcastle was becoming a seaport of some importance, the combination of its proximity to reserves of coal and the growth of steam transportation ensuring steady trade and, in consequence, a growing economy. Its life as a penal settlement and timber port was in the past. Farming had replaced the convict establishment in 1823 and timber cutting since the turn of the century had decimated the inland cedar forest along the Hunter River to a large extent.

After a brief stop at Newcastle, giving ongoing passengers just enough time for breakfast or a light meal, the vessel continued its passage up the meandering course of the Hunter River. Abundant birdlife, 'pelicans, curlews, plovers, cormorants, ducks, teal widgeons, sandilords and many others' populated the broad estuarine environment of Fullerton Cove. Further upstream, past the junction with the Williams River, the Hunter narrowed in places to not much more than the width of the steamer, the dense brush along the thickly wooded banks impenetrable and obscuring the surrounding countryside. But further on the river widened into a larger expanse of water framed by wooded hills and valleys, before narrowing again, the sequence of narrowing and widening repeated several times. Here and there along the course of the river's bank were the simple dwellings of the indigenous inhabitants and a few primitive houses of new settlers. The twenty five mile journey to the head of navigation at the Green Hills, and therefore the final destination where cargo and passengers were discharged, took about three and a half hours.[1]

In 1801 an exploration party, led by Lieutenant James Grant and Lieutenant-Colonel William Paterson, had spent four weeks exploring the Hunter valley, reaching a point a little beyond the current location of the city of Maitland.[2] The area around the village of Morpeth, 17 miles by river below Maitland, was originally occupied by an indigenous people who called the place 'Illulaung', meaning the place of the green hills and Paterson accordingly gave the place its English name.

European settlement spread rapidly. As was the case elsewhere in the colony, possession of land under British laws of ownership was paramount. The land was taken in complete ignorance of the cultural law and ownership of the indigenous inhabitants. Many of the new settlers, displaced from their traditional lands in Britain, unwittingly and in most cases uncaringly, displaced the Aboriginal people from their traditional lands. The relentless increase in areas of cleared and cultivated land with their fence lines marking out individual ownership gradually eroded the economic and social structure of aboriginal society. No longer able to freely roam over their land, they became a confused people in their restriction, subject to their own laws and practices but dispossessed of their occupation under strange laws imposed by an alien force. Acts of aggression towards the new settlers, followed by cycles of vicious retaliation, were inevitable.

The land around the Green Hills was granted in 1821 to Edward Close, a lieutenant in the 48th regiment and a veteran of the Peninsular War. The following year, Close settled on his 2560 acre grant, called Illulaung, which adjoined the government reserve for the future township of Morpeth.[3] He subsequently subdivided the land with the first batch of allotments sold in 1834.

Between 1827 and 1830, Green Hills developed as a river port.[4] After the arrival of the first steamship, the schooner rigged paddle steamer *Sophia Jane* in 1831, other steam powered ships, the *Tamar*, the *James Watt*, the *Australian*, the *Maitland*, the *Ceres* and the *King William IV* appeared. A regular if not entirely reliable service developed[5] and the commerciality of the area burgeoned. The Hunter region could now supply grain and other agricultural products more quickly to Sydney than the farms to the west of the Blue Mountains where the arduous trek over the mountains with bullock or horse team restricted transport.

About 1833 the first proper wharf was erected and two licensed inns, the Illulaung Hotel and the Wheatsheaf Hotel, were operating. A distant tortuous 17 miles upstream, along the narrow meandering river, was Maitland, developing as a commercial and administrative centre for the area. Transport to Maitland was restricted to smaller vessels operating along this stretch of river. In 1833, a road built using convict labour was completed between Morpeth and Maitland,[6] shortening the distance to three miles and facilitating a more direct route for conveying goods and passengers.

When John and Charlotte Campbell arrived in the region a small town of about 500 people had been established on the south side of the river. Officially named Morpeth after the town of Morpeth near Newcastle in England, the more regional name of Green Hills was still commonly used. An important commercial and cultural centre, much of the Hunter Valley's agricultural produce passed through its wharves en route to Newcastle and Sydney, while most of the people and goods from those major centres also passed through its wharves on their way further up the valley and to the interior beyond.

John rented a small farm of 100 acres at Phoenix Park, the area the indigenous inhabitants called 'Narragan', across the river from Green Hills. Standish Lawrence Harris, an architect and emigrant from Dublin, Ireland, who was granted the land in 1822 as part of a larger holding known as Goulborn Grove, gave it the name 'Phoenix Park' after the urban park in his home city.

Phoenix Park occupied an oval shaped peninsula of land embraced by the Hunter and Paterson Rivers where they diverged from their junction, to a point upstream where they came to within two hundred yards of each other. Comprising 1,190 acres of level, alluvial land, the peninsula contained the finest quality soil 'ever seen'.[7] The broad, deep banks of the rivers were covered with native shrubs and trees while the flat land formed a grassy plain broken into lots of 30 or 40 acres by clumps of trees or narrow belts of forest.

By the mid 1830s most of the land in the region had been granted or sold to a number of owners who had in turn sold portions of their holdings to others or let blocks of land out to tenant farmers. Tenant farming was not widespread in Australia but where it existed it gave immigrants with little capital the opportunity to commence their own agricultural business in their new homeland. Unlike the old system John Campbell had experienced on the Sutherland Estate in Scotland, tenancy came with a form of title to the land; a rental or lease agreement in his own name. He could not be removed at the whim of the landowner and was effectively master of his own destiny.

Regionally, natural vegetation ranged from thick, impenetrable, luxuriant rainforest on the lowlands along the lower reaches of the river to open grassland and savannah woodland on higher ground. Much of the lowland forest had been cleared and large areas placed under cultivation and fenced. The rich alluvial soils replenished by floods along the river flats, were continuously productive. A relatively even distribution of rainfall throughout the year gave farmers a great variety of choice in selecting produce for their agricultural enterprises, although unpredictable floods and periods of drought could be devastating. Crops of maize, wheat and barley proliferated; beef cattle for meat and hides and dairy cattle for milk, butter and cheese flourished; and potatoes, beans, cabbage, turnips, pumpkin, onions and other vegetables were grown in garden plots all providing both household and saleable produce. Horses also thrived in the good conditions.

John, an experienced farmer, initially tried raising sheep but the lower Hunter region was unsuitable for that activity. However his trade meant that he could supplement his income with carpentry jobs in the region as well as make improvements in the crude slab or bark house and farm buildings that came with the rental property. By 1839 he was a well to do, respected farmer in the community and had two convicts lodged in his house who occasionally worked for him. He had established a good reputation with several prominent citizens and had become re-acquainted with one of Charlotte's former masters and good friend, James Norris. Norris had been appointed to the position of agent for the Tamar Steamboat at Morpeth in March 1837. His instructions were to extend credit to no one except those who had made arrangements for quarterly payments in Sydney and to accept goods for shipment from wharf to wharf only.[8]

In 1839, the new Governor of New South Wales, Sir George Gipps, visited Maitland and Newcastle. The day before his arrival the town was tidied, shops illuminated, windows cleaned, clothes brushed and boots blackened. At 7 pm a meeting of the town's people was held at the Wesleyan Chapel and a deputation appointed to meet the Governor. The next morning the weather was unfavourable with frequent rain showers. Undeterred most of the population made its way to Morpeth for the Governor's arrival. The hotels were kept busy attending to customers.[9] A brand new omnibus was despatched to Morpeth to meet the *Tamar* steamer and convey his Excellency's party to Maitland. But inclement weather had forced the *Tamar* into in Watson's Bay the previous evening[10] and Gipps and his party on board the steamer failed to arrive on schedule. Many people gave up waiting and returned home. It was almost dark when he arrived later that evening, Tuesday 2nd of April, and was warmly greeted with cheers and applause from the assembled crowd, many of whom had returned to Morpeth on hearing the steamer was coming up the river. Escorted to Maitland by the official delegation, Gipps reached Maitland about 7:30 pm and took up residence in the Government cottage for the duration of his visit.[11]

In spite of the crowd's acclamation, Gipps' arrival at Morpeth was not without incident. A self appointed delegation of 'ladies' had been formed to meet the Governor. One of the 'ladies' approached Gipps to shake hands, but instead of receiving the Knight's hand received a blow from the Chief Constable, Mr. Riley, who was accompanying Gipps. The 'ladies', incensed by the incident, began shouting for Paddy Grant, the Police Magistrate and chanted 'Down with the Governor and the Chief Constable'. There was no sympathy from the officials present. Some of the 'ladies' spent the night in the watch-house and the incident gave Gipps a tainted impression of the Morpeth populace.[12]

The reason for Gipps' visit was in part due to a series of petitions received from residents of both East and West Maitland disputing the location of markets and the large amount of funds allocated for improvements in East Maitland compared to West Maitland. The ceremonial events conducted during his visit included the presentation of a memorial from the Residents of West Maitland. In the memorial they outlined their need for increased expenditure on police and funding for improvements to the town including construction of a market house, watch house and district police office.

Gipps gave a verbal reply confirming a licence to hold a market would be granted and improvements made to roads, but he could not respond to their requests for augmentation to the police force as funds were not at his disposal to do so.[13] Subsequently, the Colonial Secretary wrote to the authors of the memorial that the matters would be presented to the Legislative Council, emphasizing that no advantage was intended to be given to one division of the town over the other.[14]

The Governor departed the district on Thursday at midday and after a brief visit to Newcastle was back in Sydney on Saturday evening.[15] Unfortunately, on account of the rain, Gipps had been unable to see the beautiful valley of alluvial soil stretching from East Maitland to Morpeth, but the local farmers found the rain most welcome after the extreme drought of the past year.

Charlotte was now 36 years old. She had given birth to two male children who had died shortly after birth. Perhaps her medical history had played some part in these deaths, but at the time it was not unusual for children to die at birth or shortly thereafter. On 24 June 1839 she gave birth to a son, John, baptised on the 7th of July by Presbyterian minister, the Reverend Robert Blain.[16] Later the boy was given the middle name 'Norris', the family name of their good friends James and Elizabeth.

Notes to Chapter 14

1. SG&NSWA, Saturday, November 19, 1831, p.2, cols 3-5; The Australian, Tuesday, October 4, 1831, p.3, col.1.
2. Arthur McMartin, *Grant, James (1772–1833)*, ADB, MUP 1966, Vol.1, pp.468-469.
3. Nancy Gray, *Close, Edward Charles (1790–1866)*, ADB MUP 1966, Vol.1, pp.231-232.
4. *The Morpeth Story*, Morpeth progress Association, 1971.
5. John Bach, *A Maritime History of Australia*, Nelson, Melbourne 1976, p 88.
6. The Morpeth Story, op.cit.
7. John Dunmore Lang, *An Historical and Statistical Account of New South Wales*, Cochrane & McCrone, 1834 p.95.
8. The Sydney Herald, Monday, April 3, 1837, p.1, col.5.
9. The Australian, Tuesday, April 9, 1839, p.2, cols 6-7.
10. SG&NSW, Tuesday, April 2, 1839, p.2, col.2.
11. The Australian, Tuesday, April 9,1839, op.cit.
12. L.E.Fredman & Elizabeth Guilford (Eds) Journal of Hunter Valley History, Vol.2 No.2, Hunter Valley Publications, Newcastle 1988, p 96.
13. The Australian, April 9, 1839, op.cit.
14. L.E.Fredman & Elizabeth Guilford op.cit., pp. 96-97.
15. The Australian, April 9, 1839, op.cit.
16. Births, Deaths and Marriages, New South Wales, Baptisms, No. 314, Vol:162a. The baptismal record does not state the mother's name, only giving the father's name John Campbell and the child's first name, John.

Chapter 15

Disaster

Over the previous eight years the couple had prospered and become settled. Unfortunately this better life was not to last. On the 9th of December 1839, John was committed to trial[1] along with William Nugent, John Elgin (the two convicts residing at his house) and Edward Cotter. They were charged with stealing a large quantity of goods from the Steam Company's stores at Morpeth on the 3rd of October. On Friday, 13 December, with a measure of superstitious foreboding, they appeared in court at the Maitland Quarter Sessions.[2]

The court heard that a large part of the stolen goods, identified by the owner Mr J.H. Atkinson, had been found in John Campbell's house and particularly in the convicts' rooms. Although Campbell was described as a free emigrant of character and a well to do farmer, he was found guilty along with the two convicts. There was no evidence against Cotter who was acquitted and discharged. John was sentenced to seven years transportation to Van Diemen's Land and Nugent and Elgin were to be worked in irons for three years.[3]

John entered Sydney Gaol on 23rd December[4] to be held for transportation to Hobart. His native place was noted as '*County Sutherland*', his religion '*Presbiterian*' and his trade or calling, '*labourer*'.[5]

While in gaol there was an attempt to have his sentence remitted. A petition,[6] including character references from six prominent citizens of Morpeth, was sent to Governor Gipps. The petition read:

> To His Excellency Sir George Gipps Knight
> Captain General and Governor of New South Wales   and
> its Dependencies
> &c &c &c
>
> J.Campbell for commutation of sentence

The humble Petition of John Campbell now in Sydney Gaol

Shewith,

That your Petitioner is a carpenter by trade and a native of Scotland came from thence free with a good unblemished character to Van Diemans Land where Petitioner remained for five years or thereabouts, after which Petitioner came to this Colony and worked at his trade but for the last few years cultivated a small farm of land near Morpeth Green Hills

That Petitioner is married, that on the birthday of Petitioners wife, Petitioner was induced to spend the day out by invitation with his wife's friends and did not return home with his wife until late in evening, under the influence of drink, but unfortunately during the temporary absence of Petitioner Nugent holding the indulgence of a Ticket of leave in the employ of Petitioner, and who shortly before vowed vengeance against Petitioner in consequence of a quarrel that they had about the same time; Nugent with his vile associates availed themselves of Petitioners absence to remove goods from the Steamer Stores at Morpeth to the residence of Petitioner, in consequence of which Petitioner and wife with three others, Nugent, John Algine, and Edward Cotter were committed for trial at the last Quarter Sessions of Maitland (Nov 1839).

Placed in this distressing predicament without being able to bring home proof against the guilty party as none of them turned approver although two of them were found guilty, Petitioner with an unblemished character up to the charge for which he was tried, under advice was induced to plead guilty, and to subject himself to the consequences whatever it might be in order to extricate and acquit from the combined charge a fond and affectionate wife, and by so pleading your Petitioner has been sentenced to seven years transportation to Van Diemans Land under such circumstances and entraped as Petitioner has been by a designing set of men Petitioner humbly hopes that your Excellency may be pleased to take into your humane consideration Petitioners case.

May it therefore please your Excellency to take your humble Petitioners case into humane consideration, and to be pleased to grant a commutation of Petitioners sentence, in such manner as shall appear to your Excellency most meet and just.

And your Petitioner as in duty bound shall ever pray.

Morpeth 13 January 40/ Application having been made to me for a character for petitioner I can positively state that he was considered an honest and industrious character till the above charge was laid against him and from my knowledge of him for the last four years cannot be persuaded that he would commit the crime laid to his charge voluntary but must have been misguided into it. J. Portus

Maitland Jan 15. 1840. I hereby certify that for the last two years I have known your petitioner John Campbell for about eighteen months since his wife had a very severe illness as circumstances which induced me several times as a minister of the church to which they belonged to visit their dwelling that she in her affliction appeared a person of more than ordinary Christian feelings, that on 7 July last I was called upon to baptise his only child that on this occasion I found him visited by the most respectable persons in the neighbourhood that it was with much surprise I heard of the subject of the memorial but was glad to find on enquiry that his neighbours his character they here certify.   Robt Blain

Morpeth Janry 13th 1840 Application having been made to me for a Character of petitioner I certify I have known him for three years and up to the period of the transaction always known him to be a steady sober and industrious man.   John Chastel, Customs

I certify that I have known the petitioner (John Campbell) upwards of three years and have always considered him an honest and industrious Character and never heard to the contrary until the above named transaction for which he was convicted.   Henry Lewis. Surgeon

> *I hereby certify that about two years ago, the petitioner John Campbell- became known to me as one of my congregation, was then represented to me as a person of unblemished character, & till the late charge was brought against him, was considered an upright & honest man by me.   John Gregor, Minister*

> *Maitland January 13th 1840   I hereby certify that I have known Petitioner upwards of Eight years and always found him an Honest and industrious man and am of the opinion that he must have been brought into his present circumstances through Elgin and Nugent tried with him.   James Norris, Agent for the Steamers Morpeth*

Gipps was prompt in ruling on the matter. Hand written in the margin of the petition was his consideration:

> *I regret to say that I see nothing in this case to lead me to think that I can properly interfere with the sentence of the Law. GG Jan 22*

Perhaps Gipps' decision was influenced by the unsavoury incident he experienced at Morpeth during his visit there in 1839. But Gipps was also of the opinion that freemen were restrained from nefarious activities by the potential to be branded a convict forever. In Gipps' words 'The fear indeed of being suspected of the taint of Convictism operates in a wholesome manner as a restraint upon those who are free from it.'[7]   John Campell had acted contrary to that opinion.

Obviously the character references from prominent citizens of the district and the implication that John had been framed made no impression on Gipps. The referees were all people of some note. John Portus was a wealthy miller and machinery manufacturer. He had built the first steam powered mill in the region on the waterfront at Morpeth and sold flour throughout the colony. Henry Lewis was a young surgeon who had taken up residence in Morpeth as early as 1836. John Chastel was an official for His Majesty's Customs in Morpeth and James Norris was the local representative for the Steamships and store in Morpeth. Both Robert Blain and John

Gregor were Presbyterian ministers representing different bodies of the Presbyterian church.

Since John Campbell and his wife Charlotte appear to have been part of the Presbyterian congregation in the Maitland area, an explanation of the state of the Presbyterian Church in New South Wales at this time is relevant and consequently the reason for the character references from two ministers, seemingly in competition for the souls of the people in the same church.

Both Blain and Gregor had arrived in Sydney from Scotland with a number of other ministers, teachers and their families and a large contingent of immigrants on board the barque *Portland*, 3rd December 1837.[8] They had been brought to the colony by Revd Dr John Dunmore Lang, Presbyterian clergyman, politician and educationist. Dr Lang had first arrived in Sydney in 1823. After forming a congregation of Presbyterians in the colony, he established The Scots Church, the foundation stone of which was laid about a year later and opened for worship in July 1826. In 1837 Lang, who had been on a visit to Britain, returned to Sydney confident that he could purify what he perceived as corruption prevalent in the Presbytery of New South Wales.

However, instead of relying on his increased numbers within the Presbytery to support his purge, he decided to establish a new church court, entitled the Synod of New South Wales. He hoped the Synod would soon embrace several presbyteries and ultimately deprive the Presbytery of its influence.[9] Blain supported the Synod, but Gregor refused. Believing there was no security for his government salary if he joined the Synod, he remained with the Presbytery.[10] The Reverend John McGarvie, whom Lang had brought to New South Wales in 1826, remained loyal to the Presbytery and became its senior minister.

While Lang was considered to be a radical and all too ready to challenge the civil authorities, Revd John McGarvie representing the Presbytery was a moderate whose respect for civil authority gained him the support of the government and the General Assembly of the Church of Scotland. However, the Synod of New South Wales, while embracing the Westminster Confession of Faith, forbade appeals from its decisions to any church court overseas.[11] Much to Lang's consternation, McGarvie and the majority of the Presbytery continued to ignore his perceived corrupting influences in the church, further broadening the division between the two groups.

Lang's perception of corruption within the Presbytery was not without grounds. Two well known cases of clerical delinquency had arisen during 1834 and 1835 discrediting the spiritual guidance provided by certain ministers of the church. The drunken behaviour of Revd Thomas Thomson, of Bathurst, had become so well known in the colony that his delinquency was 'thrown in his teeth' wherever he went. With McGarvie's influence and support Thomson was allowed to resign rather than be dismissed[12] and he returned to England.

The second case of clerical misconduct was more serious and pertinent to Presbyterians in the Hunter River region. The Revd John H. Garven, who had been highly recommended to Lang and had been brought to New South Wales in 1834, had repeatedly shown a propensity, to intemperance on board ship during the voyage. On reaching Sydney, 'he was solemnly and most affectionately admonished in the presence of all his brethren'. Suitably chastised he was despatched to Maitland where he might mend his ways under more favourable circumstances. However, Garven did not reform and in fact his indiscretions became worse.[13]

Dr. Lang travelled to Maitland to determine if reports against Garven were well founded. In the course of the investigation that took place, the principal witness, a free unmarried-female immigrant and maid-servant to Garven, gave evidence that her master and the Surgeon of the village had been drinking together in a small room in Garven's house, the whole evening of a certain day in December 1835. They both became intoxicated and during the course of the evening Garven had twice presented, and attempted to fire, a loaded musket at his own convict servant.

Consequently, two enquiries were held. At the first inquiry, McGarvie refused to allow any witness to say anything that would affect the character of anyone else and Lang, realising his pursuit of the case was impractical, gave up. The second enquiry into the matter was held without Lang who had returned to England. McGarvie vigorously defended the sobriety of the Surgeon who then proceeded to discredit the character and testimony of the principal witness, whose mother, a respectable free immigrant, would not allow her to attend the enquiry without Lang being present. McGarvie characterised the drunken incident as 'an instance of unbecoming levity' and in such circumstances, it was only a matter of course that the Presbytery honourably acquitted Garven and sent him back to his people without blemishing his character.

The acquittal however served only to strengthen and confirm Garven's 'tippling propensities'. Eventually most of his congregation deserted his ministry and any respectable persons who had any regard for their own character avoided his company. Later Reverend McGarvie manipulated the investigation of a second incident of gross intoxication at William's River in such a way that the enquiry was abandoned and another chance to get rid of Garven was lost.

One of the first acts of the Synod of New South Wales, was to rectify the sorry state of the Presbyterian communion in the Hunter River region. To that end it sent the Rev. Robert Blain, shortly after his arrival in New South Wales, to officiate at Maitland. Blain, described as 'a man of apostolic zeal, of Christian simplicity of manners, and withal an enthusiast for the Temperance Society', was to endeavour to collect the congregation again 'till the good providence of God' should open up some effectual way for Garven's removal. The 'providence of God' was not long in coming.

Blain took passage to the Hunter River on the *Sophia Jane* on the evening of 11 December 1837 and, coincidentally, Garven, who was returning from a meeting of the Presbytery in Sydney, was also on the steamboat. Believing his position was assured under the protection of Rev. McGarvie, Garven showed little constraint in his drinking habit. Lacking any self control he got mortally drunk on board the *Sophia Jane* and losing all sense of propriety was rolling about the public deck throughout the night and the following morning.[14] His behaviour was not only witnessed by Blain and several others connected with the Synod, but also by another member of the Presbytery, the Reverend Mr. Hetherington of Patrick's Plains.

Whether through divine intervention or the natural course of destiny, Garven's end was soon realised. Scandalised, attacked in the newspapers and anticipating an enquiry with an unfavourable outcome, Garven resigned his pastoral charge at Maitland on Thursday 4 January 1838.[15] He was subsequently informed that he had been expelled from the Colonial Presbyterian Church.[16]

Meanwhile, the Presbytery initially sent John Gregor to Liverpool to usurp the appointment of a minister from the Synod who had yet to arrive. He was summarily rejected when the people of Liverpool realised he was not the minister the Synod had appointed.[17] He next went to Williams River, with letters of introduction from Lang notwithstanding his refusal to join the Synod. Although well accepted there, he saw that Maitland provided a better opportunity. Obtaining the signed invitation of a small number of Presbyterians of that district, the Presbytery appointed him their minister. Consequently, with Robert Blain already settled in Maitland, a battle for supremacy in the area developed between the Synod and the Presbytery.[18]

Lang had no wish to impose any particular minister upon the congregation or interfere in any way with their freedom of choice. His brother, Andrew Lang of Dunmore near Maitland, owned the land on which the Presbyterian Church stood, and through him Lang offered the Presbytery the use of the premises on alternate Sundays. But the offer was refused. Completely ignoring Lang and Blain, the Presbytery appointed Gregor and Revd George McFie (who had voted against formation of the Synod) to preach alternately, overriding the people's right to hear whomsoever they wished.[19]

The election meeting of 22nd of February 1838 was thrown into confusion when the supporters of John Gregor, realising they were in the minority, claimed that some of the Presbyterian congregation had not heard Gregor speak at Maitland. Lang proposed that in this case only those adult men and women who had heard both candidates should vote. But McGarvie countered with a motion excluding women from voting. That motion was lost by a considerable majority, but Lang did not persist in his proposal and suggested that the matter should be referred to the Government in reference to Sir Richard Bourke's Church Act of 1836. In Lang's opinion this was the only principle on which the Government could be expected to act in recognising a Presbyterian minister or allotting him a stipend. The election was deferred and the meeting broke up.[20]

Governor Gipps' attempt to mediate a resolution to the rift was to no avail. Blain and Gregor continued to practise in the Maitland area, each holding services in Morpeth on different Sundays and both ministering to John and Charlotte Campbell thus accounting for the two character references.

In 1839, the schism caused Lang to make another trip to England where he attempted to overturn recognition of the Presbytery as the controlling body of the Presbyterian Church in New South Wales. He also tried to persuade the British government that colonial Presbyterians were independent of the General Assembly of the Church of Scotland and their ministers should receive monetary support from the government. But the Colonial Office, on advice from the General Assembly, refused to interfere with the Presbytery of New South Wales, and Lang failed in his bid to assert his clerical independence and obtain government funding.[21]

Early in 1840 he sailed for the United States to investigate how its churches managed without government support and, if possible, raise sufficient money to make him independent of the General Assembly. During Lang's absence the two Presbyterian groups in New South Wales resolved their differences and combined to form the Synod of Australia in connexion with the established Church of Scotland.[22]

With the reconciliation of the two Presbyterian groups in New South Wales, the new united Synod of Australia instructed both ministers in Maitland to withdraw. Gregor, who had founded a boarding school, refused and the Synod suspended him in 1841. He then sought orders in the Church of England, and was made a deacon in September 1842. Three months later he was ordained a priest.[23] In April 1841, Blain left his congregation at Maitland and relocated to Hinton, less than 2 miles northeast of Morpeth, where he built a church and manse, the Presbyterian Parish of Hinton embracing the Lower Hunter including Morpeth.[24] Lang returned from England in March 1841 and joined the new united body, ending the three years of turmoil that had plagued the Presbyterian Church in the colony.

The petition only served to delay John Campbell's passage to Van Diemen's Land. He remained in Sydney gaol until the 31st of January 1840 when he was sent to Hyde Park Barracks with four other prisoners where it was to be ascertained whether any of them had been convicted more than once.[25] A letter from the T.C Harington of the Colonial Secretary's Office to the Principal Superintendent of Convicts requested that the report be provided quickly as it was proposed to send the men to Van Diemen's Land by the *Abercrombie* sailing on Sunday (2 February 1840).[26]

In this instance the wheels of government moved quickly. The five men were returned to Sydney Gaol and a report from J. McLean, Principal Superintendent of Convicts sent to Colonial Secretary on the 1st of February. An Indent was enclosed for Governor Gipps' signature.[27]

> *Sir*
>
> *In compliance with the request contained in your letter of the 31st last (hereof) I have the honour to acquaint you that I have caused the men named in the margin to be examined and found that Campbell arrived free at Hobart Town by the ship 'Greenock', and came up here in the 'Henry' in 1825 Nathan arrived free in 1831 by the ship 'Caroline', Henry stated that he came to this Colony as a sailor in the 'Fanny' in 1832, Jones arrived free in Van Diemen's Land with his Father when a child, and Donough came free in the 'Thames' with his mother in 1826 to join his father Philip Donough par 'Countess Harcourt' /2/*
>
> *I have the honour to be*
> *Sir*
> *Your most obedient Servant*
>
> *J McLean*

This document raises a few questions. The date of 1825 and the '*Henry*' are enigmatic. The petition submitted to Governor Gipps in Campbell's defence states that John had remained in Van Diemen's Land '*for five years or thereabouts*' suggesting he came to New South Wales at the end of 1828 or early in 1829. Furthermore no record has been found to confirm John Campbell took passage from Hobart to Sydney on any vessel named *Henry*. Perhaps the recording official misheard his answers and therefore made mistakes. Alternatively the handwritten "5" in "1825" could be transcribed as a "9" giving the more probable year of 1829 for his arrival in New South Wales.

Gipps, however, was interested only in whether or not the prisoners had been convicted previously. There being no evidence in that regard, he acted quickly to assign the convicted men over to the jurisdiction of the Lieutenant Governor of Van Diemen's Land for the term of their sentences.[28]

> *By His Excellency Sir George Gipps Knight Governor in Chief of the Territory of New South Wales its Dependencies and Vice Admiral of the Same ye ye ye*
>
> *Whereas the several persons named in the Annexed List have been Convicted of the Offences and have been sentenced to be transported for the period set opposite their respective Names, And Whereas the said persons have been embarked on board the Schooner 'Abercrombie' for the purpose Of being transported to His Majesty's Colony of Van Diemens Land, Now therefore in pursuance Of the power in me vested I do hereby Assign the Several of the Said Persons so Convicted to the Lieutenant Governor of the Said Colony of Van Diemens Land for the time being and to his Assigns during the Several periods for which the Said Persons have been Sentenced To be transported respectively*
>
> *By His Excellency's Command*
> *(Signed E. Deas Thomson)*
>
> *Given under My Hand at Government House*
> *Sydney this 1st day of February 1840*
> *(Signed) GeoGipps*

New South Wales
Assignment List of Five Male Prisoners embarked on board the 'Abercrombie for Van Diemen's land

	Name	John Campbell	Bertram Nathan	John Henry	William Jones	John Donnough
	Offence	Larceny	Rec. Stolen Property	Larceny	Felony	Cattle Stealing
Convicted	Where	Maitland Q.Sns	Sydney Q.Sns	Sydney Q.Sns	Milbrun Q.Sns	Campbelltown Q.Sns
	When	9 Dec 1839	4 Jan 1840	6 Jan 1840	4 Nov 1839	17 Jan 1840
	Sent. Yrs	7	7	7	7	10
	Age	49	26	23	26	29
Height	Feet &	5	5	5	5	5
	Inches	6½	4	1	10½	8½
Complexion			Fresh	Fresh	Man of Color	Fresh	Fresh
Color of	Hair	Grey	Dark	Black	Light	Brown
	Eyes	Grey	Grey	Black	Grey	Grey

Colonial Secretary's Office   (signed) E. Deas Thomson
Sydney 1st February 1840

 The assignment list contains the first known description of John Campbell. His age of 49 years is wrong and his height is debatable, but the fresh complexion, grey hair and grey eyes should be accurate unless the examiner had poor eyesight as well as a lack of measuring and calculating ability.

 Later that day Harington sent a letter to the Sheriff, requesting that the five men be embarked on board the *Abercrombie* sailing for Hobart Town the next day.[29] There was a slight delay in departure, but on Monday, 3rd of February, the 143 ton brigantine *Abrecrombie* under the captaincy of F.C. Carew left Sydney for Hobart Town. On board were eleven crew, the five convicts, cabin passengers J.S.

Smith, J. Smith, and Ensign Scott. In steerage were 29 rank and file of the 51st Regiment and 7 women. The brig carried sundry cargo and 2 guns.[30]

Notes to Chapter 15

1. SRNSW: NRS 2514 Sydney Gaol Entrance Books, No.3371, [4/6439], Reel 1864.
2. The Australian, Saturday, December 21, 1839, p.2, col.7.
3. Ibid.
4. SRNSW: NRS 2514 Sydney Gaol Entrance Books, No.3371, [4/6439], Reel 1864.
5. SRNSW: NRS 2514 Sydney Gaol Entrance Books , No.3371, [4/6439], Reel 853.
6. SRNSW: NRS 905 Colonial Secretary's Correspondence, Letter 40/775, [4/2513], Reel 2245.
7. Michael Roe, *The Quest For Authority in Eastern Australia,1835-1851*, Melbourne University Press, Parkville Vic.,1965, p.195.
8. The Colonist, Thursday, December 7, 1837, p.3, col.4.
9. D. W. A. Baker, *Lang, John Dunmore (1799–1878)*, ADB, MUP 1967, Vol.2, pp.76-83.
10. SG&NSWA, Thursday, December 14, 1837 p.2, cols. 4-5.
11. Baker, op.cit.
12. The Colonist, Wednesday 3 January 1838, p.2, col.6; p.3, cols.1-2.
13. Ibid.
14. The Colonist, Wednesday, January 3, 1838, p.2, col.6; p.3, cols1-2-3.
15. SG&NSWA, Saturday, January 6, 1838 p. 2, col. 3.
16. SG&NSWA Saturday, February 10, 1838 p.2, col.4 ; HRA Series I Vol.20 p. 317, Lang to the Marquess of Normanby, 7 September 1839.
17. The Colonist, Wednesday, February 28, 1838, p.2, cols 5-6; p.3, col.1.
18. HRA Series I Vol.20 ,pp.330-332, Lang to Under Secretary Stephen, 18 June 1839.
19. The Colonist, Wednesday, January 31, 1838, p.2, cols 4-6; p.3, cols 1-2.
20. The Colonist, Wednesday, February 28, 1838, p.2, cols 5-6; p.3, col.1.
21. Baker, op.cit.
22. Ibid.
23. K. Rayner, *Gregor, John (1808–1848)*, ADB, MUP 1966, Vol. 1, pp.472-473.
24. Adolphus Peter Elkin, Morpeth And I, Sydney : Australasian Medical Pub. Co., 1937.
25. SRNSW: NRS 1000, Colonial Secretary's Correspondence, Copies of Letters sent to the Sheriff, Letter 40/13, [4/3901 p.217], Reel 1064.
26. SRNSW: NRS 962 Colonial Secretary's Correspondence 1832 – 1842, Letter 40/56, [4/3687 p.426], Reel 1052.

27 SRNSW: NRS 905, Colonial Secretary's Correspondence 1832 – 1842, Letter 40/1168, [4/2486.2], Reel 1841.
28 SRNSW: NRS 1188, Colonial Secretary's, Assignment lists of convicts sentenced to transportation for Colonial Offences and sent to Van Diemen's Land [4/4523 pp.71-72], Reel 901.
29 SRNSW: NRS 1000, op.cit, Letter 40/12, [4/3901 p.217], Reel 1064.
30 AOTAS: MB2/39/5 p38, Brigantine Abercrombie arrival in Hobart from Sydney, 12 February 1840.

Chapter 16

Canadian Rebels

The passage took ten days, the *Abercrombie* arriving at Hobart early in the morning, Wednesday, 12 February in '*squally*' weather, wind from the southwest[1]. At 6 am the colonial officers boarded the brig and soon relieved it of its passengers.

Chief Police magistrate William Gunn and his clerks quickly processed the five convicts. There was more urgent work to be conducted on the convict transport ship, HMS *Buffalo*, which had arrived the same day. John Campbell was given Police number 2580 and his details recorded in the indent[2] as follows:

Height:	5' 9¾'
Age:	41
Trade or Calling:	Farm Laborer, Completer
Where tried:	Maitland QS
When Tried:	9 Dec 1839
Sentence:	7 (years)
Native Place:	Sutherland
Married or Single:	M
Children:	1
Religion:	Presb
Read or Write:	Yes
Offence, &c:	For Stealing 2 Pieces of Calico prop of Mr Atkinson he prosecuted me---
Ship Character:	Greenock & Ditto (Abercrombie, 12th Feb 1840)
Remarks:	Wife Charlott at a Farm I rented at The Green Hills NSW. She intends coming Down here. The Farm was 100 acres.

There are three things of particular interest in this document: reference to the items stolen for which he was prosecuted being merely two pieces of calico; his alternate trade as a 'completer' suggesting his carpentry work was of finishing quality; and the fact that his wife 'Charlott' intended to come to Van Diemen's Land to be with him.

Stripped of their clothing, the men were examined for any distinguishing marks and issued with a pair of trousers, two shirts and a jacket, all made of coarse, rough, murky-grey Indian cotton. To cover their heads they were given a stiff, four cornered, leather skull cap and for their feet, thick, clumsy shoes and no socks. Their own clothing was tied in separate bundles, marked with their names and taken to be stored until such time as their government service ended or they received an indulgence.

In contrast to 1823 there was little notice of John Campbell's second arrival in Hobart. The town's people were preoccupied with the arrival of the HMS *Buffalo* carrying 139 convicts, including 136 prisoners from the rebellions of 1837 - 1838 in Upper and Lower Canada. A large crowd had gathered on the shore to see the rebels and satisfy their curiosity about the appearance of the revolutionary Canadians they had heard so much about. They were mildly surprised to find the men did not look any different than themselves.

The rebellions in British North America had resulted from a number of factors, largely influenced by dissatisfaction with the system of government in the colony. Both Upper and Lower Canada governments consisted of an elected House of Assembly and an appointed Legislative Council. The Legislative Council in both provinces was controlled by a privileged few, critically referred to as the Family Compact in Upper Canada and the Chateau Clique in Lower Canada. The Governor-in-Chief, residing in Quebec, who was also the Governor of Lower Canada, and his lesser counterpart in Upper Canada, the Lieutenant-Governor, could veto or reserve all bills and prorogue or dissolve the legislature at will. There was undoubtedly friction between the two houses of government, where they existed, in the all the British colonies; but in Lower Canada there was the additional difficulty of 'two nations warring in the bosom of a single state .... in a struggle that was not of principles but of race.'³

Both provinces had suffered during the economic downturn of the 1830s further aggravated by widespread crop failures in 1837 but there were more fundamental, underlying causes for strife. In Lower Canada, French Canadians led by Louis Joseph Papineau and the Patriotes were pressed to promote their culture, rights and interests against a growing English population and an ever increasing English monopoly of the Legislative Council. The English complained that they were chronically under-represented in the Assembly. As loyal subjects of the Crown, the province belonged to them as much as it belonged to the French and as part of the British Empire it would have to become English. The ethnic cleavage drove other aspects of the struggle; the economic difference between a static and a dynamic view of society, the clash of personalities and the need for constitutional reform.⁴

In Upper Canada, the reform movement was led by William Lyon Mackenzie, a radical who favoured a society and economy based on that of the United States, and Robert Baldwin, a moderate who sought responsible government under the British system. Their resentment did not have the sharp edge of ethnic difference as in Lower Canada and focused primarily on the dominance of the Anglican Church and the Family Compact. They demanded reforms to the Legislative Council's control over revenue, expenses, land granting policies and the civil service.

On 21 February 1834, the Legislative Assembly in Lower Canada passed Ninety-Two Resolutions which included calls for an elected Legislative Council and an Executive Council responsible before the house of the people's representatives. In 1835, the British Government finally realizing that all was not well in Lower Canada commissioned Lord Gosford to report on the situation and provide recommendations. Gosford's report formed the basis of ten essentially reactionary resolutions drafted by Lord Russell, the Home Secretary, which refused an elected council and effectively closed the door to negotiations in March 1837. Their major demands rejected, the Patriotes organized mass demonstrations and began to prepare for an armed insurrection. On 22nd November 1837, a column of troops sent to arrest offenders, one of whom was Papineau, encountered a band of Patriotes at St. Denis and shooting began.[5]

After a few sharp encounters, the Patriotes, who had fought well, were forced to scatter and the affair ended. Lacking careful organisation, military experience, money and most of all the support of the masses, the armed rebellion was destined to be brief and unsuccessful.[6] Papineau fled to the United States crossing the border on November 25th.

In Upper Canada, Baldwin's constitutional approach to self government was thwarted when the Lieutenant Governor, Sir Francis Bond Head, refused to be bound by the advice of the Executive Council[7] of which Baldwin was a member, setting the Assembly and the Governor in direct opposition. Mackenzie's agitation for reforms had also failed. In the ensuing election campaign following dissolution, Head, in an unusual action for a representative of the Crown, campaigned on a platform of Loyalty and anti-Americanism.[8]

Frustrated by the Lieutenant-Governor's direct intervention in the 1836 election, which, on a wave of anti-American sentiment, secured a conservative majority in the Assembly, Mackenzie concluded that armed insurrection was the only remaining solution to achieve reform. In 1836 and 1837, Mackenzie gathered support among farmers around Toronto, sympathetic to his cause. With British forces out of the province suppressing the Lower Canada rebellion, Mackenzie and his followers armed with pikes and fowling pieces attempted to seize a Toronto armoury in early December 1837.

Failing in that endeavour the rebels gathered at Montgomery's tavern on Yonge Street. In the ensuing battle they were quickly routed and most fled to the United States. A group of rebels from the settlement of London (in the west of Upper Canada), who had marched toward Toronto to support Mackenzie, were defeated on December 13 near Hamilton on the west end of Lake Ontario. Most of them also fled across the border.

Mackenzie escaped to the United States and attempted to rally his forces on Navy Island in the Niagara River but the rally collapsed. The United States charged him with breaking neutrality laws and he was imprisoned in Rochester, New York. Sir Francis Bond Head, was recalled in late 1837 and replaced with Sir George Arthur who arrived in Toronto in March 1838. Arthur, prior to being recalled to England in 1836, had served as Lieutenant-Governor of Van Diemen's Land for twelve years. During his tenure there, Arthur, a devout Calvinist who believed that man's nature was basically wicked,[9] had proved a rigid disciplinarian of unbending conventionality.

In the United States it was not long before bands of sympathisers contemplated another attempt to liberate Canada from British rule. Joined and encouraged by rebels who had escaped over the border, they began a series of attacks on border points in Upper and Lower Canada in the autumn of 1838. Lieutenant-Governor Arthur had been given orders to deal firmly with the rebels. The raids were easily repelled and further rebellion suppressed. Many of the culprits were captured and gaoled. Somewhat reluctantly, the American government intervened to control its citizens, preventing the conflict from broadening into an international confrontation.

To find a solution to the colonial ills, the Imperial authorities appointed Lord Durham to the post of Governor-General and Lord High Commissioner of British North America. Durham was given the assignment to report on the grievances among the colonists and recommend a way to appease them. Baldwin, who had strongly disapproved of the rebellion and remained neutral during the uprising, briefly met with Durham and subsequently sent him a memorandum on his central concept of Responsible Government. Baldwin's ideas greatly influenced Durham's report, which eventually led to greater autonomy in the Canadian colonies, and the union of Upper and Lower Canada into the Province of Canada in 1840.

Most of the rebels captured were pardoned, but 29 were hanged and Arthur arranged for 150 to be transported to Australia. Nine reached Hobart on the *Marquis of Hastings* in July 1839, three of whom died shortly after arrival as a result of privations on the voyage. Four more arrived on the *Canton* in January 1840 followed by the main party on HMS *Buffalo*. The prisoners on the *Buffalo*, had left Quebec 28th September 1839. Seventy eight American prisoners were disembarked in Tasmania (one having died on the voyage) and 58

French-Canadians continued on to Sydney where they arrived on the 26th of February 1840.

Arthur had transmitted the character of each of the prisoners transported on the *Buffalo* to the colonial authorities with orders to keep the Americans separate from the French Canadians. Confirming the necessity of these orders was the fact that the two groups had been confrontational during the voyage. In pursuance of Arthur's instructions, the Americans were not landed at the wharves and conveyed as usual to the Prisoners' Barracks in Hobart, but put on shore at New Town Bay and sent directly to the public works at Sandy Bay about a mile and a half out of town.[10] The French Canadians remained on the *Buffalo* and were conveyed to Sydney.

A general pardon for everyone but Mackenzie was issued in 1845. Mackenzie was eventually pardoned in 1849 and allowed to return to Canada. He resumed his political career and was elected to Legislative Assembly of the Province of Canada for Haldimand in 1852. Strongly disillusioned after his time in the United States, he wrote to his son that 'after what I have seen here, I frankly confess to you that, had I passed nine years in the United States before, instead of after, the outbreak, I am sure I would have been the last man in America to be engaged in it.'[11] In later life however, Mackenzie advocated annexation of Canada by the United States.[12]

Baldwin became the rallying figure in rebuilding the post rebellion Reform Party, forging an alliance with Lower Canadian liberals led by L.H. Lafontaine.

Following the failure of the second insurrection, Papineau left New York for Paris in 1839 where he remained in exile until 1845 when he returned to Canada under amnesty granted to him in 1844. He was elected to the Legislative Assembly of the Province of Canada in 1848, but vehemently opposed the Act of Union and advocated annexation to the US.

Colonial sentiment towards the rebels in Australia was mixed. The Sydney Gazette reported on the 10th of March that it understood that the Canadian rebels were to be sent to Norfolk Island on the *Buffalo*:

'We are glad of this, as we have bushrangers, highway robbers, and house-breakers enough in this colony already, without having a cargo of mal-contented political incendiaries, vulgarly called Patriots (which in Canada was a plausible name for cut throats) landed on our shores.' [13]

In a rebuff to the editor of the Gazette, a correspondent to the Australasian Chronicle, who named himself only as 'Castigator', pointed out grievances in the colony of New South Wales similar to those expressed by the Canadian Rebels.

'...classing these prisoners (whose crime, at the utmost, was but petty treason) with the worst of murderers, burglars, and bushrangers? The individual who can exult at such a measure has not the feelings of a man, and his conduct is equally unchristian like with those judges, or governors of the Canadas, who passed the outrageous sentence.
... What says that important document, Lord Durham's report? Have not the colonists of the Canadas been trampled upon by the infamous Tory gangs of Downing-street? Sending amongst them their hungry place-hunters, as their officials, from the governors down to the fourth-rate clerk in their various overpaid do nothing offices? And during the last twenty-six years we have witnessed something of the kind in this colony - one of the largest revenues under the British crown squandered away in the most prodigal manner, in useless offices, exorbitant salaries; and although its inhabitants, like humble slaves, submit to be taxed at the rate of nearly £5 per head - the highest taxation of any given population in the world - they are without a voice, or anything in the shape of taxation by representation. It is true, we have men amongst us who have talent, courage, and spirit-

> who have spent thousands of their private property within the last ten years, who were joined by perhaps a thousand of the most respectable and middle classes, in demanding our rights; but the Whigs, like the Tories, fell into the same trap of corruption, in providing for their place hunting friends, so that our rights and privileges have been deferred from year to year, by the renewal of acts. But I am happy to say, even the Whigs see the necessity of granting us a House of Assembly…'[14]

In the colony of New South Wales the Executive Council was largely appointed by the Governor and included military and judicial officials. Effectively it acted as a cabinet, the Governor taking part in cabinet meetings and political decisions. The colonial Legislative Council, established in 1824, was subordinate to the Governor and the Executive Council and served more as a sounding-board than a legislative body.

Responsible government was not far off. In July 1842, The New South Wales Constitution Act 1842 (UK) created Australia's first semi-representative legislature laying the foundation for the parliamentary system. Full responsible government was not granted but it enabled the first election to be held for two-thirds of the representatives in the New South Wales Legislative Council. Not only were ex-convicts eligible to vote, they were allowed to stand for election. Full self government was enacted in New South Wales in 1856.

The Canadian convicts were not sent to the harsh penal settlement at Norfolk Island as initially surmised. However, the Americans in Tasmania spent a much more difficult time there than the French Canadians transported to New South Wales, who, for the most part, were better treated, liberated sooner and assisted in getting home to Canada. It was considered that the Canadians, particularly the French Canadians, were not so much to be blamed or punished as they had been excited to rebellion by the Americans who desired to free Canada from the tyrannical rule of the British. Fourteen Americans died as a direct result of transportation and penal servitude. Several tried to escape. Three succeeded in making it to the open sea in a fishing boat where a passenger ship picked them up. They reached America seven months later. By the end of 1844, half of those in Van Diemen's Land had been granted pardons. Nearly all were pardoned by 1848, but five remained in penal servitude until at least 1850.[15]

Notes to Chapter 16

1. AOTAS: MB2/39//5, Reports of ships arrivals, 26 December 1839 to 8 July 1841, p.38.
2. AOTAS: CON16/1 Indents of convicts locally convicted or transported from other colonies Archives Office of Tasmania, p.122.
3. A.R.M.Lower, *Colony to Nation, A History of Canada,* Longmans Canada, 1964.
4. Ibid., p.222.
5. Ibid., pp227-228.
6. Ibid., pp228-229.
7. The Executive Council, similar to a cabinet, contained members from both the Legislative Assembly and the Legislative Council.
8. Lower, op.cit., p243.
9. A.G.L Shaw, *Arthur, Sir George (1784-1854),* ADB MUP 1966, Vol. 1, pp. 32-38.
10. The Hobart Town Courier and Van Diemen's Land Gazette, Friday, February 14, 1840, p.2, col.5.
11. Carol Wilton, (2000). *Popular Politics and Political Culture in Upper Canada, 1800-1850.* McGill-Queens University Press, Montreal-Kingston, 2000, pp. 144–67.
12. Ibid., pp. 146–147.
13. SG&NSWA, Tuesday, March 10, 1840, p.2, col.6.
14. Australasian Chronicle Friday, March 13, 1840, p.2, col.5-6.
15. Albert Schrauwers, *Union is Strength: W.L. Mackenzie, the Children of Peace, and the Emergence of Joint Stock Democracy in Upper Canada*University of Toronto Press, Toronto 2009, pp. 181-184 and 192-199; *William Gates, Recollections of Life In Van Diemen's Land,* Australian Historical Monographs, George Mackaness (ed.) D.S.Ford, Sydney 1961, Part I, p.6.

Chapter 17

Van Diemen's Land

Hobart had grown considerably over the 12 years since John Campbell had been there as a free man. Now, returning as a convict, conditions were obviously going to be different and in this regard an even greater change awaited him. A transition to the probation system of convict discipline had been introduced into Van Diemen's Land the previous year by George Arthur's successor, Sir John Franklin. This system of convict management was devised in response to dissatisfaction with the assignment system which, as a form of punishment, had come to be seen as too lenient and inconsistent to be effective either for reform or deterrence. Assignment was also tainted with its suspicion of slavery.[1]

The probation system took a more punitive approach. Rather than being assigned on arrival, convicts served an initial period on a work gang or in confinement under a strict program of religious and moral instruction prior to their assignment to free settlers.

Shortly after the indents had been drafted they were delivered to the Muster Master and a convict conduct record was commenced for John Campbell, Police Number 2580, *Abercrombie*. These details of identification would remain with him during the period of his sentence. His initial record was drawn up under the old assignment format and later the information transferred to a probation period record. His crime, place and date of sentence and his appearance were recorded again with a few additional characteristics noted:

Height	*5/9¾*
Age	*41*
Complexion	*fresh*
Head	*long*
Hair	*Grey*
Whiskers	*do* (grey)

Visage	*long*
Forehead	*high*
Eyebrows	*Grey*
Nose	*med*
Mouth	*med*
Chin	*med*

His native place was stated as Dornoch, Sutherland and his trade given as a farm labourer. A single line in the record described his fate under the probation system: '*To be placed on the Roads for 6 months vide Memo of PS 24th Feby 1840.*'[2] Similarly Bertram Nathan, transported for receiving stolen goods, and John Henry, for spending £5 of his master's money without authorisation, were each given terms of six months on the roads. John Donnough, who had been convicted of cattle stealing from Mr Wilmot of Bong Bong, was placed on the roads for nine months. William Jones, who had been sentenced in Melbourne for robbing his master of £40, was sent to Port Arthur for twelve months.[3]

In compliance with the directions of the Principal Superintendent's memo, Campbell, Henry, Nathan and Donnough were escorted from the Prisoners' Barracks in Hobart Town and marched to a work station to serve their initial periods of probation on a road gang. Work stations commonly consisted of a number of huts arranged around a central square where the men were mustered. A palisade of split timber surrounded the whole compound, access and egress made through one large gate which was locked at night. Each hut was made of the same split timber as the palisade, the pieces set upright to a height of about ten feet and fastened at the bottom to logs. The roofs were thatched, the floors bare earth and there was no fireplace. The huts, of variable capacity depending on size, could accommodate from ten to fifty prisoners. Single person bunks were arranged around the walls in two tiers and a coarse cotton rug and a coarse blanket provided for bedding.

Work on the roads was hard particularly for those men unaccustomed to extreme physical labour. There was a variety of tasks. The stone had to be gathered, hauled to the road site, broken down to several different sizes, wheeled onto the road way and shovelled into place. Everything was done manually. Tools of trade consisted of shovels, pick-axes, grub-hoes and wheel barrows. Even the carts used to supply or remove materials were hauled by men, harnessed with leather collars and traces like beasts of burden. The cart's loading box measured six feet in length, four and a half feet in width and two feet in depth. Near the end of a cart's tongue was a crossbar against which the men could push, but fully laden with stone the cart could barely be moved by the four men attached to it.

Road construction employed the same technique devised by John L. McAdam at the beginning of the 19th century for the turnpikes of Britain. The roadway was first graded to a flat surface and covered with a layer of coarse stone bedded down to form a firm road bed about 5 inches thick. Eight inches of powdered stone were added on top of the road bed and covered with a light layer of earth sufficient to fill the interstices of the surface. Once compacted, the roads were smooth and often as hard as rock.

The physically demanding nature of the work and lack of comfort in the accommodation was further exacerbated by the lack of nourishment in the men's food rations. A pound of damper and a pint of gruel was rationed morning and evening and a pound of boiled mutton served at dinner. Made from coarse flour mixed with cold water and baked in the ashes of an open fire, the damper was ashen, hard and glutinous. Channelled through an army of officials, overseers, clerks, constables, cooks and wardsmen, pilfering substantially decreased the quality and quantity of the food delivered to the convicts. Consequently, the meat ration was regularly of the poorest quality, of insufficient quantity and often bad or fly-blown by the time it reached the men. Occasionally, the ration of damper was increased by half a pound and now and then a small amount of cabbage or turnip served with the mutton.

As if the work were not punishment enough, an inability to work or infraction of the rules, rendered the men subject to punishment at the hands of the overseer who, depending on his nature, could be kind or cruel. In some cases men were forced to work until they dropped. Flogging, usually 30 lashes, was administered as corporal punishment and solitary confinement 'on bread and water' served as both mental and physical punishment. It is estimated that only about one quarter of all the convicts transported to the colony served their sentences without having received some further form of punishment.

Grinding, monotonous and menial, the work dragged on from dawn to dusk, day to day, week to week, month to month, the soul destroying routine only relieved by a day of rest each Sunday and its accompanying compulsory attendance at church. For John Campbell the 6 months must have seemed an eternity. He was accustomed to hard work and perhaps there was some satisfaction in building something of value that would be used for many years to come. But the separation from his home and family and the knowledge that his skills could be put to better use weighed heavily on his mind.

By August 1840 John had served his six months probationary period on the roads and was summarily assigned as a farm labourer to Mr Halstead at Richmond. John Halstead, his wife Elizabeth and six children had arrived in Hobart Town, on the brig *Brilliant* from London via the Cape of Good Hope, on 15 Nov 1831.[4] During John Campbell's assignment, Halstead was in charge of a property owned by David Lord named 'Frogmore' near Sorell. According to the census of 1842 there was a completed stone dwelling house on the property in which, on the night of 31st December 1841, fourteen people, were present. Nine of the residents were free and there were five males in bond, three of whom were married and two single. None of the married men's wives was present. One of the married males belonged to the Church of Scotland and this was undoubtedly John Campbell.[5]

Whether or not Charlotte took passage to Van Diemen's Land is unknown. She may have remained in Morpeth or travelled to Sydney to stay with friends. But no record has been discovered to ascertain her whereabouts during the period of John's sentence. There was obviously an intention to join her husband as the remarks in John's indent suggest. It is unlikely she would have been able to join him during his six months on probation which spanned the period from his arrival in Van Diemen's Land in February 1840 to the end of July that year. But she may have arrived during his assignment to Halstead.

A Certificate of Freedom had been prepared for Charlotte on 26th of January 1841 and she was therefore free after that date. Her appearance had changed little since her arrival in Sydney in 1827. She was five feet 4 inches tall, and had a fair ruddy complexion, dark brown hair and chestnut eyes. She had lost a front tooth on the upper right side of her jaw and had a scar on her chin and another on her right eyebrow. The certificate was issued in the name of Dawson but at the bottom of the document it was noted that she was the wife of John Campbell.[6]

However, Charlotte was not present at Frogmore at the end of 1841. Assuming she had come to Van Diemen's Land, it can be assumed also that she returned to New South Wales sometime after February 1841, for on 16 November of that year Charlotte gave birth to twin daughters in Sydney.[7] Perhaps her pregnancy had prompted the Halsteads to advise her that she could no longer stay at Frogmore and she returned to Sydney where she could be with friends.

Only one of the twins survived the birth. Baptized by the Reverend John McGarvie on the 10th of December in the Presbyterian Parish of St. Andrew, she was named Sarah. The parents were noted - John Campbell, profession a carpenter, and Charlotte Dawson, their residence Sydney. Charlotte registered the child and provided the other details even though John was absent.

In Van Diemen's Land, John attempted to improve his situation. On 23 December 1841 an application for an indulgence for John Campbell of the *Abercrombie* had been presented to the Superintendent of Convicts regarding Campbell's position with Mr Halstead. It stated:

> *If this man's statement be true which I have no doubt of I should think the error has arisen in his assignment as he states he gave his name in as a farmer on arrival. If another man could be sent to Mr Halstead I should recommend his being admitted into the police.*[8]

John's conduct record was exemplary. In fact it is remarkable that there was not one misdemeanour reported against his name. The other four men from the *Abercrombie* had not fared so well. John Donnough, recorded as a 19 year old farm labourer from Dublin, was particularly unsettled and subsequent to his release from the roads he was constantly in trouble.

His infractions were numerous: neglect of duty and disobedience of orders (2 months' hard labour); appearing dirty at muster on the Campbell Town chain gang (reported); disobedience of orders (reported); failing to report having received a pass (1 month hard labour on the tread wheel); disobedience (14 days' labour on the tread wheel); gambling while on a pile driving gang (2 months' hard labour on the roads); burglary while on a Glenorchy work party and concealing two silk handkerchiefs on his person while in gaol awaiting trial (12 months' hard labour in chains and then sent to Port Arthur on probation for 12 months); misconduct (14 days' solitary confinement); misconduct in cutting palings and stealing grapes (additional 3 months' hard labour in chains); misconduct in improperly having two cakes in his possession (2 months' hard labour in chains); misconduct (4 days' solitary confinement); and misconduct (2 months' hard labour in chains).

All this took place between August 24th 1841 and May 27th 1844. Over the following sixteen months he went through three periods of reclassification and on the 7th October 1845 was granted a Ticket of leave. He was recommended for a conditional pardon in December 1847 but on 2nd May 1848 he was absent from muster and was placed in the cells for 3 days. His conditional pardon was approved at the end of November 1849 and he received a Certificate of freedom the 5th of February 1850.[9]

Bertram Nathan and John Henry also had numerous infractions, although to a lesser extent than Donnough, and they both suffered similar penalties to Donnough for their misdeeds. Henry received a Certificate of Freedom on 6 January 1847 and a Conditional Pardon was approved for Nathan on 16 December 1845. Nathan's conduct record was not carried over from the old assignment system record books to the new probation system books and there is no note recording his receipt of a Certificate of Freedom.[10]

William Jones, a groom and carter by trade, sent to Port Arthur for twelve months, was less troublesome after his release. He was first assigned to a Mr. Forster but in April 1841 was sentenced to six months' hard labor on the roads at Glenorchy for using threatening language to a fellow servant. Afterwards he was assigned to Mr. Murray in Hobart on 22 July 1842. Murray returned him to the government in March 1844, the final note in his record stating his station as 3rd Class.[11]

The blank pages of John Campbell's conduct record are a stark contrast to those of the other four men, and to many other conduct records of the time. Location notations reveal only that he was obliged to report to the authorities and shed little light on his actual location or work: 19 February 1842 Chief Police Magistrate; 4 September 1842 Police Superintendent; 21 November 1843 Police Magistrate.

However he was not admitted into the police force. Possibly another man as capable and trustworthy could not be found for Mr Halstead or John was just too valuable a servant for Halstead to lose. Sometime during the first half of 1843 he was admitted to the General Hospital in Hobartown on medical grounds and transferred from there, on 15 June, to the Colonial Hospital, several miles up the Derwent River, at New Norfolk. He was released from that medical facility prior to September. A letter from the Purveyors Office to Cornelius Gavin Casey, Colonial Assistant Surgeon at New Norfolk dated 1 September 1843 included the sum of £1 4s 0d as payment for his treatment, noting that he was the assigned servant of Mr Halstead.[12]

Notes to Chapter 17

1. Ian Brand, *The Convict Probation System, Van Diemen's Land 1839 to 1854*, Blubber Head Press Hobart 1990 p.1.
2. AOTAS: CON 35/1/1 p.131; CON 31/1/8 p.117, Convict Conduct Records.
3. AOTAS: CON 31/1/32 p.211, Nathan; CON31/1/22 p.125 Henry; CON31/1/12 p.47, Donnough; CON31/1/25 p.119, Jones.
4. The Hobart Town Courier, Saturday, November 26, 1831p.2, cols.2-3.
5. AOTAS: CEN/1/40 (Census 1842) pp.149-150; HO 10/51 AJCP reel PRO 80 p.255 *Return of Male and Female Convicts showing their distribution throughout the Colony on 31st December 1841*.
6. SRNSW: Certificate of Freedom, No.41/0108, [4/4364], Reel 1008.

7   SRNSW: Register of Baptisms, Burials and Marriages, Vol.45/1841, Nos. 3867 and 3868, Reel No. 5016; Vol.47/1841, Nos.1812 and 1813, Reel 5017.
8   Tasmanian Colonial Index, Frame: (40) ML 324, Reel: P3.9, Ref: CY11.
9   AOTAS: CON31/1/12; CON35/1/1 p.173.
10 AOTAS: CON31/22 p.125; CON35/1/1 p.279; CON31/1/32 p.211 and CON35/1/1 p.432.
11 AOTAS: CON31/1/25 p.118; CON35/1/1 p.317.
12 AOTAS: HSD285/1/353 Patient Records – Admission Papers, Reel Z275.

Chapter 18

Charlotte's Revenge

Charlotte returned to Morpeth and in July 1843 rented a house from Joseph Trickelbank. John Elgin of previous notoriety was also back in the Morpeth area. For his part in the robbery which had resulted in John Campbell being sent to Van Diemen's Land, Elgin had been sentenced to three years on a chain gang. But the sentence had been commuted possibly due to the demand for his trade as a miller and he had avoided the punishment which he so rightly deserved.

It was not long before history repeated itself. On Tuesday 29 August 1843, Elgin was indicted for stealing several monetary notes to the value of £11 belonging to Robert Battley of Morpeth and Charlotte was charged with receiving the notes. It was alleged she knew the money was stolen. They were brought before Police Magistrate, E. D. Day who committed both of them to trial and sent them to Newcastle gaol until their day in court. They arrived in Newcastle on the 2nd of September.[1]

Charlotte knew Edward Denny Day though his wife Margaret, the fourth daughter of James Raymond, the postmaster-general. Day[2] was a colourful character. In 1834 after serving in India, he had resigned his military commission as a lieutenant in the 62nd Regiment because of ill health. He migrated to Sydney where he obtained employment as clerk to the Executive Council, later serving in the office of the colonial secretary. His marriage to Margaret Raymond in 1836 produced six sons and five daughters. Day was appointed Police Magistrate of various districts including Maitland in 1837, finally settling in Maitland in 1840 where he played a major part in public life.

Under instructions from Governor Sir George Gipps, in June 1838 he led a party of mounted police to arrest white men alleged to have killed at least twenty-eight Aboriginal people at or near Henry Dangar's station at Myall Creek on the Liverpool Plains. Eleven men were caught, tried and found guilty. Seven of the convicted men were hanged.

In December 1840, Day organized a party of mounted men, to pursue a gang of bushrangers, who had terrorized settlers in the Scone district, raiding cattle stations and breaking into homesteads. In one raid the clerk of a store at Scone had been murdered. Five of the bushrangers were captured after a short skirmish at Doughboy Hollow and a sixth was arrested the next day. All were tried, found guilty and hanged on 16 March 1841. Grateful residents of the Scone district presented Day with a service of plate for his efforts.

The case of Battley versus Elgin and Campbell was heard in the Maitland Circuit Court on Tuesday, 14 September 1843, Justice Stephen presiding with assessors J.S. Ferriter and E.D. Day. Battley testified he had given some money to his wife on the night of the 25th of August. The money had been put in a buttoned, leather purse which was then wrapped in a pair of stays and placed under their pillow. He said that on waking in the morning his wife had alerted him that the door to the bedroom was open and he had exclaimed 'Oh, the money!' Putting his hand under the pillow he found the money was gone. There was only one door to the bedroom and the front door of the house was locked. But there was a trap hatch and ladder in the ceiling of an open room adjoining the kitchen, which gave access to the house.

Battley's suspicion immediately fell upon Elgin, who had been in his service as a labourer for the past four months, and who currently lived with the female prisoner. A search warrant was obtained on the 28th of August, and Constable William Crawford and Battley, went to the prisoners' house. Crawford searched the house and the female prisoner, and found a £5 note and five £1 notes upon her person. Battley identified the £5 note of the Bank of Australasia by the number 2202 on the back. He also identified two of the £1 notes from the distinguishing marks on them. The notes were produced in court, and Battley again identified the £5 note and one of the £1 notes.

Joseph Trickelbank testified that the female prisoner had rented a house from him at Morpeth for a month before she was apprehended. She had paid her rent with a £1 note on Saturday (the

26th) which he had subsequently given up to Constable Crawford. When asked, Crawford replied that he did not know if the prisoners lived together as man and wife.

In defence, Elgin said he found the money wrapped up in a piece of paper, about fifteen yards from the Battley's house, and gave it to the female prisoner to take care of. Charlotte admitted she had received the money from Elgin.

The magistrate summed up the case and the jury at once returned a verdict of guilty. Elgin was sentenced to be transported beyond the seas for 15 years. Despite there being no evidence that Charlotte knew Elgin had stolen the money she was sentenced to three years' imprisonment with labour in the 3rd Class of the Factory at Parramatta.[3] It is possible Charlotte planned the whole escapade to pay back Elgin for what he had done to her husband and to secure safe haven for herself and her children in the Female Factory.

Elgin at last received the punishment he deserved. He had been transported to New South Wales on the Morley in 1828 for stealing notes in County Down, Ireland. A miller by trade he was married, with one child. He could read and write and had no prior convictions when sentenced to transportation. Originally assigned to Andrew Lang of the Hunter River, Elgin received his Certificate of Freedom on 29 May 1834. It is of interest that in 1839 he was still considered to be a convict proving that a Certificate of Freedom did not always remove the convict label. In 1843 he was definitely a convict again, transported to Van Diemen's Land on the *Sir John Byng*.[4]

He was 40 years old when sent to Van Diemen's Land. Described as 5 feet 6½ inches tall, of brown complexion with a long head and visage and a high forehead, his nose was small, his mouth wide and his chin long. His hair and whiskers were grey, eyebrows brown and his eyes blue. A scar on the thick of the thumb on his left hand and a scar on his forehead were distinguishing marks.[5] His wife Mary, his mother Mary, a brother Tom and a sister Mary were all in New South Wales.[6] The existence or whereabouts of children was not recorded.

Initially sent to Maria Island, his first years in Van Diemen's Land would not have been pleasant. But his record shows no misdemeanours until August 1846 when he served 7 days in solitary confinement for having sugar in his possession. Subsequently in November 1847, while still on Maria Island, he was charged with larceny but acquitted. About 1849 he was removed from Maria Island. He petitioned for a ticket of leave in November that year and again at the beginning of January 1851 without success. The second refusal may have driven him to despair for on 7th January, he was found *'slovenly being in Mr Waterhouse's garden'* at midnight. For this misconduct he was sentenced to 6 months hard labour at Salt Water River, northwest of Port Arthur. He finally received a ticket of leave at Sorell in February 1852. Recommended for a Conditional Pardon in January 1854, his pardon was approved in November 1854 after serving only 11 years of his 15 year sentence.[7]

Charlotte was admitted to the Sydney Gaol on 26th September 1843 and sent to the Female Factory the next day.[8] On the day of her arrival, the Matron, Sarah Bell and her husband Thomas, who was the House Steward and Storekeeper, were discharged from their offices[9] under allegations of embezzlement. It was also alleged that amongst other things they had defrauded the government by drawing rations and clothing for an additional 50 non-existent children.[10] The Sub-matron, Mary Corcoran, implicated in the charge of embezzlement, was also discharged from her position[11] and a sub-contractor John Hamilton implicated as well. All were committed to trial for fraud and embezzlement. Bail was set at £200 each and two sureties each in the amount of £100.[12]

The Factory was placed under the superintendence of William Edward Rogers, a 3rd class clerk in the office of the Principal Superintendent of Convicts. Elizabeth Rheinhart, a Sub-matron, acted as Matron until the appointment of Lucy Knight Smyth in February 1844. Lucy's husband, George Smyth, took on the office of House Steward and Storekeeper. Rheinhart remained at the establishment as Sub-matron.[13]

Charlotte was now almost 41 years old. With age she had become stout but her complexion was still fresh, her hair brown and her eyes dark brown.[14] John Norris was 4 and Sarah, who had been given the middle name of Elizabeth, was 1 year and 10 months old.

On entering gaol Charlotte had stated her trade as a seamstress hoping to evade the horrendous task of breaking down rock from the Pennant Hills quarry for road metal. From 1839 the government had advertised that needlework could be sent to the Factory and there was a very good chance that she could be occupied in that trade. Fabric already cut for shirts, shifts, babies' clothes, pinafores, pantaloons, waistcoats and jackets, was left at Hyde Park Barracks and completed articles of clothing picked up from there. A tailor, who cut work from measurements or patterns for the women to sew, was kept at the Factory as well. The women also laundered items received from outside the Factory.[15]

In December 1843 the needle work and laundry service at the Factory came under dispute. In the Legislative Council, William Bland presented a petition 'signed by about a thousand free females' requesting the Council adopt some measure to mitigate the difficulty they experienced in procuring employment due to competition from the women in the Female Factory.[16]

The petition was considered in the Council the following day. Bland moved that the petition be presented to Governor Gipps for his consideration to expediently administer relief. William Charles Wentworth seconded the motion, arguing that the Government should do all it could within its power to prevent the Factory women from competing with respectable females who depended to a great extent on their own exertions to support their families. He contended that the factory women might be more usefully employed in dressing wool and the manufacture of cloth as they had done previously.[17]

Reverend Dr Lang reiterated Wentworth's support stating that many respectable persons were compelled by the current economic depression to depend upon the exertions of their wives and daughters for a livelihood. However he contended that the best method of enabling the factory women to regain their lost characters and become useful members of society was to distribute them to private assignment throughout the country. In this way they would be thrown into contact with 'the more moral classes of the community' and estranged 'from their old vicious habits.[18]

Richard Windeyer suggested that the petition should be sent directly to the Governor for his consideration without any motion from the Council as the Council had no direct control over the

Female Factory. Bland concurred and agreed to withdraw the motion provided the Colonial Secretary would undertake to bring the petition to Gipps' notice.[19]

The Colonial Secretary, Edward Deas Thomson, member of both the Executive and Legislative Councils, agreed to do so but expressed his regret that the matter had not initially been brought to the attention of the Executive. Expenses for the Female Factory were paid from the military chest and the Council therefore had no control over the regulation of the establishment. He stated that it was regrettable that the employment of the poor unfortunate women confined to the Factory should be to the detriment of the free portion of the community.

With his membership of both houses Thomson was often faced with a dilemma. As Colonial Secretary he had a legal responsibility to the Governor, whose instructions he was bound to carry out, but he also had a moral responsibility to the legislature.

Considering the contention that wool dressing and clothing manufacture might be a more useful form of employment, Thomson argued that operations requiring the extensive use of machinery had not been successful in the prisons and had been abandoned. As an alternative the women had been employed next in breaking stones, an activity which had come to be regarded as highly objectionable. Subsequently, at the recommendation of the Secretary of State, Gipps had ordered the women to be employed in needlework and laundry, which had proved to be very successful. When this employment was established, the price of labour was very high and the service very convenient but the labour situation had recently changed.[20]

Regarding Lang's proposal, Thomson informed the Council that since last February the number of females at the Factory had been greatly diminished. Many had been sent out to private assignment on small wages and therefore Dr Lang's recommendation for their reformation had been acted upon.[21] He had no doubt that the Governor would give the matter careful consideration if presented, but he was unwilling to recommend the subject to His Excellency. Bland then withdrew the motion.[22]

The number of inmates at the Factory was indeed in decline. Transportation to New South Wales had ceased in 1842, reducing the flow of female convicts to the Colony. When Charlotte entered the Factory at the end of September 1843 there were about 500 women and 125 children present.[23] By the end of December 1843 there were 452 women and 125 children.[24] At the beginning of June 1844 the numbers had dropped to 429 women and 94 children. Of these, 87 women were classified under colonial sentence, 313 were transported convicts, 2 were in solitary confinement and 27 were in the hospital.[25]

Around the end of May and beginning of June the Catholic Archbishop, the Reverend Dr. John Bede Polding spent 12 days at the Female factory 'with the most pitiable portion of his flock'. He gave instruction, heard their confessions and administered communion to 240 women. While Polding was in the Factory, the Bishop of Australia for the Church of England, the Right Reverend Dr. William Grant Broughton preached a sermon (which he later published) in which he inferred that the spiritual exercises performed by the Archbishop, his Clergymen and the Sisters of Charity were an attempt to convert the Protestant women in the Factory into the Roman Catholic faith. The women of the Factory stated that Broughton had 'declared that the Catholic Clergy were liars and hypocrites and whoever listened to them would be sure to go to hell with them'.[26] His words were not as dramatic as the women proclaimed but he did caution the women that there were those among them who would lead them into error and delusion in religion, placing them in danger of everlasting peril.[27]

The Catholic Clergy of course objected to these charges. They insisted that Dr Polding had given instruction only in the room devoted to the divine worship of the Catholic Church except when he visited individuals in the hospital and cells. To his knowledge he did not speak to any single Protestant woman on the subject of religion nor utter one word of a controversial nature. Anxious to discharge his duties towards the unfortunate Catholic inmates of the Factory he devoted his time to instructing them in the principles of their religion and under the influence of Divine Grace, to persuade them if possible to live up to them.[28]

A letter outlining the affront to the Catholic Church was drafted and sent to the Governor requesting that his Excellency convene a committee of inquiry consisting of two clergyman and two magistrates. One clergyman was to be appointed by Dr. Broughton and one by Dr Polding. The two magistrates, one Catholic and one Protestant, were to be appointed by the Governor.[29] But the ensuing enquiry went unreported and the dispute faded from public view.

However another controversy soon arose in the Factory. On Tuesday, 26 November a fracas developed when officers of the Factory attempted to separate children from their mothers. The Governor and Magistrates visiting the establishment at the time demanded the separation stopped and quickly restored order. The reason for the attempted separation was unknown and it appeared the Factory management had acted of its own accord.[30]

Through all this Charlotte remained quiet, applying herself diligently to her tasks in the Factory. Perhaps she was now old enough and wise enough to insulate herself from trouble. The institution also provided a modicum of security inhibiting any departure from good behaviour. Eventually she was rewarded. Having served two thirds of her sentence in good conduct, the visiting magistrate recommended the remission of the remainder of her sentence of imprisonment. Governor Gipps approved the recommendation and there being no other cause for her further detention, orders for her discharge were given on the 3rd of September 1845.[31]

Immediately prior to Charlotte's departure there were just 270 women and 95 children remaining in the institution.[32] The demography of the Factory had changed immensely since the beginning of September, 1843 when 403 of the 505 women were transported convicts and 70 were under colonial sentence.[33] By the beginning of September 1845, women not under colonial sentence numbered 198 and there were only 54 women under colonial sentence.[34] The appointment of one of the prisoners to the staff position of overseer of lunatics in 1845[35] also suggested a change in the stereotyping of inmates and heralded a new role for the institution. On the last day of March, 1848, the Female factory was 'broken up'[36] and ceased to function as a factory. The Visiting magistrate, Storekeeper and Keeper of Lunatics were transferred to the Convict, Lunatic and Invalid Establishment and by 1850 the institution was officially named the Parramatta Lunatic Asylum.[37]

Notes to Chapter 18

1. SRNSW: NRS 2373, Newcastle Gaol Entrance Books [2/2020] Reel 757, Annual Gaol Number 636; [2/2016] Reel 759 Annual Gaol Number 637.
2. Ben W. Champion, *Day, Edward Denny (1801–1876)*, ADB, MUP, 1966, Vol. 1, p.300.
3. The Maitland Mercury and Hunter River General Advertiser, Saturday, September 23, 1843, p.2, col.4; The Sydney Morning Herald, Tuesday, September 26, 1843, p.4, col.3.
4. June Reeks (compiler), They Were Here, The Convicts of Raymond Terrace, Raymond Terrace & District Historical Society Inc., Vol.2, pp.83-84.
5. AOTAS: CON35/1/2 No. 834 p.12.
6. AOTAS: CON16/1/5 No.834, p.17.
7. Op. Cit AOT CON35.
8. SRNSW: NRS 2519 Sydney and Darlinghurst Gaol Entrance Books, 1843 [2/6440], Reel 854.
9. SRNSW: NRS 1286, Returns of the Colony ('BlueBooks'), 1822-1857, Year 1843.
10. The Sydney Morning Herald (SMH), Monday, September 4, 1843 p2, col.4.
11. CO 206/85 AJCP reel PRO1174 Blue Book Statistics 1843 PFF, pp. 264-265.
12. The Australian Tuesday, October 17, 1843, pp.3-4.
13. SRNSW: NRS 1286 op.cit.; SRNSW NRS 906, Returns of the Female Factory Parramatta, Convict Registers 1829 - 1848, [4/7327], Reel 702; The Australian, Tuesday, October 3, 1843 p.2, col.6; CO 206/85 AJCP reel PRO 1174 Blue Book Statistics 1844 PFF, pp. 286-287.
14. SRNSW: NRS 2523, Sydney Gaol Description Books, [4/6302], Reel 857.
15. Carol Liston, Convict Women in the Female Factories of New South Wales, in Women Transported, Life in Australia's Convict Female Factories, p.42.
16. The Morning Chronicle Saturday, December 23, 1843, p.3, col.2.
17. SMH, Friday, December 22 , 1843, p.3, col.2.
18. Ibid.
19. Ibid.
20. Ibid.
21. Ibid.
22. The Morning Chronicle, Wednesday 27 December 1843, p.4, cols.1-2.

23 SMH, Wednesday, September 6, 1843, p.2, col.8.
24 SMH, Saturday, January 6, 1844, p.2, col.3.
25 The Australian, Wednesday, June 5, 1844, p.3, col.4.
26 SMH, Wednesday, September 18, 1844, p.1, cols.3-4.
27 The Morning Chronicle, Wednesday, June 19, 1844, p.4, cols.1-2.
28 SMH, September, 18, 1844, op.cit.
29 Ibid.
30 The Australian, Tuesday, November 26, 1844, p.3, col.4.
31 SRNSW: NRS 905, Colonial Secretary's Correspondence 1843 to 1847, Letter 45/6389, [4/2688].
32 SMH, Wednesday, September 10, 1845 p.3, col.5.
33 SMH, September 6, 1843, op.cit.
34 SMH, September 10, 1845, op.cit.
35 SRNSW: NRS 906, Returns of the Female Factory Parramatta, Convict Registers 1829 - 1848, [4/7327], Reel 702.
36 CO 206/90 AJCP reel PRO1176, Blue Book Statistics, pp330- 331, 1848 PFF.
37 Annette Salt, *These Outcast Women – The Parramatta Female Factory 1821 – 1848,* , Hale & Ironmonger 1984, p.119.

Chapter 19

Free Again

On 12 January 1844 John Campbell was granted a Ticket of Leave.[1] Almost three years later, on 9 December 1846, his period of transportation expired. A notice in the Hobart Town Gazette informed him that he could collect his Certificate of Freedom on or after that date by application at the office of the Comptroller-General of Convicts, Hobart Town or at the office of a Police Magistrate in the interior.[2]

John was now free again and at liberty to return to New South Wales. He wasted little time and on 5 January 1847 he took passage on the brig *Louisa* arriving in Sydney on the 12th of January.[3] Charlotte had been free for over a year. Reunited they returned to the Hunter River to re-establish themselves as tenant farmers along the Scotch Creek on the Lidney Estate, five kilometres down river from Morpeth.

The Lidney Estate of 2,000 acres had been granted in favour of Francis Shortt in December 1823 by the Governor, Sir Thomas Brisbane.[4] However after only six years in the colony, Shortt died in 1828 at the age of 49 years. At the time of his death he was at the residence of Simeon Lord, Macquarie Place Sydney. As executor of the deceased, Lord administered his estate later claiming a Deed of Grant for the Lidney Estate[5] which was eventually awarded to him on 19th July 1838.[6] The grant was described as:

> Two thousand acres in the County of Northumberland, parish of Alnwick; commencing at the north-west corner and bounded on the west by the east boundary of Dr Moran's farm, bearing south by compass 238 chains 30 links, and a continued south line of 20 chains ; on the south by an east line by compass of 80 chains; on the east by a north line

of 20 chains and the west to the boundaries of West's, Eale's, and Jacob's lands, being a north line by compass of 221 chains and 30 links to the River Hunter; and on the north by the River Hunter to the north-west corner aforesaid.[7]

Lord died in 1840 and the Estate was purchased by Edwin Hickey who, with his brother William, owned the Osterly Estate on the opposite side of the river. Under Hickey's ownership, John and Charlotte took out a tenancy on Lot 27, fronting onto the west side of Scotch Creek. The farm, about 30 acres in area, contained more than 20 acres of arable land and was well placed on the road which ran along the west side of the creek.

Lidney Estate contained mostly cleared farming blocks of rich alluvial land in the most fertile part of the Hunter district. In an effort to prosper, the farmers during the first half of the 19th century attempted to grow a great variety of crops, selecting the most suitable species by trial and error. Lucerne, maize, sugar cane, cotton, barley, wheat, oats, tobacco, millet, vegetables and potatoes were grown. Vineyards and orchards were planted. Pigs, beef and dairy cattle, horses and fowls were raised.[8]

From the early days of farming in the district, dairy cattle were an important necessity for milk products. A small dairy farm usually had a herd of ten or twelve cows and crops were specifically grown for fodder or pasture. A non dairy farm would most likely have a cow or two to provide milk for its inhabitants.

On its eastern side, Lidney adjoined Millers Forest originally occupied by Vicars Jacob. Lidney was often referred to as being in or part of Millers Forest but the two estates developed separately. By the 1860s, the settlers at Millers Forest owned their farms whereas a single landowner held Lidney and leased the land to tenant farmers on an annual basis. This difference in tenure was noticeable in a number of ways. Direct ownership of the land gave the farmers incentive to maintain homes, establish gardens and improve land to a greater extent than the tenant farmers who could lose tenure through non renewal of the annual lease or the sale of the property. The difference was most evident in housing. On Lidney, the farm homes were very humble, built of slabs covered with stringy bark and their cracks filled with the same material. In many cases they had dirt floors. In Millers Forest the houses were more substantial and more comfortable.[9]

Hickey eventually sold the Lidney Estate and departed to England. Prior to his departure and the subsequent prolonged sale of his Lidney Estate in the late 1850s early 1860s, the farms were sublet at a yearly rate of from thirty shillings to three pounds per acre, the more expensive land located proximal to the river. With the railroad on one side of the estate and the Hunter River on the other side, the farms had superior infrastructure for delivering all sorts of produce to market. It was expected that rents would double over the next ten years.[10]

John and Charlotte settled into farm life, John as usual supplementing his income with proceeds from carpentry work. Another son, Robert, had been born but died at 11 months old. Memory of the turbulence in their lives settled into the past. There was purpose to their lives; freedom and stability in routine. Their past experiences had taught them how to keep out of trouble. By the 1850s they were well established on their farm at Lidney. John Norris and Sarah Elizabeth had grown to an age where they were able to help their parents with the farm and household chores. But circumstances beyond their control soon impinged on their tranquillity.

Christopher Walsh, a tenant on a neighbouring farm at Lidney, was accused of brutally murdering his wife Mary in a drunken, frenzied attack, on the night of Thursday, 23rd of March 1854.[11] Walsh was a farmer of considerable means. The couple had four small children and his wife was expecting their fifth child at the time of her death. Several people from the area, including Charlotte, provided statements concerning the circumstances of Mrs Walsh's death at the inquest held at 4 o'clock on the following Friday afternoon.

During the previous three years Walsh had given way to drunkenness rather frequently. He and his wife had often quarrelled when Walsh got drunk, his inebriation making him jealous and disposed to brutal violence towards his wife. His wife also took liquor occasionally, but not often. On more than one occasion while drunk, Walsh had beaten his wife causing bruising to her body and the disfigurement of her face.

In one particular incident, after Walsh and his wife had returned from the Morpeth regatta on the evening of the 6th of March, he had beaten her, ill-used her, and turned her out of doors. The poor woman went to the house of her neighbour, John Campbell, for protection and slept with Mrs Campbell that night.

Mary's face was much disfigured, from the kicks and blows Walsh had dealt her and she showed Charlotte her legs covered with bruises. The next morning Charlotte escorted her home, but Walsh insisted that she should never again live with him, accusing her of drunkenness. Although she begged and beseeched him to let her come home he would not relent. She was forced to return to the Campbells' house where she remained for the following three nights, after which Walsh sent for her and she returned to her home.

On the evening of the twenty third, Walsh came home from Raymond Terrace in a drunken state. Prior to Walsh's arrival, Thomas Barnes, a farm servant, had returned to the house from work late that afternoon and found Mrs. Walsh drunk, and lying on the floor. He got his supper and went outside, remaining out until Walsh came home between nine and ten o'clock in the evening. Gathering Walsh's things from the boat, he brought them to the house. When he re-entered the house Walsh was standing at the table, and his wife was on the sofa. Barnes lit his pipe and seeing that Walsh was drunk, anticipated there would be a quarrel or worse. So he walked out and slept near a stump in the field about fifty rods from the house. He did not hear any noise from the house during the night and did not go to the house until the next afternoon, being away most of the day at a threshing machine.

The nearest neighbour to Walsh was Joseph Neville, living at a distance of about fourteen rods from the Walshs' house. Between one and two o'clock on Thursday night Neville and his wife were awakened by dogs barking, and heard loud cries at the Walshs' place. They could hear Walsh insisting that his wife should leave the house. His wife, in a clear, sober voice begged him to have mercy for her and her child's sake and not to murder her. Walsh was heard to say

'I've often said I'd kick the bloody bastard out of you, and now I be damned if I don't do it.'

Between each plea and vicious reply the Nevilles heard the sound of blows, as if a sack or other soft body was being struck by a weapon. Evidently from the sound of her cries, the blows were inflicted on the unfortunate woman. The sounds and noises were heard from Walsh's place for over an hour. The children were also heard crying bitterly. Neville wanted to interfere, but his wife implored him not to go. Mrs Neville thought the violence was no more than usual, Mrs Walsh having frequently in previous quarrels begged her husband not to murder her.

Next morning the Walshs' eldest daughter arrived at the Neville's place during breakfast time, and told them that her father had broken a gun over her mother's head and killed her. Neville then went to the house and saw Mrs. Walsh lying on the floor dead. Her back, shoulders, breast and legs were naked. The floor showed extensive marks of blood. Walsh was dressing himself as if he had just got out of bed. In reply to Mr. Neville's exclamation of horror he said that it was a 'pretty mess, and that his wife was dead, but that he hadn't done it; she had been out somewhere in the night, he didn't know where'. Neville, astonished at this denial, told Walsh that he had heard the row and the sound of blows during the night.

Neville quickly left the house. He went straight to the landlord, Mr Hickey and informed him of the tragic event and then went to the Raymond Terrace police. About ten o'clock in the morning chief constable Thomas Jones apprehended Walsh at his house. The blood on the floor had been partly cleaned with a mop or some rags and water. Jones observed that the woman's body exhibited extensive bruises, similar to those which would result from a blow struck with a thick stick or a gunstock. About two gallons of rum and more than £100 in money were found in the house. In a back skillion, in a dark corner, was a gun, its stock recently broken in two. On the stock was a spot of blood.

Dr John Thomas Morris examined the body and found four contused wounds on different parts of the head. He also observed bruises on the back of each arm and on the lower part of the back and injuries on other parts of the body. The injuries were consistent with blows from a gun or similar object. Death had been caused by an effusion of blood on the brain from blows delivered to the head. Morris also confirmed that the deceased was far advanced in her pregnancy. Walsh's demeanour during the inquest was most hardened and callous. He was immediately committed for trial and sent to Maitland Gaol.

The trial commenced on Monday, 24th of August 1854 before his Honour Mr Justice Therry in the Maitland Circuit Court. Mr W. A. Purefoy and Mr Peter Faucett appeared for the defence instructed by attorney, Mr Henry O' Meagher. Witnesses were Joseph and Ann Neville, Charlotte Campbell, Thomas Jones, Thomas Barnes and Dr Morris. Character witnesses for Christopher Walsh were Mr. Allan Hickey, Mr James Campbell, Mr Edwin Hickey, and Mr Samuel Dickson.

The witnesses called gave their evidence, as they had at the inquest. Mr Purefoy addressed the jury. He commented forcefully on the importance of the case and on the duty of the jury to find their verdict solely on the evidence. He expressed the opinion that although the case was presented to them as one of murder, it could be deduced from the evidence that the charge should be reduced to manslaughter. Purefoy argued that the husband had been greatly provoked which led to a sudden transport of temper and excessive violence, rather than the death being the result of a premeditated act of barbarity. Walsh had returned home sober from Raymond Terrace. Finding his wife intoxicated, her condition had driven him to madness. The evidence of Neville and his wife, that they heard the violence as late as one o'clock in the night, was of little value. People suddenly aroused from sleep had little knowledge of the real time. As well, the language heard was subject to serious doubt due to the distance between the houses.

Character witness, Allan Hickey said Walsh was an industrious man, a kind father, and an attentive husband. James Campbell and Samuel Dickson said Walsh and his wife, when in Morpeth, appeared always affectionate and familiar and Edwin Hickey gave him a character similar to that given by Allan Hickey.

Justice Therry, in summing up, instructed the jury about the distinction between murder and manslaughter. He stated that if the jury believed the evidence of Neville and his wife, they had strong proof of a deliberate act, repeated from time to time, and there was no other conclusion than that of wilful murder. If Barnes' testimony was true, he did not see how the drunken state of Walsh's wife would justify Walsh beating her till she was dead. Nor could such a death be regarded as manslaughter only. Therry read the evidence to them in full. He then repeated his previous observations, telling the jury that in his opinion their verdict must be either guilty or not guilty of murder.

The jury retired for three quarters of an hour, returned, and said they had not agreed, one member disagreeing with the opinion of the majority. The dissentient juror having explained his grounds for thinking the crime only manslaughter, Therry again explained the distinction between murder and manslaughter as applied to this case and indicated the points in the evidence bearing on the question. The jury retired again at ten minutes past nine o'clock. But by half past nine they had not agreed and were locked up. At a quarter to eleven, Justice Therry entered the court and sent for the jury. However, they were still in the same hung position. Therry patiently read over the law on the subject again and the jury shortly afterwards unanimously returned a verdict of guilty.

The prisoner called up for judgment, addressed the court in a long and incoherent speech. He said that he was innocent of any intention to kill his wife, but maintained she had been on intimate terms with Barnes. Otherwise he gave no explanation for the impulsive action which resulted in the dreadful deed he had committed that night.

In his address to the prisoner, Therry commented on the barbarous nature of the crime Walsh had committed and expressed his complete agreement with the jury's verdict. Holding out no hope of mercy in this world, he counselled the prisoner to lose no time in preparing for eternity. He then sentenced Walsh to be hanged by the neck until dead.

On Thursday morning, 28th of September at nine o'clock, Christopher Walsh was executed at Maitland gaol.[12] The prisoner, attended by The Reverend Dean Lynch through the final days of his incarceration, 'had been very quiet and penitent in his manner,' preparing for 'his death with Christian fortitude and hope'. Revd Lynch escorted the unfortunate man to the scaffold. At Walsh's request, the Reverend briefly addressed the crowd of about four hundred persons assembled, including a number of women and children. He informed the gathering that Walsh wished him to say that he had come home in a sober state but before arriving had allowed suspicions to work up a great excitement in his mind. Taking a quantity of liquor, his passion had naturally increased and under the influence of this augmented excitement he had given his wife the beating which had led to her death. He had not intended to kill her. Nor had he known of her death until the next morning. After mature consideration he had come to believe that she was virtuous and faithful to him. He deeply regretted his conduct, and entertained no animosity.

Although Walsh seemed to meet his fate with resolve, he 'suffered much in his last struggles'. The body was delivered to his friends for interment.

This distasteful episode behind them, John and Charlotte returned to their daily farm routine. But in 1857 the area was hit with three disastrous floods in quick succession during June, July and August. The last of the three floods was the worst. Before daylight on Saturday the 22nd of August the river overflowed its banks at Berry Park and almost simultaneously at the bend a little below Osterley.[13] Duckenfield and Berry Park to the west of Lidney were completely submerged and the banks of the Hunter almost completely cleared of trees. The low lying area between Duckenfield and Raymond Terrace, comprising the whole of Millers Forest including Lidney, was quickly inundated.

Residents along Scotch Creek had watched its course during the previous night and had not perceived any noticeable rise. Consequently most people in the district had gone to bed confident there would not be a problem. But during the night they were aroused by gun shots and cries of distress. When they got out of bed many found themselves up to their knees in water.

The water rose with alarming speed. One resident reported that it rose five feet in about an hour and a half. His house, being relatively higher than any of his neighbours' houses was soon filled with women and children and he was obliged to make a platform above the water line for them to stand on. However, before they were eventually rescued the water rose to a point where it covered the platform and was over their shoes.

By Saturday evening boats had picked up nearly everyone in the area and taken them to a safe place. Several persons nearly lost their lives falling into drains while making their way through the water to higher ground. One man carried his wife on his back for nearly a mile, the water up to his breast for a considerable distance.

People flooded out were relocated at various properties in the district. John Eales of Duckenfield, Mr. Humphries at Berry Park, Mrs. Parnell of Osterly and John McPherson, a farmer at Duckenfield, provided shelter and food. Their generosity was quite remarkable as many of the people given relief were not their own tenants. In particular, McPherson housed over 100 people, even giving up his bedroom to a group of women.

The most distressing part of the flood was the destruction of property. Most of the settlers had sown wheat three times during the season, but each flood had destroyed all the growing crops. An enormous amount of hay and maize had also been destroyed. In the latest flood, nearly every settler had the whole of his corn and wheat crop destroyed. As well stores of grain had been lost, whether on the straddle or stored in the house. The two earlier floods had carried away the settlers' wharves on the river bank, broken down the bridges over the creeks and made the roads impassable. For several months it had been almost impossible to get drays to any town and there was no way of getting the grain to market. But the previous floods had not reached the stored grain and it had been presumed to be safe. Now it too was lost.

All the pigs and a great number of poultry had been swept away. Almost all the cattle from the Scotch Creek were saved as they were able to swim to higher ground in the near vicinity but many died subsequently from lack of feed. Cattle in the lower part of Miller's Forest near Raymond Terrace, endeavoured to make it to the opposite bank of the river but were swept downstream in the current and lost.

The loss of personal items was also very considerable. Most people put their clothing in boxes and placed them with their most valuable articles on tables in their homes, assuming that the water as it spread out over the flat land would not rise very high. But unfortunately they were grievously mistaken. The water running through the houses rose to a level where the tables floated and overturned in the current, spilling all into the flood.

On Sunday the 23rd August, the locality was one broad expanse of water. Only the tops of houses could be seen here and there. Every person was affected to a variable extent, some much more than others, and many were entirely ruined. When the water eventually subsided everything was covered with mud and the ubiquitous smell of rotten and fermenting grain was extremely foul.

To make matters worse for John and Charlotte, Sarah, at 15 years old was seven months pregnant. She had most likely conceived around the time of the Raymond Terrace Regatta held on January 26th to celebrate the anniversary of the colony's foundation.

It had been an eventful day opened with a nine gun salute, followed by a gun fired to welcome the steamer *Fenella* loaded with passengers from Morpeth. The weather had looked threatening in the morning with drizzling rain but as the day wore on the sky brightened and the weather became more favourable.

The expanse of water at Raymond Terrace was well suited for holding a regatta, each race in full view of the spectators arrayed along the banks of the river. Throughout the day cannons were fired at intervals announcing the start or finish of races. The *Fenella*, 'a leviathon among minnows' cruised about on the river between races discharging and picking up picnic parties at Spectacle Island. At Raymond Terrace, the wharf, the public houses, and the green were thronged with pleasure seekers, all determined to be amused. Flags flying on the wharf, the public house and at other points along the river added to the gaiety of the scene.

Five match races were held for oared boats and skiffs and three matches for sailing vessels. The eighth and final race was a four man gig and dinghy race in which the bowman of the gig had to catch the man in the dinghy within 20 minutes of the start. The race provided a great deal of entertainment, the dinghy dodging and weaving around boats on the river, the less manoeuvrable gig in hot pursuit. After a succession of amusing dodges, towards the end of the allotted time, the dinghy had seriously puzzled its pursuer. The canon announced the end of the race and victory to the dinghy sailor.[14]

The day had been a great success. No disturbances of any kind were reported or cases of inebriation so frequently seen on holidays. It was hoped that this, the first Raymond Terrace Regatta, would be the precursor of many to come. However, for John and Charlotte, the delightful day was now at the end of August a mere memory overshadowed by the three floods since the regatta and Sarah's current predicament.

Notes to Chapter 19

1. AOTAS: CON31/1/8 p.117; CON35/1/1 p.131; Hobart Town Gazette, Friday, 12 January 1844, pp45 & 46; Cornwall Chronicle, Launceston, Wednesday, January 17, 1844, p.4, col.6.
2. Hobart Town Gazette, Tuesday December 1, 1846, Government Notice No.211 Colonial Secretary's Office 18th November 1846, p.1378; Cornwall Chronicle, Launceston, Saturday 5 December 1846, p.948, col.3.
3. Graeme Broxam, Shipping Arrivals and Departures Tasmania, Vol.3, 1843-1850, Roebuck 1998, p.86; SRNSW: NRS 1291, Colonial Secretary, Shipping Reports, Vol.1, 1847, [4/5231], Reel 1274.
4. The Australian, Tuesday, April 3, 1838, Supplement p.2, col.6.
5. Ibid.
6. NSW LPI E243946 Vol.142, Fol.237, Ewan Wallace Cameron.
7. The Australian, April 3, 1838, op.cit.
8. Cynthia Hunter, Raymond Terrace and District, History and Heritage, Raymond Terrace District Historical Society Inc., 1996, p.100.
9. Ibid.
10. SMH, Thursday, December 18, 1862, p.8, col.4.
11. The Maitland Mercury & Hunter River General Advertiser (MM&HRGA), Wednesday, March 29, 1854, p.2, col.2; MM&HRGA, Wednesday, August 30, 1854, p.2, cols.1-2.
12. MM&HRGA, Saturday, September 30, 1854, p.2, col.4.
13. MM&HRGA, September 12, 1857, p.2, col.1.
14. MM&HRGA, Saturday, January 24, 1857, p. 1, col.1; Tuesday, January 27, 1857, p.2, col.3; Thursday, January 29, p.2, col.3.

Chapter 20

Final Trials

The first of the next generation arrived on 24 October 1857. He was named Angus Campbell. After the birth, Sarah brought a charge of affiliation against Dugald McGregor, the father of the child. The Raymond Terrace Bench convicted McGregor and ordered him to pay a weekly maintenance of 10s retrospective to the date of the child's birth.

An appeal against the conviction was made in February 1858 on the basis that the magistrate had no power under the act to grant retrospective payment and secondly, had no power to order immediate payment of costs or imprisonment in default of payment. The Chairman concurred in the first objection but declined making an order and the court was adjourned sine die[1]

The case was resumed in the Maitland Police Court on 26th of February before Major Crummer, Mr Davidson, Mr A. Dodds and Mr A. Lang. Sarah Campbell was represented by Mr Minter and Dugald McGregor by Mr Chambers.[2]

Sarah, described as a 'sun kissed', respectable looking young girl of 17 years, deposed that she had known the defendant for 3 years. Their first intimacy arose in January 1857 at Scotch Creek. The defendant used to visit her parents, and promised to marry her. Before the child was born she told him of her condition but he would not speak to her. Afterwards, when she went to his house for support, she was told he was not at home, even though she believed he was. Cross examined, Sarah claimed that she had never walked along Scotch Creek at night with anybody but the defendant. She remembered being at a marriage in October 1856, with one of the Mitchams, but came home in the day time. The night the defendant seduced her she had not consented, but struggled to get free. His promise of marriage had influenced her.[3]

Witnesses gave statements in support of the girl. George Lancaster, of Raymond Terrace, remembered seeing the girl and defendant together one night about 9 pm on the Scotch Creek. He heard the girl ask McGregor to let her go. He had also seen them together once before alone in a paddock talking.

James Wells, a boy of 14, stated that he saw the girl and the defendant at his father's house. They had gone into an outhouse with a light and he heard McGregor say 'Will you? do!' to which the girl replied, 'No, Dugald I won't,' and she 'sung out for Mrs Wells'. About a month later he saw them at Campbell's place walking along the side of the road. Her brother John was with him at that time. He never saw any other man with her.

Sarah's brother John said he remembered the defendant going home with his sister from the Mitchams. Charlotte, Sarah's mother, said she knew the defendant 'to her sorrow'. He was in the habit of visiting her house, but discontinued coming in February 1857. At the end of January, she had sent 'her girl on a message' to the Mitchams and the defendant was there then. Before the confinement of her daughter, she had gone to Dugald who after a few minutes' hesitation said he knew nothing about the state of her daughter.[4]

Mr Chambers addressed the Bench for the defence and called three witnesses, none of whom could prove anything very damaging against the girl. Consequently the Bench ordered McGregor to commence paying 7s weekly, in advance, for the support of the child and all costs.[5]

Angus was baptised on 13 June 1858 in the Church of England at Raymond Terrace. At the same ceremony, another child, John Pywell, the son of Mary Ann Pywell, a 15 year old girl was also baptised. The father of this child was 44-year old John Henry Hawley, a dealer, who lived in Raymond Terrace. He was married and had two children of his own and three step-children.

McGregor honoured the required maintenance payment until 10th of February 1860 when he suddenly stopped payment. Sarah was obliged to sue for future maintenance.[6] Her case was heard at the Court House, East Maitland, on Tuesday the 29th of May. The bench ordered McGregor to pay 5s per week, in advance, from that date. He was also ordered to pay professional costs of £1 1s and court costs.

Later that year Charlotte and Sarah became embroiled in another controversy. Elizabeth Martin, a neighbour, and her daughter Bridget were indicted for concealing the birth of a child, at Lidney, on the 29th of August. The case was heard before the District Judge, Mr Owen at the Maitland Quarter Sessions on the Monday the 5th of November. Charlotte and Sarah Campbell, John Buckley, Allen Hickey and Joseph Wright were called as witnesses. The defendants pleaded not guilty and were represented by Mr. Simpson instructed by attorney Mr. Henry O'Meagher.

Apparently neighbours about Lidney Park had noticed that Bridget Martin, who was naturally a very slight girl, was getting very stout. When a neighbour asked if she was in the family-way, she denied it, saying that 'she wished every young woman was as clear of it as she was, for that she was as clear of it as the angels in Heaven'. But by the 13th of August, Bridget's health seemed to have deteriorated to a very bad state. Charlotte made several enquiries about her health, but Bridget's mother told her that the only thing wrong with her daughter was a headache and a boil on her leg.

On the 4th of September Charlotte went to the Martin's house with Bridget's father. She told Mrs. Martin there were rumours her daughter had given birth to a child. Elizabeth replied, 'thank God if it is so it was not by a married man'. This was possibly a back handed reference to the children born to Sarah Campbell and, in particular, Mary Ann Pywell.

Bridget called Mrs Campbell into her bedroom to speak to her alone and pleaded 'for God sake leave me alone'. Charlotte replied 'tell the truth, for if you do not by fair means you will be made to do so by foul means'. Bridget then broke down and told Charlotte she did not know what her mother had done with the child. Mrs Martin was in the next room, separated from the bedroom by only a few wooden slabs. A short time later she came in from the garden with a box containing the body of the child. It was wrapped up in two pieces of checked shirt. Its mouth was filled with earth.

Acting on information from the witnesses, the Chief Constable from Raymond Terrace visited Mrs. Martin on the 13th of September and asked her if a birth had taken place in her family. She affirmed that it had. When asked where the body was buried she led the constable outside to an onion bed. Pointing to a specific spot, she said, 'The body is buried there'. She told the constable her daughter had known she was pregnant, because she had felt the child move one day before she attended a threshing machine. After that she had not felt the child move again. She had been confined on Wednesday the previous fortnight and about eight or nine o'clock in the morning, the child was delivered, premature and stillborn. Mrs Martin had concealed the body in the bed-room, and had told no one about it, not even her husband.

Consequently, Allen Hickey, on behalf of the landlord, wrote to the coroner and an inquest was held. Being ashamed of her situation, Bridget had made no preparation for the birth of the child, but had told the father of the child that she was pregnant. He advised her to tell her friends about it. Joseph Wright said that he knew that the defendant was pregnant, but was not acquainted with any other of the circumstances.

The jury deliberated for only a quarter of an hour, returning a verdict of not guilty for Bridget Martin who was accordingly discharged. Elizabeth Martin was found guilty with a recommendation for mercy. The judge, in sentencing Elizabeth, said he approved of the recommendation for mercy since the case was not of such a nature as to require him to impose a heavy sentence. Therefore, to mark the power of the court in such cases, he should only pass the very lenient sentence of one month's imprisonment.[7]

Notes to Chapter 20

1. SMH, Monday, February 15, 1858, p.2, col.5.
2. Northern Times, (Newcastle), Saturday February 27, 1858, p.2
3. Ibid.
4. Ibid.
5. Ibid.
6. MM&HRGA, Thursday, May 31, 1860, p.2, col.4.
7. MM&HRGA, Thursday, 8 November 1860, p. 2, col.4.

Chapter 21

The Past Dismissed

As John and Charlotte passed into old age, their son John Norris took charge of the farm which had become principally a dairying enterprise. The farm carried about a dozen cows and milking took place wherever the cows happened to be standing, his stool and bucket carried to each cow. The land was worked with horses and ploughs; crops of broom millet for cash, potatoes for human consumption, and lucerne and maize for cattle feed were grown.[1]

The district was well known for the yield and quality of its lucerne (alfalfa) crop and the hay it produced, an important feed for dairy cattle. Several men wielding long blade scythes harvested the crop, cutting it into swathes and leaving it to dry. Before the advent of bailing, the hay was gathered loose in wagons and stored in stacks for later distribution.[2]

There was, notwithstanding the hard work demanded from the land, time for recreational activity. John Norris became a prominent cricketer in the district. As an example of his skill, in a match between the Raymond Terrace team and the Miller's Forest and Lidney Club on the Queen's birthday in May 1862, he led the Miller's Forest-Lidney to victory scoring 46 of their 100 runs in the two inning match to defeat the opposition by 2 runs with two wickets in hand.[3] Later he played for the Tarro club, his stonewalling tactics pulling the team through many matches.

On Christmas eve 1862, at the age of 23 years old, John Norris married Mary Ann Pywell in Morpeth. They were married according to the rites of the Primitive Methodist Church in the house of the Reverend George James. Between 1864 and 1884, John Norris and Mary Ann had eleven children; four girls and seven boys. Mary Ann's child John, born out of wedlock in 1857, was raised as a Pywell.

Prior to their marriage Mary Ann had worked as a servant on farms at Miller's Forest. She had arrived in New South Wales on the

25th of February 1855 at the age of twelve with her father Thomas aged 40, a brother Thomas, 14, and a sister Rachel, 10. They were from Weldon, Northamptonshire, England, and had come to Australia as immigrants on the ship *Bengal*.[4] Shortly after their arrival, they moved north to the Hunter River. The children were without their mother, their father's wife, Sarah Barwell, having died in Little Weldon in November 1852.

Mary Ann was well known in the district for her buttermaking and she regularly took her basket of butter and eggs to Newcastle on the Steamer *'Planet'* to sell to special customers.[5] Her butter making technique followed a centuries old process, laborious but proven. Milk was placed in large dishes and left to stand overnight. The cream would rise to the surface where it was skimmed off and hand churned into butter. In the late 1800s, the centrifugal cream separator was introduced dramatically speeding up the butter-making process by eliminating the slow procedure of letting cream rise naturally. The separation was accomplished on the farm, and the cream shipped to the local butter factory.

Mary Ann and her sister-in-law Sarah became good friends working together on the farm. In 1864 Sarah gave birth to a child she registered as Charlotte Mair, the father's name given as Alexander Mair. Sarah married Alexander in West Maitland on 20 December 1865 and they had five children; three girls and two boys including the prenuptial Charlotte. About 1870 they left Raymond Terrace, stopping for a year or so in Murrurundi and eventually settling at Gulgong, north of Mudgee, New South Wales.

Angus Campbell, Sarah's first born son, was raised in the home of his grandparents, mother and uncle. He retained the Campbell name and grew to be a fine young man. In 1884 he and his wife Ellen Masters settled on a property at Bodangora, north of Wellington, New South Wales. Together they raised ten children. Harold and Wallace (two of their five sons), and Angus' half brother, William (Bill) Mair, served in the Australian Imperial Force during the First World War, the Great War of 1914 – 1918. Harold and Bill saw service on the Gallipoli Peninsula and all three men saw action on the Western Front. Sergeant Harold Campbell failed to return from the war. He was killed in action on Anzac Ridge in the Ypres Salient, Belgium 7th October 1917.[6]

John and Charlotte's personal history faded from view as the lives of succeeding generations took precedent and their children and grandchildren became successful and respected Australians. Time dimmed the memory of the inauspicious and unpleasant events in their past. John died at Lidney on 31st of July 1870. Fredrick Ephraim Cook, a farmer at Lidney was the informant. The death certificate simply stated he had died of natural causes after being ill for 14 days. He was buried on the second of August in the Morpeth cemetery, with Primitive Methodist minister, William Kingdom presiding over the ceremony.

Charlotte lived for a further eight years passing away on the first of August 1878 at Scotch Creek, Miller's Forest. Her death resulted from an inflammation of the liver and bowels which she had endured over the last nine days of her life. The Minister and witnesses at her burial were John Foggon of the Primitive Methodist Church, Andrew Tulip and Allen Hickey. Her son John was the informant but contrary to her husband's death record her father's name (and therefore her maiden name) was recorded as Dixon.

Was this an innocent mistake or a deliberate cover-up? The latter of the two possibilities is the more likely. Beginning with the anti transportation movement in the late 1830s the convict establishment in Australia was branded as brutal and degrading, both overseers and convicts lacking in moral compass. The stamp of brutality, degradation and lack of morality cannot be applied to all officials, masters and convicts, but the detestable aspects of the system and the people within it were emphasised and indelibly imprinted on people's minds as the norm. Beneficial results were disregarded. Little was said about those men and women who, through serving out their term of transportation, had paid their debt, become free citizens and disappeared into the fabric of Australian society. They built roads and buildings, established farms, became merchants, government officials, lawyers and politicians. But their productivity, experiences and contributions which helped build and advance Australia to the democratic, commercially successful and free society we know today, largely remained unacknowledged.

With the cessation of transportation to New South Wales in 1840 and Tasmania in 1853 and an increase of immigrants, the proportion of convicts and those with convict heritage to free settlers in society diminished. By the 1860s a feeling of shame regarding Australia's convict beginnings was well developed and with it embarrassment for those with convict ancestry. The rigid moral code of the Victorian era, firmly entrenched in the hearts and minds of the population, aggravated the stigma; a concerted attempt was made to wash away the pervading stain[7] of convict history. The past was conveniently forgotten or facts distorted, family stories fabricated, connections disconnected.

Mary Ann told her children and grandchildren that John had initially tried and failed at sheep farming in the Morpeth area, so he returned to carpentry and was also an overseer of convicts. He had acted kindly towards the convicts. Charlotte would bake damper for him to give to them secretly, his employer often questioning him about the large amount of flour he used from his allowance.[8] There was no mention of Charlotte's convict past. It was assumed that both had arrived as free settlers in New South Wales, establishing themselves in the Hunter district after their marriage in Sydney. John's wrongful conviction and consequent servitude in Tasmania was conveniently forgotten or hidden under the guise of his kindness towards the convicts in his charge.

Over the past sixty years archival documents have gradually become more and more accessible to the general public. Facts about the more than 137,000 men and almost 25,000 women transported are constantly being revealed. Gradually the contribution of this group of people in building Australia is being recognised and the birthstain removed. Now, in recognition of their achievements, there is generally pride in having an early Australian convict in the family tree.

Transportation was a means of populating the fledgling colony with a cheap work force as well as diminishing a growing population driven to crime by poverty and inequality. It also provided a means to rapidly increase the colony's population as a deterrent to any would be usurper. Those transported were mainly young, their crimes in general of no great significance other than representing a will to survive in a world of poverty. A product of their environment in Britain, transportation to Australia gave them a chance to improve their condition. Charlotte was a part of this history.

John, a victim of the Highland clearances in Scotland, sought a better life in Australia only to be caught up in the machinations of the convict establishment in the colony and become a convict himself. They both led turbulent lives but their strength of character carried them through all the adversity to that better life for themselves and for their descendants. They lie in unmarked graves in the Methodist Section of the Morpeth cemetery.[9] May they rest in peace.

Notes to Chapter 21

1. Royal W. Campbell, 'The Campbells Are Still Coming', *Raymond Terrace and District Historical Society Bulletin*, Vol.7, No.2, March 1984, p.11.
2. Ibid.
3. MM&HRGA, May 27, 1862, p.2, col.5.
4. SRNSW: NRS 5316, Persons on bounty ships (Agent's Immigrant Lists), 1838-96, [4/4792], Reel 2137; SRNSW: NRS 5317, Persons on bounty ships to Sydney, Newcastle, and Moreton Bay (Board's Immigrant Lists) [4/4944], Reel 2468.
5. Royal Campbell, op.cit., p.11.
6. Maurice Campbell & Graeme Hosken, Four Australians at War, Letters to Argyle 1914-1919, Kangaroo Press, Kenthurst, M.S.W., 1996.
7. for a complete analysis of the shame about convict origins and ancestry the reader is directed to the Babette Smith, *Australia's Birthstain*, Allen & Unwin, Crows Nest, 2009.
8. Royal Campbell, op.cit., p.8.
9. Raymond Terrace Pioneer Cemetery, List of persons whose deaths have been recorded at Raymond Terrace Court House but have been interred in cemeteries other than Raymond Terrace, Raymond Terrace Historical Society Inc., 1992.

Acknowledgements

The support of the following people and organisations is greatly appreciated: Barbara Otterman, whose research uncovered significant events in the story; Margaret Bowering for her guidance and encouragement; Lynne Palmer for research assistance; Lyn and John Campbell for information about Sarah Elizabeth Campbell and other pertinent facts; Graham Campbell for photographs of John Campbell and Sarah Elizabeth Campbell; Fiona Campbell for photographs of John Norris Campbell and Sarah Elizabeth Campbell; the excellent staff and facilities of State Records, New South Wales, Kingswood and former NSW Archives Office at the Rocks Sydney, in particular Fabian Schiavo; the staff and resources of the State Library and Mitchell Library, New South Wales; Parramatta Family History Centre – Beth Matthews; Raymond Terrace Library, Family History Section – Elaine Hall; the staff and resources of the Tasmanian Archive and Heritage Office; the staff and resources of the Queensland State Archives; Family History Resources and staff at the State Library of Western Australia; John MacDonald for his knowledge and assistance in Golspie and Rogart, Scotland; Geordie and Irene Jack for their hospitality and guidance in Golspie; the staff and services of the National Library of Scotland and National Archives of Scotland; the staff and resources of the Lincolnshire Archives, Lincoln, England.

Also the internet resources of Trove-National Library of Australia for its online newspaper archive; Google digital books for - Pharmacopoeia Chirurgica; Elizabeth Fry's 'Observations'; John Howard's 'State of Prisons'; Sir John Sinclair's 'General Report of the Agricultural State'; Captain John Henderson's 'General View of the Agriculture of the County of Sutherland 1812 and 1815'; The Scottish Jurist Vol. IV, 1832; John Dunmore Lang's, 'Historical and Statistical Account of New South Wales'; and James Loch's 'Account of improvements on the Sutherland Estate'.

Bibliography

Adam, R.J., *Sutherland Estate Management: Papers*, Scottish History Society, Edinburgh, 1972.

Alexander, Alison, *Tasmania's Convicts, How Felons Built a Free Society*, Allen & Unwin, Crows Nest, 2010.

Allen, Thomas, *History of the County of Lincolnshire*, Saunders, London & Lincoln, 1834.

Atkinson, Jeff, *Mary Proctor, Convict, Pioneer and Settler*, Rosenberg, Dural, 2005.

Bach, John, *A Maritime History of Australia*, Nelson, Melbourne, 1976.

Bagwell, P.S., *The Transport Revolution from 1770*, Batsford, London, 1974.

Bangor-Jones, Malcolm, *Sheep Farming in Sutherland in the Eighteenth Century*, The Agricultural Historical Review, Vol. 50, II.

Bateson, C., *Australian Shipwrecks - vol 1 1622-1850*. Sydney, AH and AW Reed, 1971.

Bateson, C., *The Convict Ships 1787-1868*, Reed, Sydney, 1974.

Bentley, David, *English Criminal Justice in the Nineteenth Century*, Hambledon, London, 1998.

Bigge, Thomas, *Report of the Commissioner of Inquiry into the state of the Colony of New South Wales*, House of Commons, 1822.

Bolt, Frank, *Old Hobart Town Today: A photographic essay*, Waratah, Hobart, 1981.

Boyce, James, *Van Diemen's Land*, Black, Melbourne, 2008.

Brand, Ian, *The Convict Probation System, Van Diemen's Land 1839 to 1854*, Blubber Head Press, Hobart 1990.

Broxam, Graeme, *Shipping Arrivals and Departures Tasmania*, Vol.3,1843-1850, Roebuck 1998.

Campbell, Royal W., *The Campbells Are Still Coming*, Raymond Terrace and District Historical Society Bulletin, Vol.7, No.2, March, 1984.

Chambers, J.D. and & Mingay, G.E., *The Agricultural Revolution, 1750 – 1880*, Batsford, London 1966.

Clapson, R.H.R.E. & Stockdale, M., *Roads Coaches and Carriers in Barton*

Before 1900, Fathom Writers, Barton-on-Humber, 2009.

Cunningham, Peter, *Two Years in New South Wales, A Series of Letters, Comprising Sketches of the Actual State of Society in that Colony; of its Peculiar Advantages to Emigrants; of its Topography, Natural History, &c. &c.* Henry Colbourn, London, 1827.

De Freycinet, Louis, *Reflections on New South Wales 1788-1839*, Translated for Freycinet's *'Voyage autour du monde* (Paris 1824 – 1844)' by Thomas Cullity, Hordern house, 2001.

Dodgshon, Robert, *The Age of the Clans, The Highlands from Somerlad to the Clearances*, Birlinn, 2002.

Donaldson, James, *Fairwell to the Heather,* Hawthorn, Vic., 2006.

Eastgate, M., *A Guide to the pre-Separation Population Index, Moreton Bay Region 1824 to 1859*, Queensland Family History Society, 1990.

Elkin, A.P., *Morpeth And I,* Sydney : Australasian Medical Pub. Co., 1937

Fredman, L.E. & Guilford, E. (eds), Journal of Hunter Valley History, Vol.2 No.2, Hunter Valley Publications, Newcastle, 1988.

Gates, William, *Recollections of Life In Van Diemen's Land,* Australian Historical Monographs, George Mackaness (ed.) D.S.Ford, Sydney 1961, Part I.

Gowlland, Ralph W., Troubled Asylum, R.W.Gowlland, Lawitta, via New Norfolk, Tas 7450, c1981.

Hammond, J.L. & B., *The Village Labourer,* Vol. 1, Longmans, Green & Co., London, 1948.

Hay, D. and Snyder, F., (eds), *Policing and Prosecution in Britain 1750-1850,* Clarendon, Oxford, 1989.

Henderson, Capt. John, *General View of the Agriculture of the County of Sutherland, with observations of the means of its improvement*, M. McMillan, London, 1812.

Hendrikson, Gay, *Myth and Reality*, in *Women Transported, Life in Australia's Convict Female Factories,* Parramatta Heritage Centre and University of Western Sydney, 2008.

Hunter, Cynthia, *Out of the Closet, Maitland's water stories,* Maitland City Heritage Group, Maitland, 2006.

Hunter, Cynthia, *Raymond Terrace and District, History and Heritage,*

Raymond Terrace District Historical Society Inc., 1996.

Hunter, James, *The Making of a Crofting Community*, Donald, Edinburgh, 1976.

Keneally, Thomas, *Australians, Origins to Eureka*, Allen & Unwin, Crows Nest, Paperback edition 2010.

Lang, John Dunmore, *An Historical and Statistical Account of New South Wales*, Cochrane & McCrone, 1834.

Liston, Carol, *Convict Women in the Female Factories of New South Wales*, in *Women Transported, Life in Australia's Convict Female Factories*, Parramatta Heritage Centre and University of Western Sydney, 2008.

Loch, James, *Dates and Documents relating to the Family and Property of Sutherland*, 1859

Loch, James, *An Account of Improvements On The Estates of the Marquess of Stafford*, Longman, Hurst, Rees, Orme & Brown, London, 1820.

Lower, Arthur R.M., *Colony to Nation, A History of Canada*, Longmans Canada, 1964.

MacDonald John, *Rogart, The story of a Sutherland Crofting Parish*, John MacDonald, Rogart 2002.

MacMillan, David S., *Scotland and Australia 1788 – 1850: Emigration, Commerce and Investment*, Clarendon, Oxford, 1967.

MacMillan, David., *Scottish Enterprise in Australia, 1798-187', Studies in Scottish Business History*, Peter L.Payne (ed.), Cass &Co., London, 1967.

Morgan, Sharon, *Land Settlement in Early Tasmania: Creating an Antipodean England*, p19 and 21, Cambridge University Press, Melbourne, 1992.

Nicholson, Ian H., *Shipping Arrivals & Departures, Tasmania, 1803 – 1833*, Roebuck, 1983.

Osborn, Margaret, *A Forest No More, A Short History of Millers Forest*.

Reeks, June, (compiler), *They Were Here, The Convicts of Raymond Terrace*, Raymond Terrace & District Historical Society Inc.

Richards, Eric, *The Highland Clearances*, Birlinn, 2008.

Richardson, T.L., *The Agricultural Labourers' Standard of Living in Lincolnshire, 1790-1840: Social Protest and Public Order*, The Agriculture History Review, Vol. 41, I.

Robson, Leslie L., *A History of Tasmania*, Oxford University Press, Melbourne, 1983.

Roe, Michael, *The Quest For Authority in Eastern Australia,1835-1851*, Melbourne University Press, Parkville Vic.,1965.

Rogers, Allan, *A History of Lincolnshire*, Darwen Finlayson, Henley on Thames, 1970.

Sainty, M.R. & Johnson, K.A. (eds.), *Census of New South Wales, November 1828*, Sydney : Library of Australian History, 1980.

Salt, Annette, *These Outcast Women – The Parramatta Female Factory 1821 – 1848,* , Hale & Ironmonger 1984.

Schrauwers, Albert, *Union is Strength: W.L. Mackenzie, the Children of Peace, and the Emergence of Joint Stock Democracy in Upper Canada*. University of Toronto Press, Toronto 2009

Sinclair, Sir John (ed.), *Statistical Account of Scotland,* (20 Vols.) William Creech, Edinburgh, 1791 -1799.

Smith, Babette, *A Cargo of Women*, Allen & Unwin, 2nded., 2008.

Smith, Babette, *Australia's Birthstain,* Allen & Unwin, 2nd ed., 2009.

Swinerton, H.H. And Kent, P.E., *The Geology of Lincolnshire,* Lincolnshire Naturalists' Union, Lincoln, 1981.

Tindley, Anne Marie, *The Sutherland Estate, ,c.1200-1920: a Short History*, Glasgow Caledonian University, 2009.

Weaver, Rosemary, *Kirton In Lindsey, Historical Aspects, The Life and Times of the House of Correction*, Kirton in Lindsey Writer's Group, Belton Ltd., Gainsborough, 1993.

Weidenhofer, Margaret, *The Convict Years; Transportation and the penal system 1788-1868*, Lansdowne, Melbourne, 1973.

Wilson Grant, Margaret, *The Golspie Story*, The Northern Times Limited, 1983.

Wilson, J., *Pharmacopoeia Chirugica,* Cox, London, 1811.

Wright, Neil R., *Linclolnshire Towns and Industry, 1700 - 1914,* History of Lincolnshire Vol. XI, History of Lincolnshire Committee, Lincoln, 1982.

Index

Abercrombie, brigantine, 214, 215, 216, 219, 228, 232
Aberscross, 14, 15, 18, 19, 20, 23, 28, 30, 31, 32, 34, 35, 36, 39, 40, 41, 43
  removals, 39
Arthur, George Sir
  Lieutenant Governor, 67, 69, 223, 228
Australian Company
  of Edinburgh & Leith, 43, 45, 48, 49, 50, 62, 64, 67
Barnes, Thomas, 110, 112, 113, 118
Battley, Robert, 236, 237, 238
bere, 32, 36, 37
black houses, 30
Black, Mary. *Wyer, Mary*
Blain, Robert, 204, 207, 208, 209, 211, 213
Bloodsworth, James, 148, 167
Brisbane, Sir Thomas, 182, 183, 246
Broughton, Reverend Dr. William Grant, 242
Buffalo, ship, 219, 220, 223, 224
Campbell, Alexander, 34
Campbell, Angus, 257, 262
Campbell, Captain David, 18
Campbell, Charlotte (Dawson), 194, 195, 198, 232, 237, 249, 251, 258, 259
  death, 263
  description, 232, 239
  Sydney gaol, 239
Campbell, Donald, 35
Campbell, Donald (senior), 34, 35, 36, 39
Campbell, George, 34
Campbell, John, 13, 14, 16, 26, 35, 39, 41, 43, 50, 51, 60, 65, 66, 67, 69, 70, 187, 192, 193, 194, 198, 201, 205, 206, 207, 208, 209, 213, 214, 216, 220, 228, 231, 232, 236, 249, 262
  arrival in Australia, 62
  assignment, 231
  Certificate of Freedom, 246
  conduct record, 232, 234
  death, 263
  description, 216, 228
  indent, 214, 219
  petition, 205, 208, 214
  probation, 229
  Ticket of Leave, 246
Campbell, John (senior), 34, 35, 36, 41
Campbell, John Norris, 239, 248, 258, 261
  birth, 204
Campbell, Robert (merchant), 142
Campbell, Robert (son of John & Charlotte), 248
Campbell, Robert Jr of Bligh Street, 148, 193, 195
Campbell, Sarah Elizabeth, 239, 248, 257
Canada
  Baldwin, Robert, 221, 224
  Mackenzie, William Lyon, 221, 224
  Papineau, Louis Joseph, 221, 224
  rebels, 220, 221, 222, 223, 225, 226
  reform, 221, 222, 228
Cape Town, 58, 60
Casey, Dr Gavin, 234
City of Edinburgh, ship, 48
  attempted escape of prisoners, 161
convict
  food, 230
  punishment, 230

work, 163, 229
Cotter, Edward, 205, 206
Countess Elizabeth of Sutherland, 17, 18, 19, 20, 21, 22, 28, 40
Cowper, William, 186, 196
Darling, Sir Ralph, 148, 177
Davis, James, 173, 174, 175
Dawson, Charlotte, 72, 73, 74, 75, 76, 81, 85, 91, 93, 94, 108, 119, 126, 133, 155, 174, 177, 193, 232
   assignment, 148, 150, 180, 192
      transfer, 183, 186
   birth, 73
   Certificate of Freedom, 231
   description, 72
   Female Factory, 170, 175, 180
   Lincoln Castle, gaol, 99, 109
   sentence, 90
   Sydney gaol, 173, 180
   trial at Kirton in Lindsey, 88
   trial costs, 93
   trial verdict, 89
Day, Edward Denny, 236
Deal, 52, 129, 132, 138
Delaney, Lawrence, 151, 152, 154, 175
Delaney, Margaret, 148, 150, 151, 153, 154, 175, 180, 183
Donnough, John, 214, 216, 229, 232
Dornoch, 15, 19, 20, 23, 35, 39, 41, 43, 229
Elgin, John, 13, 16, 205, 208, 236, 237, 238
   description, 238
Elsham, 72, 77
emigration, 17, 43, 44
   to Australia, 44, 45
equator, 56
Falconer, Cosmo, 18
Female Factory
   Moreton bay, 163

Parramatta, 150, 151, 167, 170, 171, 172, 173, 174, 175, 176, 177, 178, 185, 187, 192, 193, 194, 238, 239, 240, 241, 242
   accomodation, 172
   classification, 177
   clothing, 178
   complex, 173
   food, 178
   hygiene, 180
   population, 242
   religion, 180
   role, 173
   work, 179
Fidell, John, 72, 74, 75, 89, 93, 94
   bond of prosecutor, 74
   prosecution, 95
Fidell, Sarah, 72, 74, 75, 76, 89, 93, 94
   bond of prosecutor, 75
   bond of witness, 75
Fidell, Thomasin, 75
   bond of witness, 74
Franklin, Sir John, 228
Franklyn, F.E. (surgeon), 99, 110, 118
Fraser, John, 16, 18
Frogmore, 231, 232
Fry, Elizabeth (reformer), 100
Garven, John H., 210, 211
Gipps, Sir George, 13, 202, 205, 208, 213, 214, 215, 236, 240, 241, 243
   visit to Maitland, 1839, 202
Golspie, 14, 15, 16, 19, 23, 28, 34, 35, 36, 39
   clearances, 20
   population, 29
Gooden, Lydia, 193
Gooden, William, 193, 194
Gordon, Ann - Matron, 176, 177
Gordon, Lady Elizabeth Sutherland, 16

Gordon, Robert, 36
Governor Ready, ship, 107, 138, 165
Grant, John, 72, 73, 74, 75, 76, 89, 90, 91, 93, 94, 99, 106, 107, 155, 159, 161, 162, 175
  absconding, 156, 159, 164
  at Moreton Bay, 163
  description, 72
  medical treatment, 163, 165
Grant, Lieutenant James, 199
Green Hills, 198, 199, 200, 201, 206, 219
Greenock, Scotland, 47
Greenock, ship, 43, 47, 50, 51, 53, 55, 66
  voyage of the, 48
Gregor, John, 208, 209, 212
Halstead, John, 231, 232, 234
Harmony, ship, 123, 129, 130, 132, 134, 140, 148, 160, 167, 173
  arrival at Port Jackson, 135
  arrival at Sydney, 139
  at Woolwich, 119, 121
  convict women, 125, 146, 147, 170, 171, 172, 176
  engagement, 119
  female servants, 146
  order to proceed, 129
  voyage of the, 129
Hawley, John Henry, 258
Henry, John, 207, 208, 214, 216, 229, 233
Hickey, Allan, 251, 259, 260, 263
Hickey, Edwin, 247, 248, 250, 251
Hickey, Ellen, 186
Hildyard, John, 74, 75, 76, 92
Hill, Revd Richard, 120, 186, 192, 193
Hobart, 47, 62, 64, 67, 68, 69, 107, 118, 119, 159, 165, 180, 205, 214, 216, 219, 220, 223, 228, 229, 231, 234, 246
  houses, 66
  population, 66
Howard, John (reformer), 99
Hubbert, Martha, 108, 119, 120, 124, 126, 133, 170, 176
  assignment, 148
  description, 108
Hunter River, 145, 167, 198, 199, 210, 211, 238, 246, 248
  floods of 1857, 253
Jervoise, Sarah, 173, 174
Jones, William, 214, 216, 229, 233
Kean, Mary, 165
Kent, Reverend George Davis (chaplain), 115, 116
Kirton Bridewell
  House of Correction, 85, 86, 92, 98
Lang, Andrew, 212, 238, 257
Lang, Revd John Dunmore, 209, 210, 212, 213, 240, 241
Lawson, Richard, 72, 75, 76, 92, 94, 95
  bond of witness, 75
Lidney, 248
  cricket club, 261
  Estate/Park, 246, 247, 259
  flood, 253
Lincoln Castle, 98, 99
  gaol, prison, 98, 100, 108, 134
  prison life, 104
Lincolnshire
  farm produce, 79
  Industrial & Agricultural Revolution, 79
  social condition, 80
  topography, 78
Loch, James, 22, 24, 26, 39, 40
Lord Durham, 223, 225
Lord, David, 154, 231
Lord, Simeon, 246
Low, Joseph, 167

MacDonald, Robert, 35
MacDonald, William, 35, 41
MacLeod, James, 35
Mann, Lilias, 34, 35
Marquess of Stafford, 17, 21, 22, 24
Marquis of Hastings, ship, 107
Marsden, Revd Samuel, 176, 177
Martin, Bridget, 259
Martin, Elizabeth, 259
Masters, Ellen, 262
McDowell, William (Naval Surgeon), 123, 124, 134, 147, 148, 149
McGarvie, Revd John, 209, 210, 211, 212, 232
McGregor, Dugald, 257, 258
McLeay, Alexander, Colonial Secretary, 146
McQueen, Mary, 72, 73, 75, 76, 85, 89, 90, 91, 93, 94, 99, 108, 110, 118, 119, 120, 126, 159, 167
  assignment, 148
  description, 72
Merryweather, John (gaoler), 103, 119, 120
Middleton, Captain Richard, 123, 139, 147, 149, 150
Miller's Forest, 254, 261, 263
  cricket club, 261
Minstrel, ship
  voyage, 180
Moreton Bay, penal settlement, 159, 160, 162, 163, 175, 193
Morisset, James Thomas, 131, 139, 140, 149, 173, 174, 175
Morpeth. *See* also Green Hills
Morvich, 20, 22, 23, 28, 34
Napoleonic Wars, 43, 44, 60, 81
Nathan, Bertram, 214, 216, 229, 233
Neville, Joseph, 249, 251, 252
Norris, Elizabeth, 180

Norris, James, 13, 180, 182, 183, 184, 202, 208
North Killingholme, 72, 73, 74, 75, 76, 77, 78, 92
  population, 76
Nugent, William, 13, 205, 206, 208
Paterson, Lieutenant-Colonel William, 199
Phoenix Park, 201
Phoenix, prison hulk, 159, 160, 161
Polding, Reverend Dr. John Bede, 242
population
  movement, 44
Port Arthur, 229, 233, 239
Port Jackson, 118, 119, 135, 159
Pywell, John, 258, 261
Pywell, Mary Ann, 258, 259, 261
Quarter Sessions
  Kirton in Lindsey, 72, 74, 76, 84, 85, 86, 90, 108
  Lincolnshire, 102
  Maitland, 205, 206, 259
  Sydney, 175
Raymond Terrace, 249, 250, 251, 253, 254, 258, 261, 262, 266
  chief constable, 250, 259
  regatta, 255
Raymond, James
  postmaster general, 192, 236
Richmond, Joshua (Captain), 48, 49, 50, 52, 54, 64
Robertson, Alexander, 53
Rogart, 15, 20, 34, 39
Scotch Creek, 246, 247, 253, 254, 257, 258, 263
Sellar, Patrick, 19, 20, 21, 22, 23, 37, 40
sheep
  farms, 19, 20
  Lincolnshire, 78, 80
  stealing, 82, 110, 111, 113

Sutherland Estate, 17, 31, 32, 36
Van Diemen's Land, 69
Sheffield, Sir Robert, 91
South, James, 72, 73, 74, 75, 76, 89, 90, 91, 92, 93, 94, 99, 106, 159
  description, 72
  in Van Diemen's Land, 165, 167
Suther, Francis, 22, 40
Sutherland, 15, 16, 17, 20, 21, 22, 24, 28, 30, 31, 34, 39, 40, 205, 219, 229
  clearances, 18
  Earls of, 15
  Estate, 17, 18, 201
  population, 17
Sydney, 47, 138
  merchandise, 143
  population, 140
  town, 140
tenant
  farmers, 14, 18, 20, 23, 28, 34, 37, 201, 246, 247
  farming, 30, 31, 32
Thompson, William, 72, 75, 94, 95

bond of witness, 75
Trickelbank, Joseph, 236, 237
Tyre, John, 50, 51, 53, 58, 64
Udale, William, 110, 112, 113, 114
  execution, 116
Uppleby, John, 74, 91, 92
Van Diemen's Land
  population, 70
Walsh, Christopher, 248, 249, 251, 252, 253
Warren, Alexander, 50, 62, 64
Watson, Elizabeth, 194, 195
Wentworth, D'Arcy, 151, 186
Wentworth, William Charles, 149, 150, 240
whiskey
  distilling, smuggling, 23, 24, 36
Whyers, William (surgeon), 108, 110
Wyer, George, 185
Wyer, Jacob, 184, 185, 186, 193
Wyer, Joseph, 184
Wyer, Mary, 194
Wyld, John, 50, 62, 64
Wynne, William, 186, 187
Young, William, 19, 20, 21, 22, 39

www.ingramcontent.com/pod-product-compliance
Lightning Source LLC
Chambersburg PA
CBHW070938230426
43666CB00011B/2476